D0878595

Reading Responsibly

A Basic Guide to Biblical Interpretation

Tony L. Moyers

University Press of America,® Inc.
Lanham • Boulder • New York • Toronto • Plymouth, UK

Copyright © 2016 by University Press of America,® Inc.
4501 Forbes Boulevard, Suite 200, Lanham, Maryland 20706
UPA Acquisitions Department (301) 459-3366

Unit A, Whitacre Mews, 26-34 Stannary Street,
London SE11 4AB, United Kingdom

Library of Congress Control Number: 2015959066
ISBN: 978-0-7618-6717-3 (pbk : alk. paper)—ISBN: 978-0-7618-6718-0 (electronic)

∞™ The paper used in this publication meets the minimum requirements of American
National Standard for Information Sciences Permanence of Paper for Printed Library
Materials, ANSI/NISO Z39.48-1992.

Contents

Preface

Perhaps, the best way to describe the nature of this book and its goals is to provide some personal background. This book is the result of years of learning, teaching, reflecting, and dialog. I suppose my interest in this subject developed over many years. Stories about David in 1 and 2 Samuel intrigued me as a young child, and certain parables in the Gospels shaped my view of the world. I developed a more well-defined interest in college during my junior year when I took Introduction to the New Testament. I had always been in the church and heard the stories, but many of them seemed distant and unrelated to concrete social and political realities. In a way, I had grown up in a social environment where people appeared to over-spiritualize the Bible making it seem unrelated to the concerns and problems of this world.

Upon learning about historical methods in college, I formed new interests in these texts. Subsequent studies at Vanderbilt and Baylor Universities only strengthened those interests. At first, I wanted to share what I had learned with others so they could study the Bible for themselves with greater awareness, understanding, and appreciation. Over time, this desire broadened. I became concerned about how people applied the Bible. Some people use the Bible in a misguided way but not necessarily in a harmful way. This benign misuse is of little concern. However, some people use the Bible to promote distrust, fear, and possible harm to an individual or a group of individuals. This use is of concern.

The majority of the book is about understanding the methods of interpretation and how one might use them. I want to empower students and others who have an interest in the Bible to study it for themselves. I suppose that is the Protestant side of my upbringing coming out. I feel that people should be able to read and interpret the Bible for themselves. However, they should do so in a responsible manner.

A responsible manner leads to the other goal of this book, which largely remains in the background until the end. The book addresses the issue of ethics or responsibility. As an interpreter, I cannot simply make the Bible say what I want it to say. One must listen to the words of the Bible and attempt to understand them in their own, unique context before responding to them in some way. The other side, however, has to do with the use made of one's interpretation. A responsible interpretation requires the interpreter to exercise critical judgment when making an application of that text. I argue that one ought to avoid using any text as a way of hurting, harming or disrespecting others.

It is at this point I think the church needs to engage in a critical dialog. The Bible has lost and will continue to lose plausibility for many people. This loss frequently happens as the result of people using the Bible as an infallible document with the primary intent to condemn and target various peoples as enemies of God. I believe there is a prophetic element in the Bible that calls people to account and repent, but this message often addresses religious people who see themselves as good and upright individuals.

Finally, this book would not be possible without the contributions of many people. Family, teachers, colleagues, students and friends have all been sources of inspiration and encouragement. I want to say a special thanks to my friend and colleague who has graciously contributed a chapter on theo-poetics in this book, Dr. Robert A. White. He has been a source of encouragement and a sounding board for much of this book's content. As always, I am deeply indebted to my wife, Ruth Moyers, for her proofreading the manuscript and her many helpful suggestions.

Introduction

This book is designed to assist and empower readers in ways of reading and understanding the Bible. The target audience is anyone, Christian or non-Christian, religious or non-religious, who has an interest in the topic of biblical studies. Since Christians come from many different backgrounds and do not share one single belief about the Bible, this book is addressed to those who believe it can be understood better with the aid of scholarly investigation.

Some readers might wonder why we should bother with a text from a bygone era. Why is it important? Moreover, why does it matter how Christians or non-Christians interpret the Bible? These are important questions and provide a good starting point for our discussion.

IMPORTANCE OF BIBLICAL INTERPRETATION

The overall claim of this book is that one's interpretation of the Bible matters. It matters regardless of whether one is a devout Christian, a Jew, Muslim, a casual reader, a secularist, or even an atheist. It matters for two main reasons. The Bible has exercised a major influence on Western thinking. Books, literature, movies, and television are full of biblical allusions, themes, ideas, metaphors, and language. A certain level of biblical literacy is needed to appreciate and understand these things. Second, the Bible matters because it can be used to motivate goodness, charity, love on the one hand—or hatred, violence, and division on the other. The Bible matters because of what it does in our hands. Does it promote good or bad? It can be a dangerous book in the hands of some people who use it to support their agendas.

It is also important because well-informed interpretive practices can help one avoid shallow and poor interpretations. Protestants and Catholics have often used the Bible as if it is a repository of proof texts. If one wants to argue A, he or she must find a biblical text to support that view. Isolated verses taken out of context can be used to support most any idea.

One should interpret biblical texts in a responsible fashion. For now, I will simply define responsible interpretations as interpretations that do not lead to or promote violence and disrespect toward others. In my judgment, biblical interpretations should never lead one person to perpetrate violence against another person. Unfortunately, biblical texts may motivate some people to less than admirable behavior. Detractors of the Bible are quick to notice this point. Some people use the Bible to promote hatred and violence.

In truth, the Bible does not always condemn violence. For example, it calls for the destruction of a people, the Canaanites. This book does not ignore the violence in the text or minimize its role in motivating violent acts. The Bible is too influential and important to ignore. Therefore, one needs to approach and interpret it in responsible ways. This book is primarily about ways to interpret the Bible, but a secondary theme is about the ethics of interpretation.

By using well-established methods to interpret biblical texts, we can also see the other side as well, turning the other cheek. The interpreter has the responsibility to articulate both. He or she needs to put these texts in their proper contexts and pay close attention to them. However, I would only endorse readings that promote respect toward others. The final chapter of this book discusses this perspective.

UNIQUENESS OF THE BIBLICAL LITERATURE

The Bible is ancient and considered Scripture by Jews, Christians, and Muslims. This fact sets it apart from modern literary texts. For that reason, methods used to interpret these texts are often unique.

The Bible as an ancient collection of writings makes interpretation a challenge. It is hard to understand a culture and society from the ancient past when all the information we have about it is limited. Archeologists have added a wealth of knowledge about the lives of these ancient peoples. It has provided knowledge about how common people of that day lived. Still, there are gaps in our knowledge. Biblical historians and biblical scholars have turned over almost every stone to gain as much knowledge about this past as possible. Still, there are gaps. Moreover, even if we knew everything, we can only imagine what it was like to live in that time and place.

Another difference derives from the difficulty of translation. Most people who read the Bible do not read it in its original language. They read translations. Translation is another form of interpretation. Translation places a layer of interpretation between the reader and the text. English translators frequently have to decide which English word to use to convey a thought written in another language. Literal word for word translations of the Hebrew Bible and the New Testament would often make little or no sense. English translators have to convey the ideas of a foreign language in language English readers can understand.

Concerning translation, another major difficulty is the fact that we do not just have one text. Translators are dealing with ancient texts that have been copied many different times. Unlike texts produced on printing presses that can reproduce texts repeatedly without variation, these texts were copied by hand. This process allowed multiple errors to creep into the text. We do not have all these copies, but many of them have survived in fragments. In fact, all the texts we do possess are copies (i.e., copies many times removed from the originals). When textual variants (i.e., two or more different forms of the same text) occur, textual scholars have to decide which text is correct and which is in error.

Another reason the Bible is different from other literary works is that many people of faith within the Judeo-Christian tradition see it as divinely inspired. Inspiration, of course, can be viewed in more than one way. Are the writers and editors inspired the way an artist is inspired by the beauty of the natural world? Alternatively, are they inspired by words from God?

Christian fundamentalists view inspiration of the Bible as "God-breathed." For them, this means that God uses the hand of a human writer to record a divine message without any input or corruption from the writer. The original words and manuscripts, not the copies, are perfect and can serve as completely factual guides to every sphere of life from science to history. This view is an extreme version; conservatives are more likely to consider the writer's personality as being involved in the process.[1]

Considering the extreme fundamentalist end of the spectrum, God is the Author of the Bible. The Bible has authority because it has God as its source. It comes to humanity through a human instrument. The human author passively records God's words; they write the words down, but it is not their words but "God's Word." In its extreme form, this view is mechanical; the human author is merely a recorder.

The terminology often used in this discussion is infallible and inerrant. Is the Bible inerrant and infallible and what does that mean? Inerrant means that the autographs (i.e. original manuscripts) are without any errors. Ancient texts have been copied numerous times before they reach us. Clearly, they contain thousands of variations when comparing these copies or manuscripts.[2]

So are the originals without error? Based on current texts, there is no reason to assume that the originals are without discrepancies. For instance, there are two interwoven stories about how Joseph ends up in Egypt. In one story, Joseph is taken from a pit by Midianites, and they sell Joseph to the

Ishmaelites. Later in Genesis 39:1, the text informs us that the Ishmaelites sell Joseph to Potiphar, who is an officer of Pharaoh. However, in Genesis 37:36 the text says that the Midianites sell Joseph to Potiphar, the officer of Pharaoh. So who sold Joseph to Pharaoh: the Ishmaelites or Midianites? Here we have two versions of the same story. This difference may pose no concern for some readers who see it as a minor difference. It is, however, a problem for fundamentalists who view the Bible as inerrant and an entirely reliable source for history. They must try to explain this inconsistency.

If the Bible contains errors or inconsistencies, can we describe it as infallible? Infallible for some people means it is true as we have it even if errors exist in later copies. The mistakes, on this view, are minor and do not affect the truths being proclaimed. For conservatives, such errors do not affect the doctrines of the Bible or hinder the path to personal salvation.

Other people reject the Bible. They do not accept the view that it is divinely inspired. It is merely a human creation. They may see the Bible as irrelevant or as a primitive text that has nothing to say to the modern world. Some may read it as literature or see it as a source for promoting violence or gender bias.

On the point of inspiration, we have extreme views. On one hand, the Bible is a human document no different from other human documents. The other extreme sees the Bible as the inerrant Word of God. A middle ground, however, is possible. One could affirm the view that God communicates to a person or group at special times and places without viewing the Bible as either inerrant or infallible.

This book does not take a particular position on whether the Bible is divinely inspired or whether it is an entirely human set of writings. I do not accept a fundamentalist view that the Bible is the very words of God in the sense that all human traits are absent. Even though the originals are not available, there is no reason to think they were perfect either. Texts are the product of human activity. I do not rule out the view that poets, writers, editors are conveying what they believe to be a divine message. Some texts, however, may have been written for entertainment or other purposes without any pretext of being divinely inspired.

From a more theological perspective, the Bible may be viewed as becoming the word of God as one reads and hears God speak through the words of the text. Theologian Karl Barth holds this view.[3] One may "encounter" the word of God in the text, which is not the same as to say that the Bible is the Word of God. The Bible is the means to hear God's word. Corrine L. Carvalho observes that we can view the Bible "as a product of true human authorship, while understanding inspiration to mean that God is encountered in an inspired text, not because the text was produced in some miraculous, otherworldly way, but because God chooses to be revealed in this humanly produced writing."[4]

This view will not satisfy everyone, but it is a good view from which to begin a study of biblical texts. Views that allow for human authorship are necessary for biblical studies. It enables us to consider the ideas of the author or editor and the time in which he or she lived.

In summary, I do not need to argue for the truth of any of these positions. Beyond rejecting the fundamentalist view, I try to keep an open mind. This book assumes the writers of the Bible reflect and respond to the thoughts and culture of their day. The biblical authors speak to the problems of their day, but these texts often speak to contemporary concerns as well. Often the writer believes and feels the message is from God and consistent with God's wishes. Therefore, biblical writers are active agents who are interacting with aspects of their culture.

THE BIBLE: A COLLECTION NOT A BOOK

People most often think of the Bible as a Book or a Sacred Book. In reality, it is not a book at all. It is a collection of books. One might characterize the Hebrew Bible, for instance, as a collection of written materials that make up ancient Israel's library.[5] It contains many different books on various topics that date from different times and come from different places.

Genesis, the first book in the collection, is, in fact, a collection itself. It is largely a collection of narrative texts dating from different time periods. There is not one author of Genesis. Biblical scholars long ago discounted the traditional view of Mosaic authorship. Genesis is a collection of materials from different sources or traditions brought together over time by editors. Some sources found in Genesis date back as early as the 10th century BCE. Other parts probably date as late as the 6th century BCE. Therefore, Genesis came together over at least five hundred years. The book has been arranged to tell a story that continues into the other four books of the Pentateuch— Exodus, Leviticus, Numbers, and Deuteronomy. In short, Genesis does not just have one author but several.

The Bible is not only a collection of individual books, but it contains many different types of literature such as psalms, gospels, and letters. The Book of Psalms, for instance, contains at least four types of psalms: laments, praises, royal psalms, and wisdom psalms. One can break lament psalms and praise psalms down into subtypes. Laments can be individual or community laments, and there are several different types of praise psalms. The Gospels contain various kinds of texts such as parables, miracle stories, and several others. We also have letters included in the Bible written by Paul and others. So the collection we call the Bible is made up of various kinds of literature spanning many centuries.

One should also recognize that certain traditions and sources once existed independently of each other. These sources and traditions were brought together in individual books of the Bible. Writers penned these books on scrolls. Scrolls were of different sizes, but a typical scroll could contain a book the size of Isaiah. Instead of copying one small book on a scroll, scribes copy several smaller ones on a scroll (e.g., the Book of the Twelve). It is common practice to refer to these writings as the Minor Prophets (Hosea, Joel, Amos, Obadiah, Jonah, Micah, Nahum, Habakkuk, Zephaniah, Haggai, Zechariah, and Malachi). Before the development of the codex or book form, therefore, it was not possible for one scroll to contain all the books of the Bible.

JEWISH AND CHRISTIAN BIBLES

It is incorrect to refer to "the Bible" as though there is only one. Not all Jews or Christians share the same canon or books in their Bible. For Jews, we may refer to the Bible as containing 24 or 39 books depending on how one divides them. What Christians call the Old Testament is known to Jews as the Hebrew Bible or TANACH (i.e., the Law, Prophets, and Writings). The different number of books (24 versus 39) reflects different counting practices. For instance, in the Jewish Bible the Twelve Minor Prophets count as one book. In Christian Bibles, they count as twelve. In the Jewish Bible, Samuel, Kings, Chronicles, Ezra-Nehemiah count as four books whereas in the Christian Bibles they count as eight (1 and 2 Samuel, 1 and 2 Kings, 1 and 2 Chronicles, Ezra, and Nehemiah). Protestants, on the other hand, combine the 39 books of the Old Testament with the 27 books of the New Testament to make up the 66 books of the Bible.

Also, the reference above to "Christian Bibles" indicates that not all Christian Bibles are the same. The Roman Catholic Bible has more books in it than the Protestant Bible. The Roman Catholic Church has Deutero-canonical books such as Tobit, Judith, 1 and 2 Maccabees, Wisdom of Solomon, Sirach, and Baruch.[6]

The change from scroll to codex allowed the books of the Bible to exist in one large document. The codex came into use at the end of the first century CE. However, the earliest codex containing the Hebrew Bible, the apocryphal books, and the oldest complete copy of the New Testament is known as *Codex Sinaiticus*. This codex also contained two additional Christian writings: The Apostle of Barnabas and the Shepherd of Hermes.

Codex Sinaiticus dates to the fourth century C.E. The Old Testament books contained in *Codex Sinaiticus* are Greek translations of the Hebrew texts. Hebrew is a Semitic language. It is also the language of the Hebrew Bible. There are a few passages in the Hebrew Bible written in Aramaic, which is similar to Hebrew. The Greek translation of these books became known as the Septuagint commonly abbreviated as LXX. The LXX also contained books from the Apocrypha such as 2 Esdras, Tobit, Judith, and the four books of Maccabees, Wisdom, and Sirach.

More than 300 years had passed after Jesus' death before the content of the New Testament was final. In the second century CE, different communities had access to different books. Not all Christian communities in the early years of Christianity possessed all the books now found in the New Testament. There were disputes over which books were authoritative. For instance, the books of Hebrews and Revelation were disputed. Some other writings existed such as the Gospel of Thomas or the Gospel of Mary Magdalene that never made it into the Bible. Today scholars and the general public have access to books that did not make it into the canon. There have been television documentaries on subjects such as the Dead Sea Scrolls, the Gospel of Thomas, The Gospel of Judas, and The Gospel of Mary. In short, many today are aware that a body of literature exists that is approximately as old as books in the Bible.

RESPONSIBLE INTERPRETATIONS

A responsible reading of the Bible promotes views that foster hospitality and respect for others. This book responds to the concerns of religious communities as well as concerns of the Other (i.e., those outside religious communities). People often view diversity as a threat challenging their beliefs. I see diversity as a potential blessing that requires openness and tolerance. Tolerance does not mean accepting the views of others uncritically. An unlimited tolerance is not a virtue. By tolerance, I refer to an attitude of respect and a willingness to hear the other person. Being open-minded makes some people feel uncomfortable. Diversity keeps things from becoming too rigid. Close-mindedness often moves one to claim more for one's views than is justifiable. Being open to the Other (i.e., what is different whether persons or ideas) suggests we can learn something new.

This openness is part of the educational process. Openness teaches us that knowledge is almost endless, and there is always more to learn. It teaches us that knowledge is provisional; it is always changing. While this insight may bring apprehension, it is also exciting; it keeps life interesting. Education keeps us moving ahead and prevents complacency. Education in all areas makes life better. It makes us better. Education can be formal or informal. Informal education is also important. Openness to learning from the world around us and from other people enables us to learn and grow. As the book of Proverbs teaches, knowledge is not the end of human endeavor but a means to a better life.

The diversity of thought and approaches can bring new energy to the discussion of biblical texts creating genuine dialogue and openness. This openness is a good thing for biblical studies. It allows the reader to explore the different possible meanings. Instead of building a fortress and looking for the one and only correct meaning, diverse approaches of interpreting biblical texts produce new and meaningful ways of reading the Bible in new and different situations. Philosopher Jacques Derrida has said that the best way to conserve a text (a way to be conservative) is to keep the text open to new and unforeseen possibilities.[7] Failing to do so could lead to a text becoming an archaic and frozen relic of the past with little to say to the present. On this view, one can never exhaust the meaning of the text due to the richness of the biblical literature and the human context, which is always changing.

Responsible interpretations pay close attention to the texts. They do not lift a verse out of context or appeal to a particular passage to condemn a group of people or a type of behavior. Such an approach is irresponsible. While there are biblical texts that justify violence for particular reasons or texts that condemn certain practices, these texts do not warrant modern acts of hatred, violence, or condemnation.

We can see an extreme example of this approach in the life of Oliver Cromwell. Cromwell equated the Catholics in Northern Ireland with the Canaanites seeing himself as the biblical Joshua.[8] In the Massacres of Irish towns, he pictured himself as the biblical Joshua fighting Irish Catholics who were Canaanites. Cromwell called for the "Irish towns to surrender and then annihilated the occupants when they refused. . . . [He] found in the biblical accounts of Joshua's massacres of the Canaanites and spoliation of their towns the models, warrants, and justifications for his military strategy of extirpation of the native Catholics of Ireland.[9] Such an example speaks for itself. Using biblical texts to justify violence, hatred, or discrimination against people and groups is not a responsible reading.

MISCONCEPTIONS OF THE BIBLE

Some false impressions might prevent a good faith effort to read and to understand the Bible on its terms. First, I have heard people say that the Bible is easy to comprehend. In some cases, a general understanding of the Bible is relatively straightforward. Even so, the reader needs to remain open and not be too quick to judge. What may seem straightforward might not be with additional thought and reflection. In my experience, such a facile view reflects a personal belief about the Bible. It is often used to dismiss or undercut the importance of a careful and well thought out study of the Bible.

Second, some have the misconception that the Bible contains one consistent view throughout. People who hold such a view see no real diversity in the Bible. Such a flawed idea brings about a misunderstanding and misinterpretation of the Bible. One who rejects diversity in the Bible has to finesse or force divergent views into a unified artificial whole. In effect, one who attempts to harmonize the Bible in this fashion is trying to impose his or her views about the Bible onto the Bible. When an individual or group asserts that the Bible says one thing or another, this is typically an indication that the group assumes the Bible speaks with one and only one voice. Such an attempt tries consciously or unconsciously to control the meaning of the text. It avoids dealing with the complexity of the different texts.

Therefore, different texts may contain different views. Paul is not always on the same page as James. The books of 1 and II Samuel are often quite different than 1 and 2 Chronicles even though they cover much of the same material. Matthew's Gospel may tell the same story as Luke's Gospel, but one cannot assume the stories have the same significance for both writers. Matthew's account may differ from Luke's in some important ways, and these differences may indicate different theologies or views. Redaction criticism, which we will cover later, is the method for making such comparisons and drawing such conclusions.

A third misconception comes from those who see the purpose of the Bible as simply a means of getting to heaven. As the saying goes, one can be so heavenly minded that he or she is of little earthly use. The Bible is not just about reaching heaven. It is a collection of writings spanning many years. It reflects many different human situations. People often over spiritualize the Bible, which separates it from the real world in which we live. The Gospels lead us to ask this question: What can we do to help bring about the kingdom of God in the here and now? The answers would have implications in the realms of politics, economics, criminal justice, social justice, and other aspects of modern life.

In short, discovering the meaning of biblical texts takes effort, and one should not reduce the possible meanings to just one. Interpreting the Bible is a serious endeavor and the implications of the Bible reach beyond the spiritual. The texts have implications for how we live this life and what we do in the present. It speaks to real social and political issues of any era.

GOALS AND CONTENT OF THE BOOK

I have three primary goals in this book. First, I want to help readers gain more from their reading of the Bible. I do not presuppose any prior knowledge of the Bible or biblical studies. To appreciate the Bible requires a broad understanding. The fact that the Bible comes from a distant past that does not share our modern day literary conventions makes it a challenge. Second, the book introduces various models of interpretation and ample illustrations of how these models work. It should prepare and empower readers to get more out of their readings of the biblical texts. The third goal is to sort out the ethical aspect of interpretation, which comes in the final chapter. It deals with the issue of responsible versus irresponsible interpretations.

The content of this book falls into two major divisions or sections. The first section is historical. It investigates the world behind the text. This book begins with a brief history of biblical interpretation. It considers the composition of the Bible as a product of a long and complex process. The historical methods discussed focus on the historical background of these texts. It endeavors to describe the historical and social setting for the different biblical texts.

The second major section of the book contains several chapters relating to the study of the Bible from a literary perspective. This approach focuses on the world of the text. We enter this world through the act of reading. The field of literary studies has changed over the years, and the approaches covered in this book focus more on the text and reader than on the biography of the author. Modern and postmodern literary approaches concentrate on some elements such as theme, plot, characters, metaphors, images, and binary oppositions. Such approaches pay close attention to the various features of language and structure.

Following these two major divisions, there is a chapter relating to an ideological approach to the Bible. This approach can take different forms. For the sake of space, I limit the discussion to a feminist interpretation. Ideology is about the world of ideas, the ideas of the text and its audiences. Readers work with certain ideologies that shape how they read texts. Ideology is defined by Merriam Webster's online dictionary as follows:

1. a systematic body of concepts especially about human life or culture
2. a manner or the content of thinking characteristic of an individual, group, or culture
3. the integrated assertions, theories and aims that constitute a sociopolitical program.

In this book, the use of the word ideology includes all three aspects.

NOTES

1. Charles Hodge, "Systematic Theology in Readings in the History of Christian Theology," *From the Reformation to the Present* ed. William C. Placher, vol. 2, (Philadelphia: The Westminster Press, 1988), 165–167.

2. Bart D. Ehrman, *The New Testament: A Historical Introduction to the Early Christian Writings*, 3d ed., (Oxford: Oxford University Press, 2004). Ehrman says there are as many variations or differences between texts in the New Testament as there are words in the New Testament. Most of the variations, however, are minor and insignificant.

3. William E. Hordern, *A Layman's Guide to Protestant Theology*, rev and expanded (New York: Macmillan Publishing Company, 1968), 133.

4. Corrine L. Carvalho, *Primer On Biblical Methods"* (Winona, MI.: Anselm Academic 2009), xii.

5. James E. Bowley, *Introduction to the Hebrew Bible: A Guided Tour of Israel's Library* (Upper Saddle River: Pearson Prentice Hall, 2008).

6. Ibid., 7–12.

7. John Caputo editor with commentary, *Deconstruction in a Nutshell: A Conversation with Jacques Derrida* (New York: Fordham University Press, 1997). 79.

8. Robert P. Carroll, "Cultural Encroachment and Bible Translation: Observations on Elements of Violence, Race and Class in the Production of Bibles in Translation," *Semeia* 76 (1996): 41.

9. Ibid., 41.

Chapter One

The Bible and Its Interpreters

Interpretation is simply a human attempt to make sense of things. The act of interpretation is passive, but it can also be active. It is an act of discovering and creating meaning. There is no sharp division between discovering and creating. It is a question of whether we discover the meaning already present in the text or whether we create the meaning. As with most things, the truth is somewhere in the middle.

Therefore, interpretation is an inevitable and necessary activity. To make sense of something is to interpret it, to determine what it means and respond as necessary. All we do in life involves interpretation. Every act of communication involves an act of interpretation. Human gestures, body language, dinner conversation, and written documents all require interpretation. Sometimes we seem to get it right as when one may receive an approving nod from a conversation partner. Other times we get it wrong leading to misunderstandings.

In oral communication or conversation, we may feel we have been successful in conveying our message to the other party. It is also possible, as I know from personal experience, that the other person may misunderstand my intent. Reading a text is no different. It is a communicative act whether the text is a sacred or non-sacred. One's well-being could even depend upon interpreting words or body language of others. Whether one realizes it or not, he or she is always trying to understand and interpret verbal and non-verbal communications. The results of our understandings may often have significant repercussions.

Those who communicate through written texts are greatly invested in the interpretive process. Biblical writers and editors produced texts from their own historical or social experiences, and they assumed their audiences would understand what they had to say. They understood the world and the will of

1

God from a particular historical and social setting, and these understandings influenced the way they communicated.

In short, every written text requires human interpretation. One might say that interpretation is part of the text from the very beginning. As the biblical authors or editors write, they are interpreting or making sense of events, of their personal experiences, of their understanding of God, and of what God wants them to do. Writers are not always happy to follow God's directions or to be God's messenger. The prophet Jeremiah, for instance, questions God (Jer 12) and wonders why he suffers. This human anguish is often expressed in the pages of the Bible. Both writers and editors ponder God's actions and words trying to understand or make sense of them.

This process is what I mean by the act of interpretation. Before the writer begins putting pen to paper, he or she engages in it. As a result, one never begins at the beginning. There is always the past that shapes the words and texts that come to us in the present. Before Paul writes his letter to the Corinthians, there is already a history, and this history of his interactions with them brings about the letters he addresses to them.

Like the biblical writers and editors, we also come to texts with concerns, doubts, needs, and various kinds of experiences. All of these things shape how we understand the text. I cannot interpret a text in exactly the same way as another person because my experiences and views are not the same. A text may always speak to one person differently than another. Consequently, the interpreter never begins his or her work fresh. The need for interpretation is always ongoing.

INTERPRETATION OF THE BIBLE

Interpretations occur even within the Bible. When we compare parts of 1 and 2 Samuel and 1 and 2 Kings with 1 and 2 Chronicles, we find an interpretative process. The books of 1 and 2 Samuel and 1 and 2 Kings are used as sources of information by the writer of 1 and 2 Chronicles writing years later. However, the Chronicler does not simply repeat the material or quote it. This writer reinterprets Samuel and Kings for a later audience.

By comparing Samuel and Kings to Chronicles, one can see a process whereby a later interpreter (i.e., the Chronicler) used and modified the older books of Samuel and Kings. For instance, the Chronicler leaves out the story of David and Bathsheba to portray David in a more positive light. By modifying these sources, the chronicler eliminates materials that present David in a bad light

Another common type of interpretation within the pages of the Bible occurs when New Testament writers interpret passages from the Old Testament and apply them to their contemporary situation. For example, Psalm 22 begins with an expression of great anguish. The psalmist feels abandoned. As one continues reading the reader encounters a writer who experiences God's deliverance. The response of the psalmist to this act of deliverance is one of praise and thanksgiving. Many people can identify with these words. The identification is possible because the language of this Psalm (and others as well) is general. The general nature of the language allows those who are experiencing difficult times to identify with the psalmist. [1]

The Gospels of Matthew and Mark portray Psalm 22 as speaking to the time of Jesus' crucifixion. While the psalmist did not envision his or her words being used in a different historical setting, the writers of Matthew and Mark apply these words to Jesus' death on the cross. Matthew 27:35 and Mark 15:24 recount the dividing of clothes and casting of lots. These words seem to come from Psalm 22:18. The ridicule of Jesus recounted in Matthew 27:39 and Mark 15:29 refers to Psalm 22:6–8. When one compares these verses and considers Jesus' last words in these two Gospels, "My God, my God, why have you forsaken me", [2] it seems clear that the writers of Matthew and Mark understand Psalm 22 as a description of what happens when Jesus is crucified. In short, then, Psalm 22 takes on new meaning with the death of Jesus.

In conclusion, interpretation is simply a human activity that plays a role in every aspect of our lives. Reading and making sense of the Bible is just one aspect of the interpretive process. Biblical writers themselves had to make sense of their world and their understanding of God before they could attempt to communicate that view to others through their writings.

EARLY JEWISH INTERPRETATION OF BIBLICAL TEXTS

In 1947, a fifteen-year-old Bedouin boy named Muhammad adh-Dhib accidentally discovers some scrolls in a cave near the Dead Sea. These scrolls are known as the Dead Sea Scrolls. There are different stories about how he finds them. These scrolls have been a source of controversy and speculation since their discovery. [3] The various types of scrolls include biblical books, commentaries on biblical texts, and documents revealing the views of a particular group of people. This group, commonly associated with the Essenes, feels that the worship in Jerusalem at the time is corrupt, and, as a result, they leave Jerusalem. The leader of this group is the Teacher of Righteousness. This group expects an apocalyptic event that would end the corruption and lead to restoration. The War Scroll tells about a coming battle between the sons of light and the sons of darkness in which the sons of darkness will be destroyed.

This group of people made a home at Qumran located on the Northeast corner of the Dead Sea. The leader of this community is to be the Teacher of

Righteousness. His job is to interpret the words of other biblical texts, particularly the words of prophetic texts and apply them to the life of that community. The Essenes believe that the words of the prophets are a mystery even to the prophets themselves. Only later would the prophetic words be adequately interpreted and understood by the Teacher of Righteousness. Moreover, the application of these words does not relate to the days of the prophets but the later Essene community.[4]

D. S. Russell discusses different ways the Essenes apply the interpretations of this Teacher. The primary application involves showing the meaning of the prophetic words for the contemporary situation, of course referring to the Essene community.[5] Applying prophetic words to their contemporary situation is important since the prophecies relate to the "end-time." The Essenes believe the end is near.[6] In their view, then, the Teacher of Righteousness provides the only correct interpretation of the prophets' words. He makes almost every word and phrase apply to the contemporary setting without regard for the original historical context of the words.[7]

EARLY CHRISTIAN INTERPRETATION OF BIBLICAL TEXTS

Our second illustration of biblical interpretation comes from the time of the early church. Saint Augustine (354–430 C.E.) provides an example of early Christian interpretation of the Bible. The most basic level of interpretation is the literal or historical interpretation. This level of meaning, according to Augustine, is only a surface level, which takes no special ability to understand. The literal meaning is valuable, but it is not as important as the deeper level. The deeper level is the spiritual one. This level is replete with mystery. It involves interpreting texts in an allegorical or spiritual fashion. For Augustine, literal and allegorical readings correspond to the letter and the spirit in 2 Corinthians 3:6.

According to Augustine, the allegorical approach is important for it reveals the mysteries of certain biblical texts that a literal approach cannot reveal.[8] Augustine did not restrict the allegorical interpretation to passages clearly intended to be allegorical. When a writer intends to produce an allegory, it is legitimate to interpret it that way. Augustine, however, is not so selective.

Allegory is a story that has a second meaning somewhat concealed behind the literal or surface meaning.[9] The underlying meaning may have moral, social, religious, or political significance. Thus, an allegory is a story with two meanings. The Bible itself contains allegories. In Ezekiel 23, the prophet tells a story about two sisters. One can understand the story literally. The real point is that the two sisters represent two nations: Israel and Judah. The criticism directed at the sisters is leveled at the two nations. At the end of the story in Ezekiel 23:31 it says that "you," referring to the southern kingdom, have walked in the way of your sister (referring to the northern kingdom). Another allegory occurs in Galatians 4:21–5:1. In Galatians, Paul uses the Greek word for allegory referring to the story in Genesis about Hagar and Sarah. These two women stand for two covenants. In these two examples, it is clear that reading the texts allegorically is consistent with what the authors intend. Augustine and others of his time, however, freely interpret texts as allegories regardless of the author's intent. For them, the meaning is not limited to what a historical author intends.

Augustine's attitude toward biblical interpretation may seem somewhat casual.[10] He says

> Whoever, then thinks, that he understands the Holy Scriptures, or any part of them, but puts such an interpretation upon them as does not tend to build up this twofold love of God and our neighbor, does not yet understand them as he ought. If, on the other hand, a man draws a meaning from them that may be used for the building up of love, even though he does not happen upon the precise meaning which the author whom he reads intended to express in that place, his error is not pernicious, and he is wholly clear from the charge of deception.[11]

So the critical issue for the interpreter is not some sense of correctness but having the right motive. Augustine's concern is for the motive and the consequences of an interpretation. Love of God and neighbor are central. Interpretations fostering a love of God and neighbor and opposing selfish desire are acceptable interpretations. The one condition to this rule is that the interpretation must be consistent with the rule of faith or the teachings of the church.[12] He believes there are several legitimate interpretations.[13]

MARTIN LUTHER AND THE BEGINNINGS OF THE PROTESTANT INTERPRETIVE APPROACH

The third instance of biblical interpretation comes from Martin Luther (1483–1546). Luther is a leader in the Protestant Reformation. By Luther's day, a fourfold method of biblical interpretation is common. The threefold method of Augustine's day involves the literal (historical sense), the allegorical (what one is to believe), and the tropological or moral sense (what one is to do). The fourth addition is analogical, which provides for hope and consolation. According to Church historian Roland H. Bainton, Luther does not totally reject the allegorical approach. He said, "it was never to be used in disputation. Luther never ceased to use it for edification."[14]

Luther affirms the literal sense as the legitimate mode of biblical interpretation. By literal, however, he does not mean historical. He identifies the literal sense with the prophetic sense. The prophetic simply refers to his view that the Old Testament is a Christian book that looks forward to Christ. [15] Clearly, Jews represent a threat to Luther. His characterization of the prophetic undermines Jewish interpretation. Jewish interpretation understands the texts as fitting into the context of God's saving actions within the life of the ancient Israelites. Jews did not see prophetic texts as foretelling the life, ministry, and death of Jesus Christ.

Modern historical scholars reject Luther's way of reading the Hebrew Bible because his method fails to respect the intent of the original writers. It is what one might call reading Christ back into the Hebrew Bible. Another emphasis in Luther's understanding of Scripture is that all Scripture proclaims Christ. The interpreter's attention should center on Christ. This emphasis accounts for his challenging the Scriptural status of James, Hebrew and Revelation. Finally, he says that the Holy Spirit has to inspire the work of interpreters. [16]

PROOF-TEXTING

Proof-texting is another common method of interpretation. The Catholic Church uses this method to support the doctrines of the Church. It collects and names all biblical texts that can be used to support Church teachings. Many Protestants also use this method to support their beliefs. For instance, one could take a doctrine of any church or denomination and ask members why they believe it. Often the reasons may come in the form of random Bible verses. One could argue that the Bible is a unity, and if one verse supports a belief, then the whole of the Bible supports that belief. There are at least two problems this view. First, a person would need to read more than one verse to determine what it means. One would need some context. Second, most scholars do not view the Bible as a total unity. One can find a variety of views in the Bible.

Beyond using biblical texts to support the beliefs of one's religious group, proof-texting is frequently used by individuals to promote their personal views. "The Bible says so" may justify a broad range of beliefs, attitudes, and behaviors. This approach often uses Bible verses as proof texts, and it fails to take the full text or context seriously. Context is essential for proper interpretations. To quote a verse to support a doctrine or belief without consideration of the total context produces defective interpretations. While it is certainly possible for a person to cite a verse and use it properly, verses are frequently cited without regard to the context in which they occur. For instance, Matthew 24:30 and other similar verses may be cited to prove that the end of the world is near. I stress this point because proof-texting is tempting. It is a lazy and often self-centered way of reading and applying the Bible to the present.

SUMMARY

In this chapter, I noted interpretations taking place within the biblical texts themselves as well as interpretations of the early Jewish and Christian communities. We saw how a Jewish sect of Essenes interpreted texts and applied them to their present situation. We also discussed the ways Augustine and Luther interpreted biblical texts. Finally, we described the use of proof-texting. In the next chapter, I discuss historical means of interpreting the Bible.

NOTES

1. W. H. Bellinger, *Psalms: Reading and Studying the Book of Praises* (Peabody: Hendrickson Publishers, 1990), 15–17.

2. Unless otherwise specified, this book uses the New Revised Standard Version translation of the Bible abbreviated as NRSV.

3. For more details see Timothy H. Lim, *The Dead Sea Scrolls: A Very Short Introduction* (Oxford: Oxford University Press 2005).

4. Ibid., 44–45.

5. Ibid. 47.

6. D.S. Russell, *From Early Judaism to the Early Church* (Philadelphia: Fortress Press, 1986), 46–47.

7. Ibid., 46–47.

8. Richard A. Norris, Jr., "Augustine and the Close of the Ancient Period," in *A History of Biblical Interpretation: The Ancient Period*, eds. Alan J. Hauser and Duane F. Watson (Grand Rapids: William B. Eerdmans Publishing Company, 2003), 392–297.

9. Chris Baldick, *The Concise Oxford Dictionary of Literary Terms* (New York: Oxford University Press 1990), 5.

10. Gerald Bonner, "Augustine As Biblical Scholar" in *From The Beginning To Jerome The Cambridge Bible History*, eds. P.R. Ackroydt and C.F. Evans vol. 1 (Cambridge: The University Press, 1970), 557.

11. Augustine, "On Christian Doctrine," in *Augustine Great Books of the Western World*, ed. Mortimer J. Adler, vol. 18 (Chicago: The University of Chicago Press, 1952), 634–635.

12. Ibid., 548–557; See also Norris' discussion of enjoyment versus usefulness 396–397.

13. Norris, 397–399.

14. Roland H. Bainton "The Bible in the Reformation," in *The West From The Reformation To The Present Day* ed., S. L. Greenslade The Cambridge Bible History vol. 3 (Cambridge: The University Press, 1963), 24–25.

15. Ibid., 25.

16. See Bainton 37.

Chapter Two

Understanding the Bible Historically

The next several chapters focus on historical aspects of studying the Bible. Therefore, it is necessary to provide a brief description of the different methods covered in these chapters. The three main historical methods are source criticism, form criticism, and redaction criticism.

1. In the Hebrew Bible or Old Testament, source criticism is practiced mostly in relation to the Pentateuch (Genesis, Exodus, Leviticus, Numbers, and Deuteronomy). In the New Testament it is primarily focused on the Synoptic Gospels (Matthew, Mark, and Luke). Source critics attempt to locate sources that make up a particular text and study them in terms of their origin, date of composition, and purpose.

2. Form criticism can be applied to any text in the Bible. It attempts to categorize a piece of literature according to its type. The types of biblical literature could be an oracle of God, a lawsuit, a lament, or a letter just to name a few. The study also attempts to analyze a text's form or structure. Paul's letter, 1 Thessalonians for instance, has greetings, thanksgiving, a body, ethical appeals and instruction, and a conclusion. The approach also considers a text's social setting and its purpose.

3. Redaction criticism can be applied to any part of the Bible that has been edited. Some confine this approach to the study of the Synoptic Gospels. I see its scope as being much broader. Redaction criticism examines how a text has been edited, and what the edits can tell us about the editor or redactor. In many texts, we can say that the author is really more like an editor. Luke, for example, uses sources to compose his account of Jesus' ministry. Yet, he did not always quote the

sources verbatim but modified them for a purpose. So what can the changes tell us about Luke's purpose?

These are not the only historical approaches, but they are perhaps the most influential. We will comment on other avenues of historical research along the way.

BIBLICAL AUTHORS AND EDITORS

Those responsible for the materials in the Hebrew Bible and the New Testament are often anonymous. Often we have books that contain materials that come from different traditions and sources. Traditions and sources may represent the work of one or more authors. The traditions and sources have been combined over the years by editors often under the name of an important individual. Even though the first five books of the Bible are referred to as the Books of Moses, mainstream scholars do not accept Moses as the author. In fact, there is no one person responsible for these works.

Since biblical texts have a long history of being passed down, they are often edited by an individual or group of individuals who help to shape the message of the text. Editors often shape, add and omit certain parts of a text before its completion. Where an editor has shaped the text, the historical critic may also want to uncover the intentions of the editor. The historical critic may ask why the editor changes or modifies the text in question. Therefore, historical critics want to know as much as possible about all stages of the growth and development of texts.

HISTORICAL READINGS

Initially, a historical reading tries to answer basic historical questions. Such questions include the following: How do biblical texts come to exist as we know them today? Who is the author? When are they written? To whom are they written? Why are they written? What are these texts about? What is the social and historical setting for the writer and audience?

One may wonder why we have to determine who wrote a text. Unlike modern texts, not all biblical texts provide the information needed to identify the author. Some texts are anonymous. While tradition assigns the book of Genesis to Moses, the Book of Genesis never says that Moses is the author of the book as a whole. So who is? The simple answer is we do not know. In fact, the book is a product of many hands. Even when the author's names are provided, scholars may sometimes question the attribution. Paul's authorship of 1 and 2 Timothy and Titus has been disputed, and the consensus is that Paul is not the author of these letters. His authorship of other letters has also been questioned. There is a strong consensus that Paul is the author of Romans, 1 and 2 Corinthians, Galatians, Philippians, 1 Thessalonians, and Philemon. There is lesser agreement about 2 Thessalonians, Ephesians, and Colossians. In short, authorship is usually a major consideration of historical approaches.

Answering these questions provides the historical backdrop for understanding biblical texts. Knowing not only who wrote a text, but also when it was written, why it was written, and to whom it was addressed are important questions. Another key aspect of historical studies involves historical reconstruction, which can be complex. It attempts to go back from what we have (e.g., the Book of Genesis as it now exists) to an earlier form of the book, which may be much shorter. A historical reconstruction endeavors to identify the oldest form of a text so one can read it in relation to its original historical setting. For example, the Book of Genesis at one time would have begun with chapter 2:4b. I discuss historical reconstruction in more detail below.

TEXTUAL CRITICISM

Beyond these historical concerns, one also has to consider the fact that the biblical books in our Bible today come from Hebrew and Greek manuscripts that are copies of copies reaching back over two thousand years. Not all of the copies survived, but many have. In this process of copying texts, mistakes occur. Even the best scribes make mistakes. The texts contain variations. The study of textual variations is known as textual criticism. The goal of textual criticism is to consider the variations and attempt to determine which text is in error and which one is correct.

Our modern English translations of the Bible derive from ancient manuscripts. These manuscripts are not the originals. They are copies of older manuscripts. We do not have any of the autographs or original manuscripts. We have copies of copies that have been passed on through countless years. There are thousands of manuscripts. Some of these manuscripts are merely fragments of a text.

Textual critics look at places where differences between manuscripts occur. They attempt to determine which reading is most likely the oldest and best reading. Textual critics follow certain rules or guidelines to recover the oldest or most original words, words that would appear in the original texts before scribes copy them.[1] Of course, this is the goal of textual criticism. Since we do not have the original or first text, the results cannot be verified or certain.

Guidelines for determining the best readings depend upon internal and external evidence. Internal evidence involves applying certain criteria to the places where variations occur. One major principle says the more difficult the reading, the more likely it is to be the original one. The reason for this principle is that scribes would try to explain and simplify a difficult reading to make it understandable. It is unlikely that the scribe would take a simple reading and make it more difficult. Another general criterion is that the shorter reading is more likely to be older. Scribes are more likely to expand a text than to delete any part of it.[2]

Other considerations concern internal and external evidence. Internal evidence concerns "style, vocabulary, and literary context."[3] If one text varies from others, one could examine the variations. Then one would determine which reading fits best with the author's language and style in the rest of the book. The external evidence relates to the evaluation or reliability of particular manuscripts. Some textual traditions and manuscripts are known to be more reliable than others. Some manuscripts are older than others. While older is not always better, it may receive special consideration. Overall, the older manuscript carries more weight. Some of the oldest manuscripts contain parts of the Hebrew Bible from the Dead Sea Scrolls. These scrolls date sometime between 250 BCE–70 CE.[4] Unfortunately, these scrolls do not contain complete copies of each book in the Hebrew Bible. Parts of the scrolls are damaged and missing. These Scrolls do contain parts of every book of the Hebrew Bible except for the Book of Esther, which is completely missing.[5]

Interestingly, there is a significant "chronological gap between the original manuscript written by a biblical author or compiled by an editor and the earliest preserved copy."[6] Take the Book of Hosea. Hosea dates to the eighth century B.C.E., but the Dead Sea scrolls that contain parts of Hosea date several hundred years later. Later still is the oldest complete Hebrew copy of the Hebrew Bible, known as the Masoretic text. This text is the product of Masoretic scholars who are active from the sixth century C.E. through the ninth centuries C.E. The earliest Hebrew manuscript of the entire Hebrew Bible dates to the tenth century C.E.[7]

The number of ancient Hebrew manuscripts is limited. According to Ernst Würthwein, the whole Hebrew Bible depends upon

> manuscripts of the tenth century A.D. and later. This is to be expected because Jewish regulations required the destruction of worn and defective manuscripts. And when scholars had finally established the text in the tenth century, all older manuscripts which represented earlier stages of its development were naturally considered defective, and in the course of time disappeared. It is also true that manuscripts were often destroyed during medieval persecutions of the Jews, sometimes by their adversaries, but sometimes also by the Jews themselves to prevent their sacred books from falling into the hands of infidels.[8]

Here, Würthwein is referring to the Masoretic manuscripts. These manuscripts are generally considered the starting point for modern translations of the Hebrew Bible into other languages.

Another early manuscript of the Hebrew Bible is the Septuagint or LXX. This is a Greek translation of the Hebrew texts of the Old Testament. The Septuagint is the product of Jewish scholars who read the Hebrew language. The Septuagint contains the entire Old Testament and other books known to Protestants as Apocryphal and to Catholics as Deuterocanonical books. Jewish scholars create this translation for the Jewish community in Alexandria, Egypt. The exact date for this translation is hard to determine. The translation is popular, and it is used by the early Greek-speaking Christian communities who view the Old Testament as Scripture. Writers of the New Testament are reading this Greek translation. The translation became so popular with the early church that the Jewish community abandoned it. As a result, books in the Septuagint known as Apocrypha or Deuterocanonical do not become part of the Jewish canon.[9]

Beyond these major manuscripts, there are many more. Some of them are fragmentary. When variations occur between different manuscripts, we can never be sure we have the original words. Textual critics must use the tools of their trade to recover what is most likely the original words of a text. Recovering the original text, however, is more complicated in the New Testament than in the Hebrew Bible. There are many more New Testament manuscripts to consider than is the case in the Old Testament. The same basic critical principles discussed above in relation to the Old Testament apply as well to New Testament manuscripts.

There are thousands of different New Testament manuscripts. These manuscripts vary in size from small fragments to entire codices. A codex or book form such as the *Codex Sinaiticus* contains more than just the New Testament. It also contains the Old Testament Books and more. In these different manuscripts, there are thousands of variations. Most of them are relatively insignificant. In Matthew 9:14, some Greek manuscripts say that the Pharisees fast often, and others leave out the word often. English study Bibles such as the New Revised Standard Version has a note that tells the reader "other ancient authorities lack *often*." Sometimes the differences are even smaller. Perhaps some punctuation or word order differs.

Quite often, however, the changes are significant. For example, the end of Mark's Gospel (i.e., Mk 16:9–20) is missing in some of the oldest and best manuscripts. Most textual scholars have concluded that the verses are additions to Mark's Gospel. As a result, they are secondary and not originally part of the Gospel. If this is the case, what does one do with this information? Should English translations omit these verses? Alternatively, should translations include them with a note? The NRSV adds a note about their absence. It says these verses are lacking in "some of the most ancient authorities."

External evidence entails comparing readings in the different manuscripts and assessing the value of each manuscript. In the Old Testament, the Masoretic text is primary, but there are others. Other key manuscripts include in order of significance the Samaritan Pentateuch, the Dead Sea Scrolls, and the Septuagint.[10] In the New Testament, there are families or groups of manuscripts. By family, the textual critics group texts into a family meaning they share certain characteristics and readings. Some groups or families of manuscripts are considered more reliable than others.

Readers without a knowledge of Hebrew and Greek or only a limited knowledge of textual criticism can make an informed decision on variant readings. Such a reader would need a translation that contains notes about variant readings such as the RSV or NRSV, and they would also need to consult the proper reference books and commentaries. Clearly, one who knows the necessary languages is in a better position to assess the evidence.

This discussion of textual criticism has been brief.[11] The experts always know much more and have superior experience at this task. But there are things the novice can do. Access to the proper tools is necessary. For those who do not read the biblical languages, a good study Bible is essential. I would recommend the NRSV Oxford Study Bible or the NRSV Harper Collins Study Bible. They have two types of notes. One type provides the reader with explanations and comments on the text. These notes occupy the bottom of the page. The second type of notes relates to the text. For instance, the NRSV Harper Collins Study Bible has a note on Genesis 9:10. At the end of the verse, there is a superscript lowercase letter "a" after the word "ark". The text note identified by the lower case "a" is found at the bottom of the right column. It says, "Gk: Heb adds *every animal of the earth.*" The note means that both the Septuagint text (Gk) and Hebrew texts (i.e., the Masoretic text) have ark, but the Masoretic text (Heb) also has the additional phrase "every animal of the earth."

Therefore, a quality study Bible can alert the careful reader to places where significant differences occur in the manuscripts. These study Bibles do not make notes on all the different variations, but only on the most important ones. For those who do not read Hebrew or Greek but want to know about significant textual variations, a commentary that observes and explains many of the textual concerns is necessary.[12]

THE WORTH OF TRANSLATIONS

Our English Bibles are translations of biblical texts. The Old Testament is written in ancient Semitic languages known as Hebrew and Aramaic. Aramaic is similar to Hebrew, and Jesus would have spoken that language. The

New Testament is written in Greek. Therefore, the Bible has to be translated from those languages into our own language.

A translation is to an extent an interpretation. A word in Hebrew may have many possible meanings. The translator has to decide which English word best renders the meaning of the text. Simply substituting an English word for the Hebrew word does not assure a proper translation. The same is true with the New Testament. Replacing Hebrew or Greek words with English words may yield translations that make little or no sense. Even when the translator tries to be as literal as possible, he or she must make decisions about how to make the text understandable to an English speaking audience. As a result, translation bleeds over into interpretation.

To illustrate this point, we can examine the Book of Ecclesiastes. In this book, the Hebrew word *hebel*[13] has a broad range of meanings. The Hebrew noun, *hebel*, can mean breath, breeze, nothingness, vanity, temporality, transitory, show, or absurdity. The exact meaning depends on its use in a particular context. The translator has to decide which English word makes the most sense of the Book of Ecclesiastes. The choice one makes affects the meaning of the book. For instance, vanity may imply an apathetic or defeatist attitude. Temporality, however, has different implications. It may simply express a view that things lack permanence. Both choices (vanity or temporality) are possible. Michael V. Fox, for instance, translates *hebel* as absurdity and reads the entire book from that perspective.[14] Clearly, translators and interpreters do not agree on which word is best. The meaning the translator assigns to this word shapes the readers' understanding of the entire book. In effect, even translations such as the King James Bible or the Revised Standard Version are also interpretations. The reader has no other choice but to try to make sense of the words before him or her.

HISTORICAL RECONSTRUCTION

The concept of historical reconstruction is actually familiar to modern readers. Imagine finding a human skeleton while walking along a path beside the river. After the shock, one would contact the authorities. The authorities would secure the crime scene and collect all the evidence they can find. The evidence is necessary because it allows police to figure out what happened. They are trying to reconstruct the events leading up to the death of this person as well as determining how the person died. Is it a natural death or murder? DNA, hair, and fiber, as we all know from detective shows, are the things that allow the police to reconstruct the events that preceded and led up to the death of the individual. Detective work is also necessary. One must look into all aspects of the death in order to learn what happened. Reconstruction is about working backward from what we have to discover and understand something in the past.

Historical reconstruction in biblical studies is an attempt to uncover the earliest form of a text. It is like peeling an onion working ones way back through the layers to the core. So it works to strip away the layers of the text to uncover its earliest form. Historical studies, therefore, describe the development of a text. In this way, historical critics can show how it came to be as we have it today. Historical critics may also tend to value the earlier form of the text over the final form. Again using Genesis as an example, historical critics may focus on the development of the book. The oldest parts of Genesis may date to the time of Solomon in the tenth century BCE. Other texts may date as late as the fifth century BCE. Historical critics can work their way back to the earliest form of Genesis dating to the tenth century B.C.E. Only after several hundred years of development do we get the Book of Genesis as it is now.

Where does the evidence for historical reconstruction come from? It comes from what the biblical texts say, from what historians can discover about the time and place these texts emerge, from what archeology can tell us, and from what other sources of that time reveal. We may have non-biblical texts and inscriptions from the ancient Near East that fills in some gaps. Archaeology may uncover artifacts or survey sites that can provide vital information about how people lived in biblical times. Sociological methods or models can help one understand the social dynamics of these past societies. Historical reconstruction attempts to learn all it can about the author and his or her audience. By employing social methods, the historian can enlarge his or her understanding of past societies by focusing on the relation between small communities in relation to the larger social world. All of this work can benefit one's effort to understand the text from its earliest history to the present.

Archaeology and the social sciences can supplement the information present in biblical texts. This supplementation is necessary because the biblical writers do not always provide modern readers with a great deal of information about the lives of common people at any given historical period. The biblical stories often focus more on the main individuals and events. For instance, 1 and 2 Samuel focuses on the exploits of King David and those associated with the royal court. It does not describe in any detail the lifestyle of the peasants living in the countryside. For modern readers, filling in the gaps can help us connect to that day and time.

From the historical perspective, the audience of interest is not modern day audiences but historical ones. Paul's letter to the Corinthians, for example, is not addressed to a modern audience; it is addressed to a group of people living in Corinth during the middle of the first century CE. The one who wishes to understand a text today must first try to understand the historical and social world of the author and audience of the past. In the case of Corinthians, the historical approach would focus on the Roman world in general and Corinth, a city in the province of Achaia, in particular.

HISTORICAL QUESTIONS

We have already noted several historical questions: How do biblical texts come to exist in their present form? Who writes the text and why? When is the text written? To whom is it written? What is the text about? What is the location or historical setting for the author and audience? To illustrate how these questions shape the historical discussion, we can look at the following topics: authorship, date, motivation, and audience.

The two most fundamental historical questions concern who (i.e., authorship) and when (i.e., date). A historical approach begins with the investigation of composition and date of a writing. Sometimes the order is an issue. Should I begin with the author or date? At times, determining the date may help to limit the possible authors. For instance, most New Testament scholars believe 1 and 2 Timothy and Titus date near the end of the first century or early second century. Moreover, most agree, even though Acts does not record Paul's death, that Paul is executed under the Roman Emperor Nero in Rome before 68 CE. If true, Paul is dead before the composition of 1 and 2 Timothy and Titus. That rules him out as the possible author of these letters.

On the other hand, the date may not be a deciding factor. The date has no bearing on whether Paul wrote Galatians or 1 Corinthians. In some cases, we never know the name of the person who composes a text. While tradition may ascribe the book of Hebrews to Paul, for example, modern scholars are not able to identify the author with certainty.

Determining the author of a modern work such as War of the Worlds is not a problem. Most people do not attempt to conceal their identity as authors. For instance, there is no problem with identifying Dan Brown as the author of *Angels and Demons*. In biblical literature, however, things are not that simple. The notion of individual authorship is not strong in the Bible. Biblical texts originate, and they are preserved in communities. As a result, their composition reflects a collective activity. In many cases, the author is not identified in the text.

Consider the superscriptions in the Book of Psalms. These superscriptions come before many of the Psalms in the Old Testament. Some member or members of the faith community in Jerusalem probably added the superscriptions to the already completed Psalms. Some people use these superscriptions as indicators of authorship. This tendency accounts for the widespread belief that David is the author of the Psalms. Superscriptions do not actually identify the author. A number of Psalms have the following superscription: "A

Psalm of David." In Hebrew, the preposition attached to David's name is l^e. This preposition can have a broad range of meanings. It can mean to, for, towards, belonging to, in regards to, according to, by, and in.[15] The Psalm of David does not rule David out as the author, but it does not identify him as the author either. It can mean Psalms written for or about David. More likely, it refers to the liturgical collection from which the Psalm comes.[16] Clearly, David is not the author of the Book of Psalms. Forty-three superscriptions do not attribute the psalm to David, and 34 psalms do not have any superscription.[17] Additionally, the language of the Psalms is so general that it is not possible to determine the author of particular Psalms.[18]

A similar example occurs in the New Testament with the titles for the Gospels. The title, "According to Matthew," reflects the tradition that goes back to Papias, an early church leader. In the early second century CE, Papias identifies the author of Matthew's Gospel as Matthew the tax collector and one of the twelve disciples. Historical criticism begins by assessing such claims of authorship. The author does not name himself or herself as the author in the body of the Gospel. The title, According to Matthew, is added later and is not part of the original text. Therefore, the Gospel is technically anonymous.

In other cases, books such as Isaiah and Genesis have more than one author. In these particular situations, biblical texts have come together over an extended period of time through a process of editing, reworking, transmission, copying, and preserving. To illustrate this point, consider the Pentateuch.

According to tradition, Moses wrote these books. Modern biblical scholarship, however, identified at least four different authors working in four different historical periods. These authors were totally unknown. All scholars could do was to describe each author in relation to his or her composition. These authors were active in four different historical periods. Portions of these five books date to the tenth century BCE, others date to the eighth century, others to the seventh, and still others to the sixth or fifth centuries. These books emerged in their present form over years of editing, copying, and preservation by people who valued these works.

Scholars adopted the practice of assigning specific designations to unknown authors. Keeping with the illustration of the Pentateuch, the four unknown authors were distinguished from each other by different letters of the alphabet. J stood for a source composed in the tenth century BCE. E stood for a source written in the eighth century. D was a source from the seventh or sixth century BCE, and the P source dated to the sixth century BCE. The letter designations were not arbitrary. They related to the time, place, style, language, and concerns of each unknown author.

For the sake of illustration, we can consider one of these four authors. P is the letter selected to identify the latest source. Interpreters call this source P because the author or authors are priest/s. Scholars identify the P source based on the use of the divine name, the style of the text, the language, and the concerns expressed in the text. P writes sometime in the sixth or fifth centuries BCE. Once the modern interpreter identifies the P source, he or she interprets it in light of the historical circumstances. Other historical questions come into play as well. Whom is this priestly writer addressing? Why does this priestly writer compose his work as he does? What is the message P wants to convey? How might the audiences respond to P?

Imagine that P wrote at a time shortly after the Babylonians had taken many of Jerusalem's inhabitants away to Babylon. These people are now exiles in Babylon. About forty-eight years later with the rise of a new and powerful nation, ancient Israel's fate turns; a new Persian king allows them to return to their homeland. Those who return experience hard times. The task before them is to rebuild what the Babylonians destroyed. P addresses a people who have experienced these hard times. What does P have to say to these people, and why is P writing to them? What is P's message for them? One could examine all of the Priestly texts in the Pentateuch and see how they might speak to the needs of these particular people.

One could pursue an answer to these questions on a small or large scale. On a small scale, one could look at specific texts and see how they speak to the situation during the post-exilic period. On a large scale, the reader could see the priestly work as a whole and ask how it speaks to that same situation. Consider here the small scale.

Genesis 1 is a well-known chapter from the Bible. It tells about the creation of the world. What might this chapter have to say to a post-exilic audience? Scholars have long noted the influence of foreign creation myths in Genesis. Some elements in Genesis 1 reflect the Babylonian creation myth. In this Babylonian myth, the goddess Tiamat battles against Marduk. In reality, this struggle is between the powers of order and chaos. Certainly the ancient Israelites could relate to the notion of the societal order giving way to chaos. They remember losing their homes and livelihood. They remember being uprooted and transplanted into a foreign land.

In Genesis 1, however, these powers of chaos are not gods. They are forces under the control of God. In Babylon, the sun, moon, and stars are gods. For the ancient Israelites, the sun, moon, and stars are objects of God's creation and under God's control. One might read this text at a time when things seem bad and find the courage to believe that the order present in creation can again be present in this new and uncertain time. It may provide motivation for people to rebuild their lives. They may see that they too have a part in renewing their community. Biblical scholar, Walter Brueggemann, identifies Genesis 1:28 as a key phrase in the Priestly text, and he suggests that this formula "be fruitful and multiply, and fill the earth and subdue it" locates the main theme for the entire priestly work.[19] Such an emphasis would speak to that historical context. This brief and general description should be enough to illustrate how the historical setting can illuminate the understanding of a biblical text.

APPLICATION

An offshoot of historical study concerns application. How can one apply an ancient text to a modern world? While historical questions focus on what the text "meant" in its original historical context, the application moves toward an understanding of what the text means for us today. Krister Stendahl distinguishes between what a text meant versus what it means.[20] The two questions are related. What did Paul's words in 1 Corinthians mean to the Corinthian church? This is a historical question. But we can move on to apply that meaning to the present. It requires one to translate the original meaning into a related meaning for the present.

Other terms like demythologizing and recontextualizing reflect the same tendency. It is all about understanding a text in its historical and social context before attempting to understand that message in a present context. Recontextualizing, for instance, means that one has to take the original meaning and transpose it into a different historical context.

Above we have focused on how to discover what a text meant in its own historical setting. If one's interest is purely historical, the discussion can stop there. If one wonders how that meaning applies beyond its original context, then, one has to apply the text to a new and different historical setting. New Testament writers did something similar when they applied Old Testament passages to their own contemporary situations. It is true that they would not have viewed what they were doing in this particular light. In ancient interpretation and preservation of texts, there is a consistent interest in updating traditions. The update allows texts to speak in new and different circumstances even if they do not stress the original meaning. The distinction between what it meant and what it means is more of a modern one. To go beyond the historical, therefore, is to press toward a theological understanding of the text.

To show how one might apply a text to the present, I return to the P source discussed above. These priestly writers tell us the story of creation. As mentioned above, this story might encourage and motivate people to start over. How would a modern reader informed by this historical information understand the message for his or her own day? The issue of Genesis 1 is creation. God creates everything and establishes order and stability allowing life on this planet to flourish. This order allows societies to emerge and exist. It allows laws to emerge that provide protection and normalcy. The created order also allows for the development of human institutions that organize human activities for the benefit of everyone. The order then is one side of life, and it provides the possibility for meaningful human relationships. In the midst of chaos or bad times, the social order provides hope for future and a goal for human activity.

The past can also serve as a warning. The P account throughout the Pentateuch makes it clear that order depends upon human choices. Laws provide the people with guidance on how to live their lives. Breaking laws have consequences. One can understand the breakdown of the created order as a result of the consequence for bad actions. While modern readers may not share this exact causal explanation for bad times, there is a sense in which one's behavior can have a good or bad effect on the social order. The actions of leaders can produce harmony and good will or conflict and hostility. Therefore, one message that we can draw from the Priestly writings is that the created order depends upon proper human action.

Also, this passage may reinforce one's trust in an orderly universe in which God is in control. Knowledge of the Babylonian story of creation may alert the modern reader to the constant threat to order. We also live in a world where the order of our lives can be shattered by the loss of a job, the death of a family member, the downturn in the economy, or the destruction of things we hold dear. In the midst of these troubles, we can find hope in a passage like Genesis 1. God cares for God's creation. God cares for us.

This creation story shows that God creates life and then provides for it so we can grow and thrive.[21] Prospering or thriving, however, does not have to be equated with material rewards of wealth. Prospering does not mean life is always easy. One may also find in this passage a sense of responsibility for taking care of this created world. Having dominion over the created world does not provide humanity with a license to exploit and destroy what God created. It is a duty to preserve and take care of God's creation. We should see ourselves as caretakers.

CONCLUSION

This chapter has described a general historical approach. The next chapter describes the basic historical background from which we can understand the stories of the Hebrew Bible and New Testament. This historical description provides a brief context to understand the basic flow of biblical history. It does not cover the details but provides a general description. The description begins with ancient Israel before the development of the monarchy and extends through the time of the New Testament.

NOTES

1. John H. Hayes and Carl R. Holladay, *Biblical Exegesis: A Beginner's Handbook* (Atlanta: John Knox Press, 1982), 35–37.

2. Ibid., 35–36.

3. Ibid., 36.

4. Lim, *The Dead Sea Scrolls*, 38.

5. Martin Abegg, Peter Flint, and Eugene Ulrich *The Dead Sea Scrolls Bible: The Oldest Known Bible Translated for the First Time into English* (San Francisco: HarperCollins, 1999), 630–631. This book translates all of the biblical texts found in the Dead Sea Scrolls.

6. Hayes and Holladay, 31.

7. Ernst Würthwein, *The Texts of the Old Testament: An Introduction to the Biblica Hebraica*, 2d ed., trans Erroll F. Rhodes (Grand Rapids: William B. Eerdmans Publishing Company, 1995), 11.

8. Ibid.

9. For a good description of this translation see Bruce M. Metzger, *The Bible in Translation: Ancient and English Versions* (Grand Rapids: Baker Academic, 2001), 13–20.

10. Würthwein, 114.

11. For more help see Hayes and Holladay, 30–41; Würthwein 105–132.

12. There are a number of good commentaries such as The Anchor Bible Commentary, Hermeneia: Critical Commentary on the Bible, and the International Critical Commentary.

13. It is pronounced *hevel.*

14. Michael V. Fox, *A Time to Tear Down & A Time to Build Up: A Rereading of Ecclesiastes* (Grand Rapids: William B. Eerdmans Publishing Company, 1999).

15. Francis Brown, S.R. Driver and C.A. Briggs, *Hebrew and English Lexicon of the Old Testament With An Appendix Containing The Biblical Aramaic*, ed Francis Brown (Oxford: Oxford Press 1906) 510–518.

16. W. H. Bellinger, *Psalms: Reading and Studying the Book of Praises* (Peabody: Hendrickson Publishers, 1990), 8–12.

17. Bernhard W. Anderson with Steven Bishop, *Out of the Depths: The Psalms Speak for Us Today*, 3d ed. Revised and expanded, (Louisville: Westminster John Knox Press, 2000) 17.

18. Bellinger, 15–16.

19. Walter Brueggemann and Hans Walter Wolff, *The Vitality of the Old Testament Traditions*, 2d ed., (Atlanta: John Knox Press, 1982), 101–113.

20. Krister Stendahl, "Biblical Theology, Contemporary," in *Interpreters Bible Dictionary* vol. A-D (Nashville: Abingdon Press, 1962), 418–432.

21. Claus Westermann, *Elements of Old Testament Theology*, trans. Douglas W. Stott (Atlanta: John Knox Press, 1982), 102–117.

Chapter Three

A Brief History of Biblical Times

HISTORICAL VALUE OF THE BIBLE

Historical descriptions of the biblical material depend upon the one telling the story. Some people naively recount the stories of the Bible as actual history. Those scholars on the other extreme see limited historical value in the biblical stories. Neither extreme is desirable. An approach that avoids the extremes seems best. A modern historian focuses on cause and effect. Focusing on why something happened leads to the question of cause. What caused things to happen a certain way? To understand why things happen, they need all the information available.

The first challenge for the historian is the lack of sources. Imagine how much video, audio, and written material we possess on modern day presidents. By contrast, we have meager information on ancient Israel and the rise of Christianity outside the Bible. Without the Bible, the historian would not even know Abraham, Isaac, Solomon, or hardly any other biblical figure existed. We would know almost nothing about Jesus. Without the Bible or other literature related to it, only the archeologist or historian might know of a David or Jesus and they would know precious little. The Bible, therefore, is indispensable as a source for a history of ancient Israel and early Christianity. Without it, one might not even care to write such a history. This fact points to the immense influence of the Bible on the world.

Yet, how does the Bible measure up as a source for history? Fundamentalists simply accept every word of it as literal Truth. They read it as a book on history and science. Historians who study ancient Israel or Rome, however, have to follow certain guidelines. These guidelines make them historians rather than theologians. Historians must seek earthly causes to explain historical events. Otherwise, they move away from the field of history toward something else.

Is the Bible a book that can tell us what actually happened? Is the entire Bible meant to be history? These are not simple questions. To keep the discussion brief, I would say that the Bible contains history. Nevertheless, the Bible is not a history book. What is the difference? The Bible is not a history book in any modern sense. It does, however, contain history (i.e., real events and actions of real people). Its purpose though is not to produce an objective and neutral account of what actually happened. Strictly objective and neutral reporting is more of a modern concern.

Consequently, we can say that the biblical writers are not historians in the modern sense of the word. They tell stories for some of the same reasons we do. The stories functioned to entertain, warn, teach, inform, and call people to repent. The stories may reflect real events. Some stories may not have happened at all or not the way they are related. Regardless, biblical writers are not investigators trying to determine what actually happened. Often they may come closer to being theologians. They attempt to communicate what events mean.

Modern historians, however, want to know what happened, when it happened, the circumstances surrounding the event, and why it happened. The modern historian cannot be faithful to his or her discipline without looking for the chain of cause and effect. Moreover, the modern historian cannot explain events by recourse to supernatural causes. As a historian, he or she must look for natural explanations. A historian may believe as an act of faith that God caused certain events. As a historian, however, he or she must stick to the mundane.

Historians must be able to provide evidence from the material world that one thing influenced or caused another. Faith alone cannot establish historical reality or probability. Therefore, these two areas need to remain separate. A historian must try to remain objective and neutral. These are goals that one can approach. By separating the natural from the supernatural, one may be able to be more objective than if the two areas mix.

If, then, the Bible is not a history book what is it? The Bible is a collection of literature that contains historical information. The literature contains both poetry and narrative. Some of the writings express the faith of a people. In other words, some of the biblical material is theological in nature. This theological nature is conveyed through historical and non-historical materials. Biblical writers may tell a story to promote a theological, social, or political perspective.

So, biblical writers do not write history for the sake of history. Still one might describe some of the writers as historians in a pre-modern sense. John Van Seters identifies certain sections of the Hebrew Bible as history in this ancient sense. Ancient historians include myths, legends, and symbolic stories in their historical accounts. They fit these events into a "genealogical chronology."[1] Van Seters argues that Genesis as a whole is a type of ancient history. It is similar to other Ancient Near Eastern accounts of its people's past. These ancient histories explain the present situation by reference to the past.[2] Early or pre-modern histories of this type have no problem with including myths or legends in their accounts. They have no problem with supernatural causality. In these ways, and perhaps others, ancient histories differ from a modern historical description of ancient Israel and the Greco-Roman world of the first and second centuries CE.

Consequently, from a modern perspective the Bible is not a book of history. Its writers did not seek to establish all the facts and create a neutral and objective description of these facts. They did not attempt to access the historical value of their sources. Biblical writers relate stories and information from their own life experiences and faith perspectives. The Bible is simply not a literal account of what happened in many cases. Sometimes they are concerned with teaching moral lessons or theological ideals, and other times they may set out to tell a good story that entertains their audiences. Parables, for example, are not literally stories of what happened. They contain truths about God and humanity, but they are not historical stories.

Truths that emerge from biblical stories and poems are not necessarily historical in nature. Stories and myths may transcend actual chronological accounts of what actually happened. Stories and myths, however, can convey truths. The creation account in Genesis 1 affirms the view that God is responsible for all creation. Whether creation occurred in an instant or over seven days or even over a much longer period does not really matter. Scientists may be concerned with what happened in the first second of creation, but the biblical texts are not concerned with scientific or historical accuracy. For the biblical writers, it is more about the meaning of creation. What does it mean to be part of God's created order? And what is the nature of this creator and his or her creation? What does it all mean for us? What does it teach us about our place in the world? These are questions that are not dependent upon historical or scientific accuracy.

Finally, one should also keep in mind that what modern historians say about ancient history is rarely certain. While there are things that are fairly certain, a complete and accurate description of life in Palestine or Rome during biblical times is a goal that one can only partially obtain. It is based on the facts at hand. Nevertheless, it is a human interpretation of those supposed facts and, therefore, it is subject to error. Paula McNutt says, "History is what historians can convince us 'probably' happened. But this 'probably' is always subject to revision."[3]

Modern historians of ancient Israel and early Christianity must consult every possible source of information that can help provide an acceptable history. Sources include the Bible, extra-biblical materials, and archeological findings. The Ugaritic texts, for instance, constitute significant sources of information. Found in Syria on the Mediterranean Sea, they help scholars of the Hebrew Bible understand specific biblical texts better. Additionally, the Ugaritic language is similar to biblical Hebrew. The Ugaritic materials can help scholars improve modern translations of the Hebrew Bible. They may also draw from archeology and the social sciences to gain a complete picture of life during biblical times.

HISTORY OF ANCIENT ISRAEL

Where should the historian begin writing a history of ancient Israel? At what point are there sufficient sources for a historical description of ancient Israelite society. Scholars do not agree on the beginning point. Some begin with the patriarchs, others with the time just before the monarchy, others with the monarchy, and others even later. Historians debate whether the patriarchal period reflects real historical circumstances in Palestine between 1700–1300 BCE. For some, it may be disturbing to find out that even the historical validity of the exodus is now in doubt although some traditions about the exodus may reflect actual historical circumstances.[4]

Whether the exodus happened as described in the Book of Exodus or whether these traditions are only partially anchored in history, the story of the exodus is crucial for ancient Israel's faith. That much is fact. This tradition tells how Moses brings the people of ancient Israel out of Egypt and into the wilderness. It continues with their taking of the land of Canaan and becoming a nation. This theme of God and Moses as liberators is one of the major theological themes in the Bible. It is possible that a significant liberation experience serves as the basis for this powerful story. While the biblical account may exaggerate the details, a liberation event of some kind may stand behind the exodus story. With that in mind, I begin our story of the Bible's history with the period after the exodus and before the emergence of the monarchy.

PRE-MONARCHIC ISRAEL AND THE PERIOD OF THE JUDGES

The history of the pre-monarchic period in ancient Israel is a rather complex topic and requires more explanation than many of the other periods of time. Scholars and archeologists are not in complete agreement concerning the origin of the people we call Israelites. Some would begin the story of ancient Israel with the patriarchs beginning with Abraham. Abraham's family left "Ur of the Chaldeans to go into the land of Canaan" (Gn 11:31). John Bright, an American biblical historian, has attempted to show how the stories about the patriarchs are consistent with what we know of the world during that time. According to Bright, Abraham was a part of the Amorite movement of peoples who entered Palestine from the outside.[5] He dates the patriarchs after 2,000 B.C.E. likely around 1700 B.C.E. The end of the patriarchal period would occur when the Israelites end up in Egypt around the around 1300 B.C.E.

This older view is not widely accepted today. It seems likely that the early Israelites originate sometime in the latter years of the thirteenth century BCE or the twelfth century BCE. Many of the events recounted in the book of the Judges take place during this time. This period precedes the establishment of a united monarchy around 1,000 BCE. There is broad agreement among biblical scholars and archeologists that the ancient Israelites are indigenous to the land of Palestine. They do not come into the land and conquer the peoples living in it. Sometime in the twelfth century BCE, these people came together forming a new people known as Israelites. These early Israelites initially settle in what is known as the central highlands of Palestine.

Some scholars suggest that these peoples come together around a common set of ideals or ideology. The nature of this ideology would include a rejection of certain oppressive practices associated with the Canaanite city-states, and it may also have had a religious component. If the exodus traditions played a part in bringing certain indigenous Canaanite elements together, then their God would be a liberator. Yahweh sides with the poor and oppressed. In short, their rejection of certain values and practices associated with the city-states may have helped them develop a common identity.

The cooperation takes place locally where several extended families live together with others forming small clans or villages. In some ways, these villages may remind one of the ways modern day Amish communities live together in close proximity and often work together for the sake of the whole. New technologies such as cisterns for catching water and terrace farming help the villages make the most of the land on which they settle.

Cooperation would also be necessary for defense purposes. Small threats may have been dealt with by the villages, whereas more severe threats may involve a larger association of people at the level of the tribe. At a broader level, different tribes in close proximity may come together for defense or perhaps on occasion for religious ceremonies.

There are, however, other views concerning the origins of the ancient Israelites. Israeli archeologist, Israel Finkelstein, posits a view of early Israel based solely on the archeological evidence. Based on his interpretation of this data, early Israelites were local peoples in Canaan. They were originally of nomadic origin. When the Canaanite city-states and villages were no longer able to create a surplus of grain for trade, the early Israelite nomads had to settle down in the central hill country and produce the grain for themselves around 1200 B.C.E.[6]

According to Finkelstein, there is not much that one can say about ancient Israel's uniqueness. It is not even possible to say with certainty that the settlements in the highlands are Israelite settlements. The only archeological evidence for an ethnic connection between these peoples and the Israelites is the lack of pig bones at any of these sites.[7]

Another place where many people expect to find Israelite uniqueness is in the area of religion. There is almost no information from the archeological record about the religion of such persons. That is not surprising. These peoples did not produce written texts. They would have been illiterate like most peoples of that day. Consequently, there would be no firsthand accounts of their religious beliefs and practices in the archeological records. We can assume that religion would have been significant to them as it was to every culture of that day.

Also, no weapons have been found suggesting that these people were peaceful agrarians. They were relatively isolated. The population estimate for these villages of the hill country is 45,000 people. There is no evidence that this society was stratified since the material finds indicate a relatively equal distribution of wealth among the families.[8]

Regardless of how the early Israelites arose, one can describe them as peasants or subsistence agrarians living off the land. They live in a three-tiered society. The smallest level is the *bêt 'āb* or extended family. The extended family includes the nuclear family living in one house in connection with one or two other individual houses. Together this grouping makes up a "family organization and residency at the level of the extended family."[9] The next level would be the village or clan (*mišpāḥâ*). The village would consist of several extended families living in close proximity to one another. The largest grouping occurs at the level of the tribe.[10] The tribe would include a group of villages or clans located in a particular geographical region.

In this kind of social setting, no significant disparity exists between rich and poor. That is not to say that ancient Israel is strictly an egalitarian society. Some distinctions in social status do exist. There are elders or those who have a leading role in that society. Still, these people would share similar social statuses and cooperate on joint projects for the benefit of the community.

American archeologist, William G. Dever, concludes that the general picture of the "proto-Israelites" in the 13th-12th centuries is consistent with the narrative accounts in Judges and much of 1-2 Samuel.[11] The general cultural picture and the view of the family in Judges are consistent with what is known about the proto-Israelites from the archeological record.[12]

In this early social setting, judges play a key leadership role at the tribal level. Elders serve in the smaller groupings of villages to help manage the affairs of the people. Therefore, the elders have an important role in the time before the monarchy. People who had developed a common identity and a common set of beliefs and values cooperate with each other when necessary for survival whether that requires fending off enemies or helping one's neighbor. Over time, however, the growing division between the poor agrarians and the wealthier landowners helps bring about the conditions that initiate ancient Israel's development into a state or nation.

THE UNITED MONARCHY

Over time, the biblical texts say that many of the people in ancient Israel call for a king so they can be like the other nations (1 Sm 8:5). This initiates a period of time known as the united monarchy. We can begin our story with King David. The story below is largely based on biblical texts. Nevertheless, one should keep in mind that the actual history of the united monarchy may be less impressive than the picture depicted by the Bible. Jerusalem, for example, at the beginning of the monarchy would have had a relatively small population. Proof of monumental architecture during this time is disputed. Outside of the Bible, there is only one mention of David during the period of the monarchy and none for Solomon. Below is the story as portrayed mostly in the biblical books of 1 and 2 Samuel and 1 and 2 Kings.

David is the first real king in ancient Israel. According to the biblical texts, disagreement occurs over the issue of kingship. Some of the population wished to maintain the old ways where judges and elders plan and organize the small communities. According to 1 Samuel 8, other people want a king like the other nations. While this text seems to pit Samuel against all the elders of Israel, surely many people side with Samuel's views. The premonarchic social structure would have likely been more beneficial for the majority of the ancient Israelite population of that time. Samuel tells the people gathered at Ramah all the bad things that come with kingship, but they still call for a king.

The emergence of the monarchy in ancient Israel, however, brings a growing social stratification and an increasing economic difference between people. The interests and values of those living in the rural communities at subsistence level would have been at odds with those persons who were associated with the more advanced towns. The king would help to protect the small groups scattered throughout the rural areas of the central highlands (i.e., Galilee in the north, Samaria in the center, and Judah in the south). Yet, he would also begin practices that benefit some peoples with land, wealth, and status. The peasants or poor agrarians would remain poor.

Samuel sees the emergence of a king as a rejection of his own leadership (1 Sm 8:4–9). Nevertheless, the text says that God instructs Samuel to be part of the process of choosing a king. This process leads to the selection of Saul.

With David, the united Monarchy emerges. This event takes place around 1,000 BCE.

This arrangement, however, does not last long. With the death of David's son, Solomon, the united monarchy ends around 920 B.C.E. During this time, David has established the city of Jerusalem as the capital of the kingdom. David's son, Solomon, has followed or succeeded his father as king. According to 2 Samuel 9–20 and 1 Kings 1–2, his succession meets with considerable opposition. With the help of key people, Solomon is successful in gaining the throne over his elder brother. This is no small accomplishment since people in that culture expect the elder brother to take over for his father in both the family and political settings. [13]

The stories about David's sons suggest that there is a tension not only in the royal family but also between the northern and southern regions of the country. One of David's sons, Absalom, tries to benefit from that division to no avail. His attempt to take the throne ends in his death (2 Sm 18). As pointed out, Solomon's succession to his father's throne is contested by his elder brother Adonijah. The tension between northern elements and the people of Judah comes to a head later at Solomon's death. Before his death, Solomon engages in a number of building projects including the construction of the temple and his palace. These projects put a heavy burden on the people in terms of forced labor and taxes. As a result, the people call for change.

THE DIVIDED MONARCHY

At Solomon's death, the kingdom splits into northern and southern kingdoms around 920 B.C.E. The division occurs because of Solomon's oppression of the people. Solomon divides the kingdom into twelve administrative districts responsible for the needs of the king (1 Kings 4:6–7). He not only taxes the people but also uses forced labor of the people (1 Kings 5:13) for his building projects such as the temple and his palace. These actions lead to problems. The people ask Solomon's son, Rehoboam, to ease their load. Rehoboam, after consultation with his advisors, declines. In fact, he promises to make things harder. This response leads to rebellion and the split of the kingdom. Rehoboam manages to hang on to the southern part of the kingdom.

The first king in the new northern kingdom is Jeroboam (i.e., Jeroboam I). The northern kingdom is known as Ephraim or Israel while the southern kingdom comes to be known as Judah. According to archeologists, the northern kingdom is much more powerful and wealthy. This period in ancient Israelite history is often referred to as the divided monarchy. Both the north and south had their own kings and the two kingdoms never again united even though hopes for a united monarchy continued.

The two separate kingdoms remain intact for about two hundred years. In 722/721 BCE, the kingdom of Assyria is the major power in the region. The Assyrians are a threat to both the northern and southern kingdoms along with Syria and other countries in the area. Syria and Israel forge an alliance and try to bring Judah into their coalition. Jerusalem manages to stay neutral. Israel and Syria's actions lead to their own destruction. The northern kingdom, Israel, falls to the Assyrians in 721 BCE. The inhabitants of the north are taken off and scattered by the Assyrians. The reference to the ten lost tribes stems from this event.

The southern kingdom manages to survive over a hundred years longer. Their refusal to join the northern kingdom extends their existence. After the fall of the Assyrians and the destruction of the capital (Nineveh) in 612 BCE, the Babylonians emerge as the dominate power. By 586 BCE, the Babylonians destroy the Jerusalem temple and the city of Judah taking many of its inhabitants into Babylonian captivity. This action begins the period known as the Babylonian Exile. The southern kingdom falls in 586 BCE, and with it the monarchy comes to an end. The promises made to David in 2 Samuel 7:11–29 about always having an heir to the throne is dead. It is a period of great soul searching for the Jewish people. A belief in a future messiah who will be from the line of David, however, takes on a prominent place in Jewish and Christian thought.

THE EXILIC AND POST-EXILIC PERIODS

The Babylonian Exile lasts until 538 BCE. This year marks the beginning of the restoration, a period when the Persian King Cyrus allows Jews to return to their homeland. Cyrus is a tolerant ruler for that day, and he is described by Isaiah 45:1 as a Messianic figure. Isaiah 40–55 dates to the time of Cyrus, and they view this Persian king as an instrument of Yahweh, literally Yahweh's anointed.

In 538 BCE, Cyrus issues an edict that allows the Jewish people to leave Babylon and return to their homeland (2 Chr 36:22–23). Many Jews, however, decide to remain in Babylon; many of them had made a life for themselves there. They do not look forward to returning to a land in ruin and starting over again. By 515 BCE, the Jews who did return rebuilt the temple in Jerusalem and tried to restore life to normal. The monarchy, however, is over for good.

The remaining years of the Persian control over the Palestinian region are sometimes referred to as the restoration. Men like Ezra and Nehemiah try to rebuild the lives of people in Judah. Ezra may have been active on into the first part of the fourth century B.C.E. Nevertheless, not much information exists about life in Judah during these years and beyond.

From a broader perspective, the Greeks and Persians engage in continued conflict. Greek sources do provide us with historical accounts of these conflicts. Alexander the Great defeats the Persians in 331 BCE. Alexander himself does not have much of an effect on Judea, but his successors do. They set in motion a process known as Hellenization that has a significant impact on this region.

After Alexander's death, his empire is divided. Two groups of rulers are important in relation to biblical history: the Ptolemies and Seleucids. In the third century, the Ptolemies control Egypt and the land of Judea. During this time, conditions in Palestine are stable, but there is a growing Greek influence. The Seleucids gain control over Judea by the end of the third century. This occurrence brings about a crisis and a clash of cultures. At one time, people in Palestine accept and adopt aspects of the Greek culture. That is not the case later.

The Seleucid leader Antiochus IV Epiphanies forces the Hellenization process on the Jewish people (see for instance 2 Maccabees 6:7–17). Antiochus IV defiles the Jerusalem temple, ends sacrifice, bans the observance of the Sabbath and traditional feasts, destroys copies of the Torah, and stops the long-held Jewish practice of circumcision.

The book of I Maccabees provides a description of his acts. The biblical book of Daniel may also have been written during this period, and much of its content reflects this historical situation. The harsh actions of Antiochus IV lead to a Jewish revolt led by Judas Maccabaeus. The Jews win their independence against Antiochus IV in the second century BCE. Before the successful revolt concludes, the temple is rededicated in 164 BCE. The Jewish people are commanded to celebrate and remember this event each year. The event is known as the Festival of Lights or Hanukkah.

THE ROMAN EMPIRE AND THE RISE OF CHRISTIANITY

The next considerable foreign influence on Judea is Rome. Pompey, a Roman general, takes possession of Jerusalem in 63 B.C.E. In the Roman provincial system, Rome brings the people of the Mediterranean region into a unified whole. The Romans value and maintain a strong sense of order. The region of Palestine during this time includes Judea, Samaria, and Galilee.

THE LIFE OF JESUS

Jesus comes from a small town in Galilee. This region has also experienced the Hellenization process. As a result, Jesus experiences Greek thought and customs. Even though Jesus grows up in the small town of Nazareth, he is not far from Hellenistic cities such as Sepphoris and Gadara. Sepphoris is only about four miles away from Nazareth, which is a one to two-hour walk.

Outside Christian literature, there is almost no information about Jesus. Jewish historian Josephus refers to Jesus' brother, and in another place, he describes Jesus as a wise person and as one who performs amazing works. He also calls him a teacher and says that he has Jewish and Gentile followers (*Antiquities* 18:63). Clearly, a Christian editor expands Josephus' comments. This Christian editor presents Josephus as one who believes that Jesus is the Messiah. He or she indicates that Josephus accepts the truth of Jesus' resurrection. It is uncertain that Josephus actually holds such views.

Except for Josephus' brief comments on Jesus, there is almost complete silence outside Christian writings on him. The Roman senator and historian, Cornelius Tacitus (20–117 CE), mentions Christ (*Annals* Book 15 verse 44). He dislikes Christianity and his reference to Christianity, and Christ is particularly negative. It is not surprising that Rome did not mention Jesus because neither Jesus nor his followers are viewed as important to non-Christians except for the disturbances they may have caused.

The information in the canonical Gospels focuses on Jesus' public ministry and says little about his childhood years. Matthew 13:55 and Mark 6:3 tell us that Jesus is the son of a carpenter or woodworker. The word woodworker or *tektōn* in Greek locates Jesus economically in a low socio-economic class. Jesus would have encountered other peoples from this socio-economic group. He knows and speaks to their concerns.

Jesus lives and relates to peasants and agrarians. His ministry is largely directed to rural areas and small towns in Judea and Galilee. The apostle Paul, on the other hand, travels and works mostly in larger urban settings. While the images and metaphors of the Gospels have much to do with agrarian life, Paul works and lives in the cities, and his language reflects this reality.

Jesus, Paul, and all the people discussed in the pages of the New Testament lived under the hand of the Romans. The Romans were tolerant in some ways, but they resisted and punished disruptive speech and actions. Anything that threatens the normal workings of the Empire was considered dangerous to the Roman order. For example, calling for the end of slavery or for equality between men and women would have been dangerous acts. Many New Testament scholars believe that is why the New Testament is almost entirely silent on slavery and cautious in other areas as well. Slavery and male dominance were normal in Roman society.

PAUL'S ACTIVITIES

Even though many Roman aristocrats and leaders would have negative views of Christianity, Paul sees the Roman authorities in a positive light. He does not call for civil disobedience and neither does the writer of I Peter. The patrolling of Roman roads made Paul's missionary travel possible. His being able to travel in relative safety allowed for the spread the Gospel throughout the Roman Empire. Things change at the end of the first century and the beginning of the second. The author of Revelation compares Rome to Babylon. By this time, Babylon is described as "Babylon the great, mother of whores and of earth's abominations" (Rv 17:5). Whatever that means, it does not sound good. In short, Christians have to choose between God and Rome at this point. Revelation is generally dated to the end of the first century C.E. or the beginning of the second century.

On the whole, then, Rome with its roads and order makes the spread of Christianity easier and safer. Christianity emerges as a universal religion in the Roman world in the first century C.E. Many Gentiles and Jews become Christian. Other than the Book of Revelation, there is no compelling evidence to suggest that it was the official policy of the Romans to persecute Christianity. In cases where it occurred, it was not based on Roman policy.

Christianity originally was a faction or group within Judaism. Jesus did not set out to create a new religion but to renew the faith of his people. Jesus was Jewish and participated in Jewish life. Scripture for him was the Hebrew Scriptures. His followers and his primary audience were Jewish. Jesus was not rejected by all Jews. He was a threat to many of the traditional Jewish leaders. Eventually, however, Christianity became a separate religion, but it remained closely tied to the Jewish Scripture, faith, and traditions. Jesus and most of his followers were Jews as was Paul and many other church leaders. Christianity retained much of its Jewish flavor even though many anti-Semitic sentiments have fueled attempts to drive the two faiths apart.

Even in the first century CE, the tension between Gentile and Jewish Christians exists. Acts 15 recounts a disagreement between some Jewish Christians and Paul. Some of the Jewish Christians believe that non-Jews have to follow the Torah and be circumcised. Paul rejects this view, and the council at Jerusalem decides the issue. The result is a compromise. The council says that Gentiles do not have to be circumcised to be a Christian. They say, "We should write to them to abstain only from things polluted by idols and from fornication and from whatever has been strangled and from blood" (Acts 15:20). Over time, the gap may have widened, but the two faiths remain closely related. In short, one has to understand Jesus in a Jewish Palestinian context. Other New Testament writings, however, have to be understood in the framework of an urban setting in Rome during the first century.

NEW TESTAMENT BOOKS

The New Testament texts cover a period of at least fifty to sixty years. Paul's letters were written to congregations that he had initiated on one of his missionary journeys. They date from a period of around 12 years or more. The date of Galatians is in dispute, but some would date it to 48–49 C.E. Others date it around five or six years later. If he died in Rome at the hands of Nero, then his work ended in the 60s. The Gospels actually date after Paul's letters. The earliest Gospel is Mark dating perhaps to the late 60s. Some writings such as Revelation date to the end of the first century C.E. or into the first part of the second century C.E.

The above historical description is brief. It provides a general background for the discussion of biblical texts in subsequent chapters. It has painted with broad strokes a look at the general historical and social settings for biblical texts. I have tried not to become too entangled in the details. The next chapter engages an interpretation of several biblical texts using a basic historical approach.

NOTES

1. John Van Seters, "The Pentateuch: Genesis, Exodus, Leviticus, Numbers, Deuteronomy," In *The Hebrew Bible Today: An Introduction to Critical Issues* (eds., Steven L. McKenzie & M. Patrick Graham Westminster John Knox Press, 1998), 22.

2. Ibid.

3. Paula McNutt, *Reconstructing the Society of Ancient Israel* Library of Ancient Israel ed., Douglas A. Knight (Louisville: Westminster John Knox Press, 1999), 214.

4. For details of one possible way of understanding the Exodus traditions see Israel Finkelstein and Neil Asher Silberman, *The Bible Unearthed: Archaeology's New Vision of Ancient Israel and the Origins of Sacred Texts* (New York: Simon and Schuster, 2001), 48–71.

5. John Bright, *A History of Israel*, 3d ed., (Philadelphia: Westminster Press, 1981), 92–96.

6. Finkelstein and Silberman133–118.

7. Ibid., 119; and Dever, *What Did The Biblical Writers Know?*, 113.

8. Finkelstein, 107–110.

9. Ibid., 67 and 107.

10. For more information on how the ancient Israelites lived out their everyday life see Paula McNutt, *Reconstructing the Society of Ancient Israel.* For a helpful description of the houses of this period see Lawrence E. Stager, "The Archaeology of the Family in Ancient Israel." *Bulletin of the American Schools of Oriental Research* 260 (1985), 1–35.

11. Dever, *What Did the Biblical Writers Know?*, 267.

12. Ibid., 123–124.

13. See Claus Westermann, "Zum Geschichtsverständnis des Alten Testaments," in *Probleme biblischer Theologie: Gerhard von Rad zum Geburtstag*, ed. H. W. Wolff, München: Chr. Kaiser, 1971, 611–619.

Chapter Four

Basic Historical Approach

This chapter discusses two biblical passages. The discussion shows how one might use historical information to address basic historical concerns such as authorship, purpose, date, message, and audience. Each historical method discussed later incorporates these elements, so this discussion is foundational to the methods. The discussion below also addresses application. How can we apply the message of these texts to our modern situation?

JUDGES 3:7–11

Judges 3:7–11 comes from the part of the canon often referred to as the former prophets. Biblical critics refer to this body of literature as the Deuteronomistic History (DH hereafter). The DH is made up of Joshua, Judges, 1 and 2 Samuel, and 1 and 2 Kings. The adjective "Deuteronomistic" refers to the fact that these books contain the same style, vocabulary and thought present in the book of Deuteronomy. A German scholar, Martin Noth, views the DH as the work of one writer living during the Babylonian Exile. Moreover, he identifies the work as historical. Others believe the DH is the work of a school of writers. Some scholars view the book of Deuteronomy as an introduction to this larger work. Whether this work is a history or theology is debatable.

One theory about the DH is that it appeared in two editions. The first edition concludes sometime during the reign of King Josiah. This edition has an optimistic character. After its appearance, events quickly changed with the death of King Josiah. As a result, optimism turns to confusion. Why did God allow Josiah, a completely faithful and good king, to be killed by the Egyptian King Neco at Megiddo in 609 B.C.E. (2 Kgs 23:29). A later edition, therefore, attempts to explain this event.

The second edition dates to the exilic period (586–538 BCE). It provides an explanation for the death of Josiah and the fall of Jerusalem. 2 Kings 23:25 says there was no king in ancient Israel that could match his faithfulness. Josiah had "turned to the LORD with all his heart, with all his soul, and with all his might." Moreover, he was completely faithful to the "law of Moses." In short, he received the highest possible praise. The second edition, therefore, has to provide an explanation for why God allows the death of Josiah, the destruction of Jerusalem, and the exile of its population.

The explanation comes in 2 Kings 23:26: "Still the LORD did not turn from the fierceness of his great wrath, by which his anger was kindled against Judah, because of all the provocations with which Manasseh had provoked him." This second edition, therefore, emerges during the exilic period.

Regardless of this theory, the final form of this work dates to the Babylonian Exile. The work as a whole incorporates older materials. Our text, Judges 3:7–11, fits the general theological perspective of the DH. It reflects the Deuteronomistic view that if one is faithful to God he or she will be blessed. Disobedience, however, brings about punishment. In the stories about the judges, a picture emerges of their role in ancient Israelite society. Some are military leaders. Others are minor judges who take care of lesser matters. Judges also possess the spirit of Yahweh. They do not serve consecutively, but their activities probably overlap.

Judges 3:7–11 contains material much older than the Deuteronomistic writers. These writers or editors took the older materials and incorporated it into their own theological pattern. The content of Judges 3:7–11 is introduced in Judges 2:11–3:6. Judges 2:11–3:6 contains this theological pattern for the reader. It begins with the sin of the people. Next, the reader is told that Yahweh allows Israel's enemies to threaten and oppress them. After this happens, the people cry for help. Finally, Yahweh sends a judge to deliver the people. This cycle repeats itself through much of the Book of Judges.

Judges 2:22–3:1 also says that God leaves the nations in the "promised land" to test Israel. In reality, there was no total conquest. There are still enemies of ancient Israel in the Promised Land. The editors interpreted this situation as a test. Besides testing Israel, Judges 3:1 says the other nations remain so that Israel may know war. These explanations reflect the writers' interpretation of past events. They have taken the incomplete conquest and the older stories interpreting them in light of their current situation; the writers are living through the years of the Babylonian Exile. This interpretation is theological in nature rather than historical. It calls on an exilic audience to learn from the failures of these early Israelites and be faithful.

With this background, we can now consider Judges 3:6–11, which is straightforward and does not need much explanation. The editors of this material see the incomplete nature of the conquest as a test to a new generation who does not know war (Jgs 2:22, 3:1). The language of Judges 2:11–14 is similar to the language and story line of Judges 3:7–11. The source of Israel's evil has to do with her deviant worship. The verb translated into English as serve or worship in Judges 3:7 has to do with performing religious rituals. Verse 7 says the people are "worshipping the Baals and the Ashe-rahs." The plurals likely indicate that Baal and Asherah are being worshiped at different shrines. Baal is a Canaanite god and Asherah a Canaanite god-dess. Asherah is the consort of Baal and a cultic object of some sort. Baal is a god of fertility. The people are tempted to trust in Baal and serve him and Asherah for their well-being.

Why would they do so? A fertility religion such as the Canaanite religion is a good fit for those who earn a livelihood from farming. Early Israel is an agrarian society where fertility of crops and offspring is essential to survival. Jeremiah 3:1–22 makes it clear that it is not Baal that is in control of fertility but God. However, many ancient Israelites probably feel that Baal is the proper god to provide fertility. So, disobedience in Judges 3:7–11 is a matter of misplaced trust in other gods. The Deuteronomistic editors here and in various other places view other gods as a danger to ancient Israel because they stand between the people and Yahweh.

Because of the people's sins, Yahweh is angry with them. Yahweh sells them into the hands of their enemy, King Cushan-rishathaim of Aram-naha-rim (Jgs 3:8). Scholars do not know this King Cushan-rishathaim other than the reference provided in this text. The verb translated "sell" means Yahweh gives them up or hands them over to their enemy as punishment for their disobedience. After eight years, the people cry out to Yahweh. Yahweh hears their cries for help and raises a savior to deliver them from their enemy. The judges are those saviors; they deliver the people. The name of this deliverer is Othniel.

Verse 10 makes three important statements about Othniel. First, the spirit of Yahweh comes upon him; this spirit possesses him. Next, he judges the people. A judge engages in administrative kinds of duties and decision mak-ing. Finally, he is a military figure going to war against the Cushan-risha-thaim, and he saves the people from their enemy. Verse 11 concludes the section with the comment that the land is at rest for forty years. The forty years is a rather common number in biblical literature and, on the whole, should not be taken as a literal figure.

This story and other similar ones address particular historical audiences. The DH addresses the people in Babylonian Exile (586–538 BCE). The exiles hear about these old stories. What do the Deuteronomistic editors want this audience to understand? They want them to make a connection between their situation and the situation of the ancient Israelites. In these patterns, we find an imperfect people who suffer the consequences of their bad choices.

They do not suffer because their enemies are stronger but because of their disobedience.

The exiles are in the same situation. They suffer because they have disobeyed God and ignored God's prophets who warned them. They share the fate of those earlier Israelites. On the bright side, the stories provide room for hope. If God came to the rescue of disobedient Israelites before, he might also come to the exile's rescue. These stories explain how God works and shows that God forgives and delivers in times of trouble.

Finally, what might this story have to say to a modern audience? It reflects the tendency of people to cry for help in times of trouble. Furthermore, it highlights the human tendencies to forget lessons from experience. Soon after trouble has passed, we often return to our old ways. The story tells us something about human nature. We read the stories in Judges and wonder how these people can be so slow. However, we are those people. We fail to learn from the past and often repeat it. This story is not just ancient Israel's story; it is our story as well.

It also shows that God allows people to suffer the consequences of their bad decisions in hopes they may learn something. For modern people, the disobedience may not come in the form of worshipping other gods; it may come in a multitude of other forms. The consequences of ancient Israel' disobedience reminds the people of their obligations to Yahweh. Their desperate situation moves them to cry for help. Yahweh's willingness to respond reminds one of God's willingness to forgive. God's discipline results from God's love. There is a message of forgiveness and a second chance in this text.

ISAIAH 40:1–11

Isaiah 40:1–11 is our second passage. It begins a second major section in the Book of Isaiah. Isaiah 1–39 reflects a different historical setting than chapters forty and following. One's first impulse might be to assume that the author of the Book of Isaiah is Isaiah. That makes sense. Why would anyone doubt Isaiah's authorship? A close reading of the book suggests that Isaiah is probably the author of much of the material found in Isaiah 1–39. However, is one writer responsible for the entire sixty-six chapters? Internal evidence indicates the contents of the book spans at least two hundred years or more. The mention of Cyrus king of Persia (Is 44:28) means that parts of the Isaiah date over a hundred years after Isaiah's death.

Most scholars divide the book into three major sections: Isaiah 1–39, Isaiah 40–55, and 56–66. Recent scholarship has shown a unity that brings these different sections together suggesting a long history of editing and expanding the original words of Isaiah in light of changing times. This history may reflect the activities of a school of writers or prophets. They would in part have been interpreting Isaiah's message to different times and situations.[1]

Generally speaking, the three divisions above correspond to three different historical settings. Biblical scholars usually associate the first 39 chapters with the eighth century prophet Isaiah often referred to as Isaiah of Jerusalem. Some of these chapters, however, date much later. Chapters 40–55 date to the time of Cyrus King of Persia in the late sixth century B.C.E. Cyrus, who allows the exiles the opportunity to return to Jerusalem in 538 B.C.E, is mentioned by name. The reference to Cyrus dates the book to the exilic period just before the fall of the Babylonians to the Persians. This text portrays Cyrus as a messianic figure; he is God's anointed (Is 45:1). He is the one who makes it possible for the exiles to return to Jerusalem. The final section of the book (i.e., Is 56–66) dates to the post-exilic period which begins in 538 B.C.E.

The Book of Isaiah contains differences in historical situation, style, language, and theological ideas indicating more than one author. Chapters 40–55 do not address the eighth century historical situation but the sixth century one. The opening chapter of the second section (40–55) looks forward to the return of the people to Jerusalem. The note of comfort in these chapters is a fitting message to those in exile. This passage describes a second or new exodus. As with the first exodus where God delivers the people from the hand of the Pharaoh, this time God anoints Cyrus, a foreign king, to deliver the people from Babylonian captivity. Cyrus is a second Moses of foreign descent.

Chapters 56–66 come from an author or authors speaking to a later time. These chapters appear to date to the post-exilic period. It speaks to the situation of the returning exiles and perhaps also to the time of the rebuilding of the temple in Jerusalem several years later.

Other reasons for considering multiple authors for the book of Isaiah include different styles, language, and new religious ideas. There are similarities between 1–39, 40–55, and 56–66, but there are also key differences. The poetry in chapters 40–55 and 56–66 is different from chapters 1–39. Isaiah of Jerusalem (Is 1–39) contains short prophetic sayings. By contrast, Isaiah 40–55 and Isaiah 56–66 contain long lyrical oracles. The mood has also changed in chapters 40–55 and 56–66. In Deutero-Isaiah (the named given to the anonymous prophet of chapters 40–55), the mood shifts from one of prophetic warning and anguish (Is 1–39) to one of hope and liberation reflecting the changed historical situation.

Chapters 40–66 introduce new ideas. The suffering servant is one of the key concepts introduced in these chapters. This servant is suffering for others, and this suffering is part of God's plan. Along with this suffering servant figure, chapters 40–66 express a note of universalism. God or Yahweh is not just a god for the Jewish people. Isaiah 42 describes the "suffering servant" as a "light to the nations." God is not just the creator of the Jewish people but the entire world. God is the God of the Gentiles as well. If, one interprets the servant as Israel, then Israel's mission extends beyond the Jewish people.[2] God, therefore, does not belong to just one people. Isaiah 56:3 and verse 6 indicate that the foreigner can be part of God's people. Isaiah 51:16, however, shows that the people of ancient Israel continue to have a "special place in Yahweh's historical plan."[3]

In short, the content of the book witnesses to a fundamental tenet of the Judeo-Christian faith. God is active in the life of God's people. We see this activity beginning with the life of the eighth century prophet and extending beyond the destruction of Jerusalem in 586 BCE and continuing down to the return of the people from Babylon to rebuild their beloved city, Jerusalem. Moreover, we see the scope of God's concern moving from a concern for the Jewish people to a concern for everyone. The suffering servant in Isaiah 40–55 is to become a light to the nations. The view anticipates the Christian concern to spread the "good news" to all nations.

Now that we have looked at the background information, we can begin our historical reading of Isaiah 40:1–11. An unknown writer familiar with the message of the eighth century prophet Isaiah of Jerusalem proclaims a new word from God. The writer extends the message of the eighth century prophet Isaiah to a new situation. This passage dates before the end of the exile in 538 B.C.E. when Babylonian captivity is near an end. The Jewish people in Babylon are near the day of their liberation. Deutero-Isaiah introduces a message of joy with the words "Comfort, O comfort my people, says your God." (Is 40:1)

Deutero-Isaiah is addressing a people in exile. They are people suffering the loss of homes, temple, and country. Some of them prospered in Babylon, but the question remains: Why would God allow this to happen? Obviously, some prophets say it is due to their disobedience, but they must feel confused and abandoned. It is during this time that some important Israelite traditions are brought together such as the Torah and the DH. Some people may have given up hope of returning to their homeland. Nevertheless, Deutero-Isaiah addresses them with good news. Isaiah 40:1–11 presents them with hope.

The message begins with beautiful words. God tells Deutero-Isaiah to speak tenderly to the people. He announces the imminent end of her punishment. The words comfort, speak, and cry are all plural imperatives. Comfort is repeated for emphasis; it indicates a sense of urgency.[4] "Speak tenderly" or literally "speak to the heart" is an attempt to convince the exiles that God is now ready to save them. Many of those addressed may have been skeptically thinking the message is too good to be true. The prophet announces that Israel has now paid fully for her sins.[5]

Verses 3–5 express the idea of a second exodus. The first exodus tells how God delivers the people of ancient Israel from Egyptian bondage and leads them into the Promised Land. God instructs the prophet to "prepare the way of the Lord, make straight in the desert a highway for our God." In Babylon, there is a highway for the gods and for the king. The imagery would have inspired the exiles. These highways are symbols of Babylon's power. The highway refers in this context to the way home for the exiles. It makes the way back home easy. The road is going to be straight, the valleys lifted up, and the hills made low. The way back is on level ground. The rough places become smooth and level.

Is this highway for the people or for God? The imagery of the highway is important. In Babylon, the function of the highway is to show Babylon's power and splendor. It demonstrates the supremacy and splendor of the gods. Concrete images of these gods were publically displayed on the highway. The glory of the Lord described in these verses, however, is not visible in the same way. It is not a visible image but the work of God in history that reveals God's glory. The presence of God is not an image that people can see or hold in their hands.

Isaiah 40:5 speaks about the "glory of the Lord." Ezekiel 11:23 describes the glory of God as departing Jerusalem. Now in Isaiah, the glory of God appears to the exiles on their way back to Judah. In short, the people's traveling on this highway reveals God's glory; it reveals God's acting in history on their behalf.[6] Therefore, the way of the Lord (Is 40:3) is also at the same time the way of the people. They are the result of God's work in history.

Verses 6–8 contrast the finite nature of human existence to God's word, which stands forever. The writer is instructed to "cry out" to the people. The writer uses the image of grass for all flesh. The grass eventually fades and dies. All flesh may refer to humanity, in general, but it may also refer to Babylon and its control. Neither flesh and blood nor Babylon's domination endures forever.

Verse 7 contains a textual problem. The Masoretic text is the standard text used for English translations of the Hebrew Bible. The Septuagint or Greek translation of the Hebrew does not have the words "when the breath of the Lord blows upon it; surely the people are grass." The Septuagint (LXX) just says, "The grass dries up and the flower falls away." English translations favor the Hebrew text. Verse 8 contrasts the grass and the flower withering to the word of God that lasts forever.

The Greek text, however, may reflect the older form of the text. Verses 7–8 in the LXX say that "the grass dries up and the flower falls away, but the word of our God remains forever." This is the simpler reading. More likely, however, it may result from a simple scribal mistake known as *homoioteleuton*.[7] This error entails the scribe's eyes skipping from one occurrence of a word to a second occurrence of that word or a similar one thereby missing the words in between the two occurrences. In the Hebrew, verses 7 and 8 both begin with the same verb, "to wither." The Greek text may reflect a Hebrew text where the scribe who copied it overlooked verse seven. His or her eye skipped from the end of verse 6 to the second occurrence of the verb "to wither" at the beginning of verse 8. If this is the case, the longer Hebrew text is the preferable one. Still, it is likely that the words "the people are grass", was added to the text.

In verses 9–11, Zion and Jerusalem are personified; God commands them to speak to the population of Judah. The message is about God, who possesses great power and rules by it. Nevertheless, this same God cares for the people as a shepherd cares for the flock. The acts of this caring is expressed beautifully in the words of the RSV: "He will feed his flock like a shepherd, he will gather the lambs in his arms, he will carry them in his bosom, and gently lead those that are with young" (Is 40:11).

One could apply this text to modern times. By focusing on the theme of comfort, people today may also find themselves in an exile of some kind. Exile may refer to a literal event in the life of an individual or group, but it may also refer to a state of mind or being. One may feel separated and cut off from all he or she loves and cherishes. One may feel like the Jewish people who had been taken from their homeland; they feel abandoned and lost. This text is an expression of renewal, hope, and promise. God provides for us in good and bad times. That is not to say that God has promised a "rose garden" to use the words of a popular song. Life has more than enough thorns. Still the good news or good tidings (Is 40:9) to the people of Israel and to everyone past and present is that God is like a shepherd who watches over us and cares for us. God is like a parent who acts in our best interest. God punishes, forgives, protects, and nurtures all at the appropriate times.

Caring for us, however, does not imply, as some modern religious figures claim, that God will make us rich or give us whatever we want. People who have experienced great pain and suffering have a problem viewing God as a shepherd. The problem of evil and suffering leads many to wonder if there is a God. If God does exist, does God really care about human misery? The image or metaphor of shepherd in Isaiah 40:11 or in Psalm 23, for instance, encourages one to put his or her trust in God. That requires trust since we do not have all the answers to life's troubles. I would suggest one may be able to find blessing even in dark days. It may be the small things that help us make it through the day that we can be thankful for.

CONCLUSION

This chapter has demonstrated how a kind of contextual approach can help us understand and appreciate the biblical texts better. It can help us apply ancient texts to new and different historical settings. In the application, I resisted any interpretation that cannot be tied to the historical context. Now we can discuss the particular historical methods used to study the Bible.

NOTES

1. For more details see Michael D. Coogan, *The Old Testament: A Historical and Literary Introduction to the Hebrew Scriptures* (New York: Oxford University Press, 2006), 331–332.

2. See Coogan, 411–412. Sometimes the servant seems to be an individual and other time a group.

3. Bernhard W. Anderson, *Understanding the Old Testament*, 3d ed., (Englewood Cliffs: Prentice-Hall Inc. 1975), 454.

4. Claus Westermann, *Isaiah 40–66*, The Old Testament Library, trans. David M. G. Stalker ed., Peter Achroyd (Philadelphia: Westminster Press, 1969), 34.

5. R. N. Whybray, *Isaiah 40–66*, New Century Bible Commentary, ed. Ronald Clements, (Grand Rapids: Wm. B. Eerdmans Publ., Co., 1975), 49. Double could be overstatement or it could mean that she has paid enough or the right amount.

6. Westermann pp. 38–39.

7. Whybray, 51.

Chapter Five

Introduction to the
Historical Critical Methods

Readers by now have an idea of the nature of historical approaches. The methods discussed in the following several chapters are meant to help the reader formulate his or her interpretations. The methods provide guidelines and strategies enhancing one's ability to read and understand the Bible. They assist one in understanding the text in a neutral and objective fashion. These methods discourage one interpreting the Bible based on his or her biases. There will always be some bias whether intentional or unintentional. Critical approaches, however, try to be objective and determine the meaning of the writer's words. It is not about what one wants the Bible to mean but what it does in fact mean.

A primary task of the historical approaches concerns historical reconstruction, which is the attempt to recover the original historical background from which one can make sense of the text. It includes questions of authorship, date, audience, purpose, and other areas of historical concern. Reconstruction is necessary because many biblical texts have grown through the centuries before being finalized.

Historical methods lead to a better understanding of what the text meant in its original setting. By understanding the historical meaning, we can apply that meaning to other contexts. For instance, one could try to understand how a text from Isaiah's time was understood by New Testament writers or how it can be applied today. If one does this properly, a connection is established between the original meaning and the extension of that meaning to different historical contexts.

The methods discussed in the remainder of the book are often referred to as critical methods. Biblical criticism does not mean that scholars are intentionally criticizing the Bible. To some people, it may seem that way. Critical is a way of referring to the practice of biblical scholarship. This scholarship applies critical methods to the study of the Bible. These methods provide guidelines that help us understand texts better. The guidelines work against our natural tendency to read our prejudices and biases into the text. These methods draw heavily on human reason. While these approaches are not faith-based, they are frequently pursued on behalf of the faith. Many biblical scholars are working in the name of the church. Still, they rely on a systematic and logical approach that values reason and experience in the interpretation of the Bible.

Even though rational inquiry is highly valued by biblical critics, one must realize its limits. A critical reading is never free of bias or prejudice, but it should strive to be as objective as possible. Objectivity is a goal; some readings are more objective than others. Ideally, a biblical scholar seeks the truth. In an academic setting, the search for truth should not be about what I believe personally or what my community of faith believes; it is about what a critical analysis shows to be true or false. Such an approach tends to see interpretation as a passive activity. The meaning is there; the interpreter does not create the meaning. The critic has to apply the proper method to extract it. The meaning is what the author is trying to communicate.

THREE IMPORTANT AREAS OF KNOWLEDGE FOR HISTORICAL APPROACHES

The historical methods covered below are not primarily for the purpose of writing a history of ancient Israel or early Christianity. The discussion in this book is not about writing history but using historical methods to interpret specific biblical texts. The historical approaches employ historical information that comes from at least three different sources.

First, biblical scholars draw on evidence from biblical and non-biblical texts to understand the history of ancient Israel and early Christianity. The Bible provides the most information for the critic. Imagine what we would know about ancient Israel and early Christianity without the Bible. Our knowledge would be severely limited. We would know almost nothing about Joshua, David, Solomon, Jesus, or Paul. As a result, these biblical texts are absolutely essential for any historical reconstruction of the Bible. There are, however, many non-biblical texts from the ancient Near East and the Greco-Roman worlds that shed more light on the biblical texts.

Historical critics are interested in epigraphical writings, which are short writings on various kinds of material. Some may be found on pottery handles, seals, and ostraca (i.e., pieces of clay with writing on them). Longer non-biblical texts provide stories and information that supplement what we know from the biblical texts. The Gilgamesh Epic, for example, is an ancient story that contains a flood story similar to the story of Noah in the Bible. Knowing both stories is important for the interpreter of the Bible. There are many other texts from the ancient Near East that can help one understand the Bible better.

An example of such a longer text is the Moabite Stone discovered in 1868 at Dhiban. The story written on the stone provides a parallel account of a battle between Moab and Israel. Being able to compare the two stories is helpful. Although the details between the two accounts differ, the main point matches. Both texts say that Moab won the battle and that it was due to the help from the Moabite God (2 Kgs 3:27). [1]

A second important resource for biblical critics is archeology. Archaeology can provide us with a direct glimpse of past societies. The data is not always abundant, but it helps to fill in the gaps of our information. It may also provide a larger context from which we can study specific texts. Archaeology has provided a great deal of valuable information for the biblical critic. It further explains the evidence we have. It can tell us about the general population and their ways of life, which are not described or only briefly described in written texts. It provides information about the elites and non-elites in ancient societies. It supplies population estimates and other information that helps reconstruct and understand aspects of social and economic structures in ancient Israel. It informs us about their technology.

Archaeology can provide us with information coming from the distant past unedited and unfiltered by generations of peoples. While biblical texts have been edited over the years, archeological artifacts remain the same. Of course, many artifacts are broken or incomplete, so they are not literally the same. All of this information helps one connect to that past.

A third area that supports the work of historical critics is sociological models and theories. The models and theories come from the fields of anthropology and sociology. They can help the historian provide a fuller picture of society. Often information is lacking, and the scholar may resort to conjecture based on models, theories, or analogy. While these models should not be used to fill in the gaps in existing historical data, they can provide ways of looking at and analyzing the data in a meaningful fashion. For instance, one may infer that if a neighboring society had certain institutions, then, other related societies would likely have similar institutions. Models and theories from the social sciences can provide insight that leads to a better description of life in ancient Israel or first century Rome. Consequently, historical critics need to keep up and be acquainted with these different fields of study.

All of this shows that the biblical critic today needs to be aware of several different fields of studies. Studies today are often inter-disciplinary meaning they draw on various disciplines in the humanities and social sciences. Social scientific theories such as functionalism or conflict theory offer fresh avenues for understanding the Bible. Such theories focus on social, religious, and political institutions, issues of power and authority as they relate to groups or individuals. History may tell us that an event happened and perhaps what caused it. Sociological approaches add depth. Good histories do not ignore the social world. Sociological approaches may simply provide the historian with additional insights and questions. It cannot replace the need for hard evidence, but it can offer valuable social awareness of how the historical events fit into a larger framework.

HISTORICAL METHODS

The primary and most influential historical methods are source criticism, form criticism, and redaction criticism. Besides these, there are other approaches. The use of a sociological perspective to write a social history is one such approach. Another approach would be called tradition-historical criticism. While there is a chapter on social approaches, I do not devote a separate chapter to traditio-historical criticism. I will discuss this approach briefly at the end of this chapter since it has implications for the other historical methods.

Source criticism attempts to identify and isolate sources in biblical texts. This is the main task of this approach, but once that has been accomplished source criticism can address other issues. It seeks to answer basic questions raised earlier concerning the identity of the author, the date, the location of the author, the message and purpose of the text, and the identity of the audience. These questions are then addressed to the different sources.

One cannot use source criticism on every text in the Bible. In the Hebrew Bible, one uses source criticism primarily on the Pentateuch. It has also been employed in the DH and the Book of Ecclesiastes. In the DH, the editors of that material have employed older sources into their own theological framework. One could try to separate the sources from the editorial framework and examine the sources as a literary whole. Some find an early and late source for the composition of 1 and 2 Samuel. In the New Testament, scholars use source criticism mostly with regard to the synoptic Gospels (Matthew, Mark, and Luke).

Form criticism, however, can be used on all the texts in the Hebrew Bible and New Testament. It is perhaps the most influential and useful historical method. The main idea is that identifying a text as a particular type of literature can help one understand it better. Knowing, for example, that a text is a creation psalm shapes our expectations of that Psalm and focuses our attention on it in a particular way. As a result, one expects to find a certain kind of vocabulary, a set of ideas, structures, and content. Form criticism focuses on identifying boundaries of a text, and it also examines a text with regard to its structure, type, setting, and purpose.

Redaction criticism is used on texts that have a history of being edited. Redaction criticism focuses on making comparisons. Consequently, if this is the goal, one has to be at least able to identify edited materials. One can then draw conclusions about why the editor has made changes to the text. In many cases, it is based on possessing two texts that can serve as a basis of comparison. Following a comparative approach, one would have to be able to identify intentional additions or alterations made to a text by a writer who is using that text as a source for his or her own text. The redaction critic then evaluates any changes made by the redactor to his or her source. Evaluating the changes sheds light on the viewpoint or theology of the editor/writer. For instance, if Luke uses Mark as a source, then we can compare the changes Luke has made to Mark. The goal is to understand the meaning of the editor's work and see why Luke added to Mark, omitted material from Mark, or changed Mark in any way.

The editor then is viewed as more than an editor; he or she is often seen as a creative author or theologian. Redaction criticism is frequently used in the Synoptic Gospels in the New Testament, but it can also be applied to some books in the Hebrew Bible. We have already discussed the notion that the DH came into its current form through two editions involving later editors to rework and reinterpret the original earlier edition.

STRENGTHS AND WEAKNESSES
OF THE HISTORICAL METHODS

The historical methods that emerged in the Enlightenment period maintained their dominance for a long time. They are still widely influential even though they no longer dominate the field of biblical studies. These approaches are valuable. Historical methods can help us understand a text on its own terms. By focusing on the background, we can gain valuable insights that allow us to understand what the writer is trying to communicate. Its strengths are geared to providing as much information as possible that makes texts more understandable.

The historical approaches, however, do have several weaknesses. This type approach is limited by several factors. First, it cannot recover the intentions of the author with certainty. This criticism causes some interpreters to abandon the historical approach for a literary one that finds meaning in the text. Second, our sources for reconstructing the past are limited. Most of the surviving written material provides selective information. The historian is often in the dark about how the common people live their lives. Information is often lacking. Third, there is always a subjective element to the work of historical critics. While I do not necessarily find this a weakness, it would be for those historical critics who cling to a strong notion of objectivity and insist that the only legitimate meaning derives from historical approaches. Fourth, many interpreters find it neither valid nor desirable to engage in historical reconstructions of the text. They are happy to stick to the final form of the text that we now possess. They do not see the value in trying to uncover an earlier version of the text. I agree that reading texts as they are now is valuable, but it is not the only way to read them. A historical approach that values a historical understanding must push behind the existing texts even if the result does not lead to certainty. Such an effort is necessary for a historical reading. Such a reading rightly respects the most ancient voices of the text refusing to ignore them for later ones.

Regardless of the weaknesses, historical approaches are essential if we want to understand the texts within their own historical contexts. There is no other way to travel back in time than by traveling back through the imperfect tools of historical and related investigations in the areas of sociology, anthropology, and archeology. In short, biblical texts contain words of peoples over many years. If we take the final form of the text as our authoritative text, then we accept the words of the latest editor or editors. Instead of letting this be the only word, I would argue that our understanding is enriched when we can look at all layers of the text from the oldest to the most recent ones. From a historical perspective, all these layers need to be studied before looking at the final form of the work produced by the editors. In sum, I would contend that the weaknesses of the historical approach only suggest that it can no longer be seen as the only legitimate way to interpret texts.

THE IMPORTANCE OF HISTORICAL RECONSTRUCTION

Even if historical reconstruction is seen as a weakness, it is an important and essential part of the approach. Since nothing in life is certain, I am not sure I would really call it a weakness. Historical reconstruction allows us to recover voices in the texts that have been muted or transformed by editors or later additions to the text. The edits and additions that go into making the final form of the text are important, but so is the oldest form of the text. Suppose, for example, archeologists found a text produced by an ancient culture that had a long-standing debate over the rights of the underprivileged. Suppose further that the text we found was heavily edited over the years by elites who had little sympathy for the poor and oppressed. Elites may have edited the texts in ways sympathetic to the views of the wealthy and powerful elements in society. Historians will want to recover the other voices in the text if they are interested in an overall assessment of the history of that culture.

Historical biblical scholars, likewise, want to recover the earliest form of the biblical texts. Some historical scholars prefer the previous form of the text over the edited texts we now have. An example of how this reconstruction works in biblical texts can be demonstrated in regard to Genesis 1–11. According to the standard source critical hypothesis, there was a time when Genesis 2:4b would have been the first verse in what we now call the Book of Genesis. Genesis 1:1–2:4a was written hundreds of years later. The older creation narrative in Genesis 2:4b–25 has been identified as the J source, and it is interspersed with texts from Genesis through Numbers. This J source has become part of a larger narrative that contains the work of at least two other sources. The other sources are labeled P (the priestly source) and E (the source that uses Elohim for God instead of the Yahweh). The E and P sources date later than J.

What does this mean? First, it means that J represents the oldest tradition or source in the Book of Genesis. Second, it means that the form of the text we now have represents a long history of sources being merged together over an extended period of time. This process involved different generations of editors working over long periods. Eventually, this work becomes the books we know and recognize today. Thirdly, each source, with the possible exception of E, told their own stories and represented independent traditions. Over time, however, these stories merge and become part of a larger story. Historical reconstruction would be about working backward from the text we have now to recover these three sources.

Granted there is value in resisting the primacy of historical reconstruction as a means of proper interpretation. There is room for both kinds of studies. Studies of earlier stages of the text in both form and source criticism are important. There is also value in redaction criticism and literary approaches that focus on the final form of the text. Historical approaches, in my judgment, have made many valuable contributions to our understanding of the Bible. At a basic level, without an understanding of the historical circumstances from which biblical texts emerge, we would have an impoverished understanding of biblical texts. The shortcomings mentioned above provide no reason to abandon it. It is more than fair, however, to resist the historical approach as the only legitimate way of reading the Bible. Historical information can have value even for literary criticism. It can inform literary readings. David Rhoads and Donald Michie's literary study of Mark 1:14–28 says that historical information about Israel in the first century is useful for literary study.[2]

THE ODD NATURE OF SOME BIBLICAL LITERATURE

Much of the Bible, particularly the Hebrew Bible, does not come from what we traditionally think of as an author. Biblical scholars may use words like a collector, a redactor/editor, or a tradent to refer to those responsible for many biblical texts. Source criticism attempts to isolate individual sources. These sources have authors even though they may remain anonymous. Scholars find labels for referring to the source such as J, but they do not know the identity or name of the author or editors of those sources.

In the Pentateuch, the works of anonymous writers are brought together with other unknown writers by editors over time. If one can identify a source that runs throughout the Pentateuch and read just that one source, one may find new insights and see the story in a different light. Reading the source as an independent story would allow for the possibility of new readings and understandings. When, on the other hand, one reads the source as part of the larger narrative, the individual source merges into the larger narrative. Therefore, the message of that source may be modified or shaped in some ways. It would be similar to having several novels written by unknown writers about similar subjects being skillfully combined into one larger novel. If the identity of the authors and redactor is unknown, it makes it difficult to understand the work's message. That is one thing that makes biblical interpretation so different from the interpretation of more modern literary works.

Redaction criticism is a historical method that focuses on the final form of the text. It does, however, assume and take the complex development of the traditions and their development seriously. Redaction criticism looks at how texts have been edited and for what purposes. It does engage in historical reconstruction in its attempt to identify the final editor's work. Once the editor's work has been identified, the redaction critic can analyze the editor's activity and determine why he or she has modified the text. Ultimately, the redaction critic is interested in the text as we now have it.

This complex nature makes the study of biblical texts a little intimidating for beginners. Imagine the challenge of explaining this to one who wants to know who wrote Genesis. That is why it is necessary to discuss the importance of tradition and editing before continuing to source, form, and redaction critical approaches. A discussion of traditions prepares one for a better understanding of these historical approaches.

TRADITION HISTORICAL CRITICISM

While source criticism focuses on documents, many scholars concentrate more on traditions rather than written sources. In biblical studies, tradition refers to written or oral communications about peoples, events, and practices passed down from one generation to another. This definition would "include proverbs, riddles, songs, poems, epics, and various kinds of folk narratives."[3]

The first two chapters of Walter Rast's book, *Tradition History and the Old Testament*, discuss the history of this approach and its four key aspects. His discussion shows how the method relates to the other historical methods.[4] In the study of the Pentateuch, this method moves the discussion away from sources and documents to traditions either oral or written. Source critics described a process whereby certain individuals joined different materials together producing larger texts. They did not, however, attribute any creativity to these individuals.

Tradition critics, however, see authors or editors as collectors. These editors may compose some stories, and they may also incorporate stories that have been passed from generation to the next. They collected them and passed them on in connected narratives. Part of their contributions may have come in how they connect the stories and how they place the stories into a larger story. These narratives, therefore, from the beginning contained traditional materials.

According to Rast, tradition criticism focuses on four different aspects of biblical traditions. The first aspect relates to those who are "responsible for the shaping and transmission of a particular tradition."[5] The priestly circle, for instance, may collect, shape, preserve, and pass on certain priestly traditions. German biblical scholar Gerhard von Rad employs tradition criticism to demonstrate "how the Book of Deuteronomy makes use of old sacral and legal traditions, which are presented, however, in a preaching or homiletic style."[6] He identified a Levitical circle as the "preachers."

A second aspect of this approach has to do with the location of the tradition. Is there a point of origin for a particular tradition? Discovering the place where a tradition began can provide valuable insights into that tradition. Shechem, for instance, was a major religious site and may have been the home of certain biblical traditions related to the covenant. If a tradition can be traced to Shechem, then a study of that tradition along with a study of that location may reveal new insights. Dating these traditions is also important. Martin Noth discusses how one might be able to distinguish early traditions from later ones.[7]

The third area identified by Rast has to do with the role that certain social, political, and religious features play in the creation and transmission of traditions. This speaks to the setting of the tradition which is also a concern for form criticism. The covenant tradition, for example, may derive from a religious agreement between God and an individual or group or it may relate to an agreement between the king and the people or the king and other kings. It functions as a contract. These features may have influenced and affected those responsible for preserving and passing on these traditions. Von Rad employed tradition criticism to demonstrate that the Book of Deuteronomy is based on the "ancient covenant form," and he concluded that "Deuteronomy . . . must have had its ultimate roots in an annual feast of covenant renewal celebrated at Shechem."[8]

The fourth feature of tradition criticism concerns themes and subjects found in the traditions. Noth identified five basic themes in the Pentateuch:

1. "Guidance out of Egypt"
2. "Guidance into the Arable Land"
3. "Promise to the Patriarchs"
4. "Guidance in the Wilderness"
5. "Revelation at Sinai"[9]

According to Noth, these themes had their own independent history associated with particular traditions. Over time, these independent traditions come together.[10] Arranged in a chronological fashion, they represent the core of ancient Israelite faith.[11] These five themes contains "the actual historical experience or immediate historical knowledge of some proto-Israelite group or tribe; however, the present connection of the themes . . . is the interpretive work of the Israelite community in the creative oral period before Israel became a state."[12]

Moreover, Noth maintains that these five themes were passed on in a "cultic" or worship setting in ancient Israel. They emerged from certain historical experiences of the people. In their worship, they recollect, relive, and retell various stories organized around these themes, which are "crucial for the existence of the people and its knowledge of God."[13]

The tradition history approach, therefore, can tell us something about the growth and development of the traditions that later became part of the Bible. Its usefulness is not limited to the Pentateuch. The Bible is full of traditional material. It is useful to consider the process that examines a tradition and its transmission. Tradition criticism provides a window into the past and helps us understand the words of the Bible as unfolding over time. The Bible did not just fall from heaven; it was part of the ongoing life of the people.

Noth's insight that themes may be products of particular groups is illuminating. We might have a case where stories associated with one tribe eventually find their way into the story about the nation of Israel as a whole. As more people become part of the family or nation of Israel, their stories become part of the larger story. As a result, the stories are no longer tied to just a small group or band of people. This approach, therefore, adds richness to our understanding of texts that would not otherwise be possible. This understanding should also inform the discussion of source, form, and redaction criticism as discussed in the next three chapters.

NOTES

1. 2 Kings 3:27 does not in any way refute such an interpretation of the event. Verse 27 indicates that after the king of Moab offers his firstborn as a burnt offering on the wall, a great wrath came against Israel.
2. David Rhodes and Donald Michie, *Mark As Story: An Introduction to the Narrative of a Gospel* (Philadelphia: Fortress Press, 1982), 79–80.

3. Pauline A. Viviano, "Source Criticism," in *To Each Its Own Meaning: An Introduction to Biblical Criticisms and Their Application*, ed. Stephen R. Haynes and Steven L. McKenzie (Louisville: The Westminster Press, 1999), 91.

4. Walter E. Rast, *Tradition History and the Old Testament*. Guides to Biblical Scholarship Old Testament Series, ed. Gene M. Tucker (Philadelphia: Fortress Press 1972), 1–5, 16–18.

5. Ibid., 19–21.

6. Ibid., 21.

7. Bernhard W. Anderson, "Introduction: Martin Noth's Traditio-Historical Approach in the Context of Twentieth-Century Biblical Research," in *A History of Pentateuchal Traditions*, trans. Bernhard W. Anderson (Atlanta: Scholar's Press, 1981), xxiii–xxviii.

8. Ibid., 26.

9. Martin Noth, *A History of Pentateuchal Traditions*, trans. Bernhard W. Anderson, (Atlanta: Scholar's Press, 1981), 46–62.

10. Rast, 29.

11. Anderson, xxi.

12. Ibid.

13. Ibid.

Chapter Six

Source Criticism

SOURCE CRITICISM IN THE HEBREW BIBLE

Simply put, source criticism attempts to identify sources found in biblical texts. In the Hebrew Bible, the practice is mainly limited to the Pentateuch. While the books of Joshua, Judges, and 1 and 2 Samuel have also been included in the discussion, here the focus is primarily on the Book of Genesis in the Hebrew Bible and the Synoptic Gospels (Matthew, Mark, and Luke) in the New Testament.

In the Hebrew Bible, writers do mention sources. The Book of the Wars of the Lord (Nm 21:14) and the Book of Jashar (Jo 10:13) are just two examples of sources mentioned in the Bible. These sources are used and referred to by biblical writers. Other sources are also mentioned. In 1 Kings 14:19, the writer says, "Now the rest of the acts of Jeroboam, how he warred and how he reigned, are written in the Book of the Annals of the Kings of Israel." Source critics, however, focus on sources not identified by the biblical writers.

One might rightly wonder why scholars look for sources in biblical texts if they are not mentioned by the writer. Why would they suspect the existence of different sources in the first place? There are several reasons to believe the Pentateuch contains sources. The most obvious is that the writers themselves are not eyewitnesses to the events they describe. As a result, they must have had access to sources containing information and stories about patriarchs, matriarchs, their children, and various events. Even if Moses had been the author of the first five books of the Bible, he would not have been present for the events occurring in Genesis so he would depend upon other sources for his information.

Since modern scholarship has rejected Moses' authorship of the Pentateuch, we might begin our discussion by asking: Who did write Genesis and
the other books of the Pentateuch? To answer that question, one must determine if Genesis and the other books are written by one or more persons. If
the books are products of more than one writer, then one has to determine the
date of each author's work. Over time, scholars build up a picture of how the
Pentateuch came to exist as we have it today.

Scholars conclude that the Pentateuch is the product of multiple authors.
A source in this context refers to the work of an unknown author. So source
criticism is focused on identifying the source, determining its author or authors, establishing its date and defining its purpose. After a close examination of Genesis, for instance, scholars discover different versions of the same
stories, different perspectives, differences in vocabulary usage, and different
styles of writing. All of these things indicate the existence of more than one
writer. Source critics also find inconsistencies. Source critics find duplicate
stories (i.e., two stories of the same events) in the Pentateuch and these
stories contain certain inconsistencies. Such inconsistencies indicate the existence of more than one writer or source. Typically, we assume writers strive
for consistency, so inconsistences indicate different authors.

Early observations focused on the various names used for God. Certain
texts seemed to prefer Elohim (i.e., God) and others Yahweh (i.e., Lord).
This observation led to the identification of a source that used one name for
God and a second source that used another. Over time, a picture emerged
leading to what scholars refer to as the documentary hypothesis. This hypothesis identified four separate sources labeled J, E, P, and D. Together these
sources made up the Pentateuch.

A few brief examples of what this approach introduced to the study of the
Pentateuch may provide an overall idea of how it works.

1. Genesis 1–2 seems to contain two different creations stories. One
   comes from the time near David and Solomon and the other several
   hundred years later. The oldest account is from the J source (Gn
   24b–25). The more recent one comes from P (Gn 1:1–2:4a). This story
   (Gn 1:1–2:4a) contains priestly language and concerns that are absent
   from the older creation account in Genesis 2:4b–25. There are differences in style, vocabulary, and perspective in these two creation accounts indicating that an editor has combined these two stories.

2. The same is true of the flood stories beginning in Genesis 6. A close
   reading of the flood narrative reveals two somewhat different stories
   containing different vocabulary, style, and perspectives. They have
   been combined in a way that makes the differences less obvious. I
   imagine the editing and combining of the two different accounts is a
   way to preserve both versions of an important story. Interruptions in

the flow of the story signal a change of source.[1] Texts may break off at one point and continue later indicating material has been inserted. Close readings by those familiar with source criticism can detect these shifts. Once the two sources of the flood are separated each source tells a consistent story.

3. Another example can be found in the story of how Joseph ends up in Egypt (Gn 37:12–36, 39:1). This story reveals two different versions of the same basic story indicating two sources. Like the flood stories, the critic has to use the principles of source criticism to isolate or disentangle the two different versions of how Joseph gets to Egypt. Once the two stories are read separately the main points do not change even though some of the details do change.

One could see this process working in different ways. One explanation could be that a single writer/editor pieces different sources together to create a continuous narrative moving from creation in Genesis 1 to the death of Moses in Deuteronomy 34. In this scenario, the writer uses the JEPD sources to create his or her own account of these events. This writer may have arranged, commented on, or explained things at various places along the way. He or she would not share modern sensibilities about citing sources. R. N. Whybray sees this writer as a historian writing during the Babylonian Exile between 587–538 B.C.E.[2]

A second way the sources could have come together involves a long process. One begins with the oldest source and tries to explain how other sources supplemented or were combined with the earlier ones. The editors combined sources over the years until it reached its current form. At first, the Pentateuch would have consisted of J. Then E material was added, and we had a version consisting of J and E or JE. Later, an editor or editors added the D material. Finally, a priestly editor or editors may have taken JED, and combined it with their own writings giving us what we now have.

SOURCE CRITICISM IN THE PENTATEUCH

The story begins with individual sources or documents referred to by the letters JEPD. This story continues with studies of how these sources combine into the final form. In other words, there was a time when the Pentateuch was much smaller. The earliest source (J) would have included parts of Genesis, Exodus, and Numbers.

Modern readers can read this form of the Pentateuch. However, to do so one would have to reconstruct the various texts of the Pentateuch to isolate and extract the J passages. Even better, one can read this form of the text in Harold Bloom's *The Book of J*. The book includes a translation of J by David

Rosenberg.[3] J being the earliest version of the Pentateuch is enlarged over time by additional sources.

One might wonder why scholars refer to the author as J. We do not know the real name of this author. All we know about this person is subject to what we can surmise from the J material. Scholars referred to this source as J for at least two reasons. First, the writer has a strong preference for the divine name Yahweh. Yahweh is translated in most English versions as Lord.[4] It is called J instead of Y because the Hebrew letter *yod* (i.e., the "y" consonant in Yahweh) is "J" in English. For example, in Hebrew Jerusalem is *Yerushalim* or Judah is *Yehudah*.

Second, J not only stands for the connection of this source with the use of the divine name, but it also refers to its origin or location. It most likely emerged from the southern kingdom known as Judah referring to the tribe of Judah. In short, J indicates the use of the divine name and the location of where the source emerged. According to the traditional documentary hypothesis, J is the oldest source dating to the 10th century BCE. This date would place it in the time of David and Solomon.

Bloom sees J as a great literary work. He suggests that the writer may be a woman.[5] Most biblical scholars view J as more of a theological or historical source. Nonetheless, J becomes the backbone of a larger work from Genesis through Numbers, but in so doing, its distinctiveness is modified by other sources. The other sources are merged with J over time.

This information is important because it allows us to see this source in both its social and historical settings. Remember that source criticism is a historical method. Historical methods are concerned with who wrote a text, when it was written, why was it written, and to whom it was written. Identifying the sources then is just the first step, and it allows for further historical study.

The second source is called E. Like J, the name of the source reflects the source's preference for the deity's name and the source's place of origin. The E source uses the divine name Elohim instead of Yahweh, which is translated into English as God. In addition, scholars view E as a northern source associated with the northern tribe of Ephraim.

Once E has been identified, historical concerns can be addressed such as location, date, the identity of the audience, and purpose of the source. According to the new documentary hypothesis, this source dates to the eighth century BCE. J and E are probably combined sometime before the end of the 7th century B.C.E. Critics refer to this amalgamation as JE.

German scholar, Hermann Gunkel, does not view JE as authors but collectors. They collected older traditions and worked them into a larger narrative. They did not change these traditions in any significant way. J and E represent "schools of narrators."[6] This view is at odds with source critics who consider J and E as authors rather than editors or collectors.

Richard Elliott Friedman asks why both sources are preserved. Why not accept one and reject the other? There are different possible answers. Friedman suggests it was because both versions were "sufficiently well known that one could not get away with excluding one or the other."[7] Or perhaps the sources had gained an elevated status that ensured their survival. It is also likely that E had attained a high regard in the northern part of the country. Editors, therefore, worked these important stories into the existing narrative.

The third source, in chronological order, is called the D and is associated with the book of Deuteronomy. The D source may have originally been composed in the north, and it was later brought south after the fall of the northern kingdom to the Assyrians in 721 B.C.E. It is possible that later the priest Hilkiah discovered portions of this source in the Jerusalem temple, which served as the impetus for the reforms of King Josiah in 621 BCE (2 Kgs 22:8–20). This source serves as an introduction to a larger work known as the DH containing Joshua, Judges, 1 and 2 Samuel, and 1 and 2 Kings. Once this source is added, the Pentateuch is again enlarged.

At this stage, the Pentateuch would begin with Genesis 2:4b. There would be no book of Leviticus. Much of what we find in Genesis, Exodus, and Numbers would not yet be there. According to the standard theory, the latest source is P. Scholars call it P because it is clearly concerned with priestly matters. This source comes from a priestly writer or writers working during or after the Babylonian Exile. While the P source dates to the sixth or fifth centuries B.C.E, it still would likely contain priestly material much older than the exile.

Concerning the process by which we get the final form, German scholar Martin Noth provided one way to understand how this process worked. He suggested an old foundational source, which he called G or *Grundlage*. Both J and E drew material from this older source. Whether he is correct or not, the notion that J and E actually worked with older traditions is possible. For Noth, J was the original narrative that provided a continuous story from Creation of everything to the death of Moses. Later, an editor would use parts of the E source to supplement J's story. The P source later provided a broader framework for JE. "Priority was given to P, with the result that the older sources appear as enrichments of the priestly narrative."[8]

Noth's view is really a description of the process that explains the final form of the Tetrateuch (Genesis-Numbers). But what about the D source and the book of Deuteronomy? The D source would have been added at some point, probably before P, as an introduction to the larger DH.[9] Deuteronomy functions as a bridge taking us from the stories in Genesis through Numbers to the conquest stories in the book of Joshua. Therefore, the process of composition reaches from the tenth century B.C.E (900's B.C.E.) down to the fifth century B.C.E. (400's B.C.E.)

The above account, then, provides a general description of four independent sources and how they came together over time. Scholars still disagree on a number of issues. Some describe the process as one source supplementing another. Others allow redactors or editors to play a much larger role in shaping the final form of the text. Some source critics no longer view E as an independent source. The date of J has also been disputed, and other scholars even question the existence of J and E altogether.

HOW THE METHOD WORKS

Source criticism in the Pentateuch is largely about properly identifying and assigning specific texts to specific sources. Source critics have attempted to do this with every passage in the Pentateuch. For students wishing to use source criticism much of the work is about reading a text, drawing conclusions, and looking at what other source critics have said about the passage. This sort of information is readily available in the Anchor Bible Commentary, the Old Testament Library Commentary, and the Interpreter's Bible Commentary. The research in this area has been extensive. German scholar Gerhard von Rad said almost a century ago that this area of study was coming to a "dead end."[10] He felt that source criticism had completed its task for the most part in being able to identify the sources correctly. Nevertheless, some designations may still be questionable. As a result, one who wishes to engage in a source critical study has several tools at his or her disposal.

How can we read the Pentateuch with the help of this method? First, we have to read the texts. As stated above, the reader does not have to begin from scratch. A great deal has been written to provide plenty of help for the beginner. I suggest that one works through a passage as much as possible before consulting commentaries. It is best for one to follow a few simple steps. Pauline A. Viviano provides six criteria for identifying sources.

First, one may look for different styles. Different writers have different styles of writing. That is not to say that one writer cannot vary his or her style. By itself, style is not overly convincing. Yet, it may indicate significant changes in a text. The priestly writer, for instance, follows a more rigid style than the J source.

Style, however, is one consideration. A closely related distinguishing factor concerns vocabulary. Different writers may use distinctive vocabularies in their work. P uses Elohim, and J uses Yahweh. This usage can be an indicator. There are other words or phrases consistently used that can point to one source or another. In Genesis 1–11, the following differences are significant: "image and likeness" versus "living being," "male and female" versus "man and woman," and "create" versus "form."[11] Looking for key terms, one could identify the source responsible for Genesis 1. One might note the use of the divine name God (i.e., Elohim) as well as the use of the verb "to create." Both terms are characteristic of P. This is enough to indicate the source is not J, which would use Yahweh and the Hebrew verb "to form" or "to shape" (wayyîṣer) rather than "to create" (bārā').

The third criterion concerns perspective. Different groups or writers have different perspectives. Variance does not always mean inconsistent, but it does mean that one person or group expresses his or her views differently than others. The perspectives of the priests living in the time of exile would be different from the point of view of one writing in a different time and place. P in Genesis 1 views God as transcendent. God speaks creation into existence. God is not really engaged in the act of creation nor does God have any personal relationship with humans. In Genesis 2, however, the Lord (Yahweh) shapes and forms humans and all the other animals. God forms the world and shapes living things with divine hands. Yahweh is not portrayed as transcendent, but as one who interacts with the man and his wife along with the other animals and the plants in the garden.

A fourth criterion identifies inconsistencies in a text. The view that there are inconsistencies in the Bible offends some people. Many feel a duty to resist any notion that the Bible has inconsistencies. Fundamentalists have gone to great lengths in trying to explain away inconsistencies or contradictions. In relation to the Pentateuch, many inconsistencies are the result of different versions of the same story. They are indicators of different sources. For example, J is consistent, and P is consistent. Therefore, discrepancies indicate the presence of more than one source.

Since the Bible was written by many different individuals and groups over hundreds of years, it is no surprise that one finds inconsistencies. If J and E, for example, represents a northern and southern source then one should expect the two sources to relate the same stories with slightly different details. This is what we find in Genesis 37:12–36 and 39:1 where both J and E recount the story of how Joseph ends up in Egypt.

Two criteria remain that can help one distinguish one source from another: interruptions and repetitions. Interruptions often occur, particularly in Genesis. It is as if a story stops, sometimes abruptly, and then picks up at a later point. For instance, the creation story in Genesis 1 continues through the first part of Genesis 2:4a. The "a" indicates that the creation story of chapter one continues through the first part of verse 4. The second part of that verse interrupts the story and begins a new account of creation. The second story continues through Genesis 4 until it is interrupted. After this interruption, the first story of P is continued. Genesis 5:1 picks up where Genesis 2:4a leaves off. Try reading Genesis 1–2:4a and then skipping to chapter 5 verse one. 5:1 simply continues the story that paused in Genesis 2:4a.

Repetitions are also common. Repetition is a common literary device, so it is not always an indicator of another source. But in certain circumstances and in certain texts where different sources occur, it may indicate different sources. For example, there are two stories of Abraham taking his wife to Egypt, one in Genesis 12:10–20 and the other in Genesis 20:1–18. In J, Sarai is Abram's wife. Abram tells Sarai to say that she is not his wife but his sister. He was afraid that Pharaoh would take her and kill him. The parallel account in the E story found in Genesis 20 relates some different details. One point of interest is that the story emphasizes that Sarah is in fact Abraham's half-sister. This detail is not mentioned in J. The difference may be significant only because it tells us something about E.

Concerning repetition, one needs to ask the following questions: Did a writer purposely repeat something for a particular literary effect or for emphasis? If so, the repetition is not evidence for different sources. If this does not seem to be the case, repetitions in certain places may point to different sources.

METHOD DEMONSTRATED IN GENESIS

To demonstrate this method, I have selected a passage from the Genesis creation account. Genesis 2 continues the topic of creation. Genesis 2:4a brings the first story to a conclusion. A second account begins in the second half of verse 4. The first task is to identify the sources in Genesis 2. The D source is not an option here since it primarily makes up the book of Deuteronomy. That leaves JE or P. The use of the divine name Elohim or God in verses 2 and 3 as opposed to Yahweh Elohim in verses 4b–5, 7–9, 15–16, 18–19, and 21–22 is helpful. The switch from Elohim to Yahweh Elohim suggests we may be looking at the J source.

When one considers the content of 2:1–4a, we find vocabulary associated with the P. The reference to the seventh day, which connects these verses with the first chapter of Genesis, the verb "to create", and the noun "generations" all point to P for the first creation account. And when considering Genesis 2:1–4a, it is evident that these verses conclude the story of the creation in Genesis 1. The style, vocabulary, perspective, and structure all indicate a connection to P.

The first account of creation in Genesis 1:1–2:4a employ the divine name Elohim for God. In terms of style, Genesis 1:1–2:4a is highly structured with regular repetition of key phrases such as "And God said … Let there be …."[12] This style is not present in Genesis 2:4b–25. The repetition in the first account is simply part of the Priestly style of writing. Also, one can find a number of Priestly terms and vocabulary in these verses. The verb create (Heb., bārā'), the phrase "these are the generations," the words images and likenesses, male (Heb., zākār) and female (Heb., nᵉqēbāʰ) are all present in Genesis 1:1–2:4a and not in 2:4b–25. In Genesis 2:4b–25, we have terms used by J such as "living being," "man (Heb., 'iš) and woman (Heb., 'iššāʰ), and the verb to form (Heb., yāṣar) instead of the verb to create.

Genesis 2 begins with the statement that the creation is now complete on the seventh day. Genesis 2:1 brings the seven days of creation to an end. Now on the seventh day, the Sabbath day, God rests. The verb "to rest" (Heb. šābat̲) is the verbal form of the noun Sabbath. 2:4a introduces another aspect of the story: "These are the generations of the heavens and the earth when they were created" (NRSV). One would then expect a listing or genealogy to follow, but this does not happen in the next verses. Instead, there is a second account of creation. The story that begins in 2:4a breaks off and does not continue until Genesis 5:1 where we get the genealogy. "This is the list of descendants of Adam. When God created humankind, he made them in the likeness of God" (NRSV). What follows is what one expected after 2:4a. Consequently, Genesis 2:1–4a clearly comes from P.

Genesis 2:4b begins a second story of creation rather different from the first one. The presence of Yahweh suggests that it comes from J. The vocabulary, perspective, and style all point to J as well. It is possible that the chapter could contain other sources. Therefore, one has to make sure that every verse in 2:4b–25 belongs to J. Editors often intertwine sources.

The divine name used in Genesis 1–2:4a shifts from Elohim to Yahweh. In 2:4b–3:24 the compound name Yahweh Elohim (Lord God) appears. In 4:1, the name becomes just Yahweh. It is likely a redactor added the divine name Elohim to Yahweh in chapters 2 and 3 to create continuity connecting these two accounts. [13]

In Genesis 2:4b–25, there is no indication of a shift to another source. The verses proceed smoothly and consistently telling the story of the creation of the world, plants, human beings, and the other animals. God planted a garden for the man and then sought to find him a "partner." [14] None of the animals Yahweh made is suitable as a partner for the man. Therefore, Yahweh takes a rib from the man and fashions it into a woman ('iššāʰ) who is found to be a suitable partner. This account begins in Genesis 2:4b and continues into chapters 3 and 4. There is no clear reason to doubt that the J account continues through the end of chapter 4. Genesis 5:1 returns to the Priestly narrative.

Now that an analysis of sources has been completed for Genesis 2, we might move on to ask historical questions. Identifying the sources is not an end, but it should lead to a more in-depth study. How does this text fit into the larger J narrative? What would this text mean to people living at the beginning of the monarchy, assuming J dates to the 10th century B.C.E.? How would it function as the beginning of J's story?

Source criticism, therefore, may serve as starting point for historical analysis. If J is the author of Genesis 2–4, then who is he or she and when did this author live? Other questions concern the audience and purpose. Whom is J addressing? This question also relates to the date. One must know the date and setting before being able to identify the audience. What is J trying to accomplish? Is this meant as entertainment, explanation, history, or theology? These are important historical concerns.

HISTORICAL AND THEOLOGICAL ASPECTS
OF THE SOURCE THEORY

Hans Walter Wolff and Walter Brueggemann make a case for J and the other three sources (E, P, and D) being theological works. Wolff and Brueggemann address both the historical and theological aspects of JEPD. They view JEPD as traditions rather than sources. Correspondingly, many scholars see editors playing an important role in combining traditions together. John Van Seters, however, sees J as an author and historian not an editor of traditions.[15] He thinks that P supplements the J material.[16] Wolff and Brueggemann's focus is on the historical setting for each tradition, and then they examine the theology expressed by each tradition. Each tradition has a message for a particular historical audience.

For Wolff, each tradition has a specific historical setting. Understanding the setting helps one understand the message of the text. To do this, one must date each tradition and locate its audience. Wolff published his findings for JE and D. Brueggemann brought Wolff's work together in a book, *The Vitality of Old Testament Traditions*. He added the chapter on the P source using Wolff's methodology. Wolff conceived his work as being relevant to his own contemporary situation, the time and events surrounding World War II. His work is an example of how a particular academic pursuit can have practical results for the church. He thinks that each tradition had a message for its own time that can also speak to the present.

For Wolff, J and the other traditions reflect a theological outlook. This view is not universally accepted. Some see the writing as a work of history,[17] and Harold Bloom views J as a great literary work of art.[18] Perhaps, this just reflects a bias in that a literary critic sees J one way, a historian another, and a theologian in still another.

According to Wolff, these biblical traditions are not just "collection of stories." They contain "confessions of faith." These confessions have sometimes been "refashioned to bear meanings not originally intended."[19] In other words, texts may be refashioned to speak to new situations. Moreover, the confessions are not "universal" or "timeless." They are always related to a specific "historical crisis."[20] It would seem that the historical approach is essential for recovering this message. The confession is known as a kerygma, a theological term meaning proclamation. The term refers to the normative part of faith. So he is trying to determine what each tradition is proclaiming in a particular historical setting. What is it calling its audience to think and do?

Wolff saw his work as speaking to the present day church. He stood among those German biblical scholars who opposed the National Socialist movement in Germany in the 1930s. The faithful church has always "protested against and called into question dominant cultural values. The task of exegesis then is to locate in any given text the confessing stance of the faithful community—a stance which will be both protest and affirmation."[21] Study of the Bible took on a new urgency to "hear the Word of God in the text."[22]

For Wolff, the four traditions come from a particular historical setting and relate to a particular crisis. The crisis calls forth the work. The purpose of the text is to deal with that crisis. To do a proper exegesis of a text, one must first identify the crisis that prompted the tradition.

Wolff came to the following conclusions about J, E, and D. J was a tenth century southern tradition that offered a critique and apology or defense for the monarchy. Wolff locates several key passages in J that articulate the proclamation for a tenth century audience. A key passage is Genesis 12:1–4a.[23] The tenth century was a time of change particularly in relation to the area of economics. With the monarchy, many people had become disadvantaged. It is also a more secular period where wealth and power become a problem. J's critique of the monarchy entails a denunciation of pride and self-centeredness. It is in part about an overly exalted view of the monarchy. The monarchy's sole purpose is to be a "blessing" (Gn 12). J argues that the Davidic dynasty is the "chosen bearer of blessing."[24] Yahweh grants this blessing first to Abraham and extends it to the monarchy. The status of this blessing is in danger since the monarchy is not living up to Yahweh's ideal.

The E tradition was a ninth century tradition that called for obedience to the God of Israel and a proper respect for God. It also called for a rejection of other gods. Even though E appears fragmentary, Wolff believes the fragments belong to an independent tradition.[25] Fear of God is the key phrase for E. The E tradition comes from the north and addresses the mixing of ancient Israel's religion with fertility religions of Canaan.[26]

D dates to the exilic period. D or Deuteronomy introduces a larger work—the DH. The kerygma or proclamation is a call for the people to repent. This idea comes from the Hebrew verb—šûb. Repentance provides a possibility for their future. The crisis is related to the Babylonian Exile. The people have been punished for their sins. The call is for the people to repent and turn to God in the hope of a new future.

Brueggemann writes the essay on P. Focusing on P's narrative traditions, he identifies the kerygma as "be fruitful and multiply, fill the land and subdue it and have dominion."[27] The audience would be those in Babylonian exile. The message is one of comfort and promise. They will again enjoy the land. P assures the people of Yahweh's promise of land. He says, "God has not forgotten his promise, and therefore Israel's history has not ended."[28]

The work of Wolff and Brueggemann shows how source criticism lays the foundation for additional historical and theological work. Their work provides a possible reason for the traditions, but there are problems. Dating the different traditions is now in dispute. This fact alone would require a new assessment of a tradition's kerygma.

Literary critic, Harold Bloom, rejects the view that J was a theologian or historian. For Bloom, J is not a confession of faith but a great literary work.[29] J is a woman whose "cognitive power is unmatched among Western writers until Shakespeare."[30] She lived and wrote during the tenth century BCE in or around Jerusalem. For him, J is a literary work that has become through the "process of religious canonization" a "sacred text."[31] His book begins with the translation of J by David Rosenberg. Bloom pays close attention to irony and other literary techniques used to produce this great work.

SOURCES CRITICISM IN SYNOPTIC GOSPELS

Source criticism in the New Testament is practiced primarily but not exclusively in the Synoptic Gospels. It could also be applied to the "literary relationship between Colossians and Ephesians and between 2 Peter and Jude" where one writer made us of another.[32] In regard to the Synoptic Gospels (Matthew, Mark, and Luke) the source critic attempts to recover the sources used by the authors of Matthew and Luke to write their accounts of Jesus' ministry. Matthew and Luke are not the names of the authors; they are titles of the Gospel that were added to the manuscripts sometime after they were written. The identities of the actual writers are unknown. The writer of Luke's Gospel makes it clear he or she used sources. Luke 1:1–4 says,

> Since many have undertaken to set down an orderly account of the events that have been fulfilled among us, just as they were handed on to us by those who from the beginning were eyewitnesses and servants of the word, I too decided, after investigating everything carefully from the very first, to write an orderly account for you, most excellent Theophilus, so that you may know the truth concerning the things about which you have been instructed.

By the time of Luke, there were many other accounts. The writer of the Gospel decides to write another account for Theophilus whose name means (lover of God). His investigation involved reading other accounts. We can assume that the writer used written and perhaps even oral sources in the writing of this Gospel. The situation would likely be much the same for the writer of Matthew's Gospel. If the writers were eyewitnesses, they would not have needed to rely on other sources except on certain occasions. Applying source criticism to the Synoptic Gospels requires one to identify the sources used by the writer of Matthew and Luke's Gospels.

There are two common theories. A two-source theory says that the writers of Matthew and Luke used Mark as one source. That would mean that Mark is chronologically first. Scholars commonly date Mark between 66 to 70 C.E. Matthew may have been written between 80–90 C.E. and Luke five to fifteen years later. Consequently, passages that occur in all three Gospels indicate that both Matthew and Luke used Mark as a source.

This accounts for one of the two sources. There are passages, however, that Matthew and Luke share that are not found in Mark. This fact indicates the presence of a second common source for Matthew and Luke. This source has been named the Q source. Q comes from the German *Quelle* meaning well or source. No one knows this author's identity.

The so-called Q source is primarily sayings of Jesus. It may be similar to the non-canonical Gospel of Thomas. Q is thought to be a written source that pre-dates our earliest canonical Gospel. In 1993, Burton Mack provided a reconstructed text of Q in his book *The Lost Gospel: The Book of Q and Christian Origins*.[33]

Another theory supplements the two source hypothesis to account for all of the materials in Matthew and Luke. It proposes two additional sources. Both Matthew and Luke had access to the special material unique to their own Gospel. They are referred to as proto-Matthew and proto-Luke or simply the M and L sources.

METHOD DEMONSTRATED ON LUKE 4:1–13

To illustrate this approach, I have selected Luke 4:1–13. To keep the discussion brief, I just describe the logic behind the identification of the source. Luke 4:1–13 is about the temptation of Jesus. The event is found in Mark 1:12–13 but it is limited to two verses. Mark's version of the story is remarkable because of its brevity. It tells of Jesus' going into the wilderness for forty days to be tempted by Satan. It also says that Jesus was with the wild beasts and that angels took care of him. The temptation in Mark 1:12–13 comes just before Jesus' entrance into Galilee. Luke 4:1–13 tells the story with many more details than Mark. The author of Luke must have had access to a fuller account in the Q source.

Once a proper identification is made, one could ask historical questions about Q. We might ask about Q's date, audience, social and historical circumstances, purpose, and its message. If Q is earlier than any of the canonical Gospels, then it is an important historical source for helping us understand the Jesus movement. Mack's book on Q attempts to understand Q in relation to a particular historical community. The Q source helps us understand the Jesus movement at an early stage.

The story of Q is recounted by Mack in his book, *The Lost Gospel: The Book of Q and Christian Origins*. Mack, influenced by the work of John Kloppenborg, does not view Q as a random collection of Jesus' sayings. Kloppenborg identified two layers or collections of sayings in Q. The first collection consists of wisdom sayings. At a later stage, these wisdom sayings "were incorporated into a composition that developed the theme of judgment by using prophetic and apocalyptic discourse."[34] One of Mack's main interests in this book is to understand the community that produced this Q document.

Mack produces a translation of the earliest layer of Q and then the complete book of Q. He divides Q into three layers: Q^1 consists of wisdom sayings, Q^2 adds an announcement of judgment, and Q^3 contains a few later additions.[35] One implication of this work on source criticism is that the historical scholar has to recover the Jesus of history from the earliest sources. The Gospels are sources for history, but they are primarily theological in nature. What we have in the New Testament is primarily about the Christ of faith. The Christ of faith is the picture we get of Jesus by reading the texts as they are now. The Gospel writers did not necessarily seek to present a historical account of Jesus' life and ministry; their portrayals of Jesus' ministry reflect their own theology. We have their interpretations of Jesus's actions and teachings. Neither Q nor Mark, the earliest canonical Gospel, is a historical account interested in the historical Jesus. Q and Mark are theological reflections on Jesus.

New Testament scholar James D. Dunn has made an interesting proposal about the Jesus traditions that can shed light on the historical Jesus.[36] He is interested in oral traditions as opposed to written documents. He asks: Do oral traditions give access to the historical Jesus? He believes they do. He compares storytelling in rural Palestinian villages today to understand the storytelling process in the past. He believes this type of comparison is valid since it has not changed much over the years.

His thesis is that we find variance/flexibility and stability in the way information is related to oral traditions. Some materials remain stable and exhibit little or no flexibility in the retelling. Other types may reveal flexibility. The community would control the process of transmission and allow for flexibility in some instances and not others. Proverbs, for example, remain fixed. Parables, on the other hand, have some flexibility.[37]

He discusses a number of passages in Matthew and Luke. The centurion's servant in Matthew 8:5–13 and Luke 7:1–10 is usually assigned to Q even though it is not a saying of Jesus but a narrative. Why should it be attributed to Q just because it is not in Mark but common to Matthew and Luke? He does not question the existence of Q, but he is asking if Matthew and Luke share a common oral tradition not found in Q. He concludes that this is the case. Matthew 8:5–13 and Luke 7:1–10 bear the marks of oral storytelling. The story shows enough flexibility to argue against the view that Matthew and Luke copied it from Q. It is likely, he thinks, that the story represents an oral tradition that both Matthew and Luke drew upon. He comes to the same conclusion on other passages as well.

Source criticism in both the Hebrew Bible and the New Testament has continued to raise the issue of tradition. Are we talking about written sources or traditions? Traditions can be communicated in writing and passed down from generation to generation as opposed to sources that may be more rigid and are the creations of an author. Sources may contain traditional materials as part of their content. Dunn holds out a place for oral tradition in his study of the Synoptic Gospels. In the Pentateuch, some scholars view JEPD as traditions rather than written fixed documents. Correspondingly, many scholars see editors playing an important role in combining these traditions. Others disagree. John Van Seters sees J as an author and historian not an editor of traditions. [38]

All of this begs the question: When does an editor become an author or when does an author become an editor? In modern thought, an author is someone who creates a work. The work is primarily original. Nevertheless, editors may be inventive and creative as well. Today editors proofread works to correct mistakes or make decisions about what is to be included and excluded in a book, journal or newspaper. In the time of the Hebrew Bible or the New Testament, however, an editor may have functioned like an author in some ways.

For biblical studies, one could generally define an editor as one who works with older materials, employing and shaping those materials to create a finished work bearing the editor's own perspective. Therefore, Gospel writers worked with older materials, but they added their own theological views and perspectives. The same is true to a lesser degree with the Hebrew Bible. Editors in the Hebrew Bible did not always edit materials for theological reasons. Since the editors did not feel any obligation to cite sources, it often appears they were authors and eyewitnesses. In short, author and editor are not as distinct in biblical times as they are today.

ONGOING RESEARCH

The German scholar Julian Wellhausen brought together several different views of his day into what has become known as the new documentary hypothesis. The dates used above for JEPD have primarily come from his work. Today, however, a number of his conclusions have been challenged. Van Seters dismisses a 10th century date for J dating it instead to the sixth century B.C.E. making it later than D and prior to P.[39] Moreover, he dismisses E as an independent source, which is a relatively common view today. Van Seters sees J as an "antiquarian history."[40] D, J, and P are sources, not traditions. Instead of a long process of editing, he argues that one source supplemented another (i.e., new supplementary hypothesis).[41] Therefore, he defends the source theory in a modified form.

There have been those who reject the classical documentary hypothesis altogether. The book, *A Farewell to the Yahwist*, is a book of essays.[42] Most of the writers question the very existence of J. It does seem that the essays accept P as a source with other filler materials at a later date. Konrad Schmid concludes there is no J. He also rejects any connection between the stories of the patriarchs in Genesis and the stories of the exodus from Egypt prior to the priestly writer.[43] The priestly writer made this connection, a view which is strongly rejected by van Seters in a later essay.[44] P connected the promises of the patriarchs with the exodus and covenant traditions in the other four books.

These are areas of ongoing discussion and debate. Credibility for J and P is bolstered by the fact that once they are identified these sources can be read as complete independent works. However, E at best seems fragmentary. D is different from the other three in that it is largely contained in one book. Still, it appears to stand as a source introducing a larger work.

One trend is emerging. Biblical scholars are dating materials later rather than earlier. Questioning sources in no way is leading back to an older view of Mosaic authorship. There is still some general agreement that the Pentateuch derives from different sources or traditions.

In the New Testament, source criticism also has a long history. It has mainly taken place in regards to the Synoptic Gospels. A renewed interest in this topic came about with the Seminar on the Historical Jesus, which focuses on the Synoptic Gospels as a source of information about the historical Jesus.

In short, source criticism is still a useful tool for historical research. It raises important historical questions. It helps one understand how inconsistencies and duplications made it into these biblical books. It alerts us to the fact that the text we now have once existed in different forms and served different purposes. It shows that the Bible has a rich and complex past. The Bible did not fall from heaven, but it came about through a long process involving people's growing understandings of themselves, their fellow human beings, and their God. This approach is, however, just one of many legitimate ways of reading these biblical texts.

NOTES

1. Pauline A. Viviano, "Source Criticism," 42–48.
2. Ibid., 52.

3. Harold Bloom, *The Book of J*, trans. David Rosenberg (New York: Vintage Books, 1991).

4. Bloom maintains the author is a woman. Richard Elliott Friedman also discusses this possibility. See Richard Elliott Friedman, *Who Wrote the Bible*, (New York: Harper & Row, 1987), 86–87.

5. Bloom maintains the author is a woman. Richard Elliott Friedman also discusses this possibility. See Richard Elliott Friedman, *Who Wrote the Bible*, 86–87.

6. Hermann Gunkel, *The Legends of Genesis: The Biblical Saga and History*, (New York: Schocken Books, 1964), 130.

7. Friedman 88.

8. Anderson, xvii; and Noth 248–251.

9. Noth, Martin. *The Deuteronomistic History*. Journal for the Study of the Old Testament Supplement Series, ed. David J. A. Clines, 15 (Sheffield: JSOT Press), 1981.

10. Viviano, "Source Criticism," 41.

11. Ibid., 43.

12. Ibid., 42–43.

13. Gerhard von Rad, *Genesis*, The Old Testament Library, ed., G. Ernest Wright (Philadelphia: The Westminster Press, 1972), 77.

14. See Phyllis Trible, *God and the Rhetoric of Sexuality*, Overtures to Biblical Theology, eds. Walter Brueggemann and John R. Donahue, S.J. (Philadelphia: Fortress Press, 1978), 90.

15. John Van Seters, "The Report of the Yahwist's Demise Has Been Greatly Exaggerated!" in *A Farewell to the Yahwist? The Composition of the Pentateuch in Recent European Interpretation*, ed., Christopher R. Matthews, no. 34, Society of Biblical Literature Symposium Series, (Atlanta: Society of Biblical Literature, 2006), 143–147.

16. John van Seters, "The Pentateuch: Genesis, Exodus, Leviticus, Numbers, Deuteronomy, in *The Hebrew Bible Today: An Introduction to Critical Issues* eds. Steven L. McKenzie and M. Patrick Graham (Louisville: Westminster John Knox Press), 14.

17. Robert Coote and David Robert Ord, *The Bible's First Historian: From Eden to the Court of David with the Yahwist* (Philadelphia: Fortress Press, 1989).

18. Bloom.

19. Walter Brueggemann. "Wolff's Kerygmatic Methodology," in *The Vitality of Old Testament Traditions*, 2d ed., (Atlanta: John Knox Press, 1982), 32.

20. Ibid.

21. Ibid., 31.

22. Ibid.

23. Hans Walter Wolff and Walter Brueggemann. *The Vitality of Old Testament Traditions*. 2d ed., (Atlanta: John Knox Press, 1982), 46–55.

24. Brueggemann, 33.

25. Wolff, 80.

26. Ibid., 80–82.

27. Brueggemann, 37.

28. Ibid., 37.

29. Bloom, 9–14, 35.

30. Ibid., 16.

31. Ibid., 35.

32. Christopher Tuckett, *Reading the New Testament: Methods of Interpretation* (Philadelphia: Fortress Press, 1987), 78.

33. Burton L. Mack, *The Lost Gospel: The Book of Q and Christian Origins* (San Francisco: Harper Collins, 1993).

34. Mack, Lost Gospel of Q, 37.

35. Ibid., 44.

36. James Dunn, "Jesus in Oral Memory: The Initial Stages of the Jesus Tradition," in *Seminar Papers Society of Biblical Literature Annual Meeting 2000* no. 39 (Atlanta: Society of Biblical Literature, 2000), 287–326.

37. Ibid., 294–296.

38. John Van Seters, "The Report of the Yahwist's Demise Has Been Greatly Exaggerated!" in *A Farewell to the Yahwist? The Composition of the Pentateuch in Recent European Interpretation*, ed., Christopher R. Matthews, no. 34, Society of Biblical Literature Symposium Series, (Atlanta: Society of Biblical Literature, 2006), 143–147.

39. John Van Seters, "Deuteronomy between Pentateuch and the Deuteronomistic History," *HTS Theological Studies* 59:3 (2003): 947–949; John Van Seters, *The Pentateuch: A Social Science Commentary,* (Sheffield: Sheffield Academic Press 1999), 58–86.

40. Van Seters, "Report of the Yahwist's Demise," 144–147.

41. Van Seters 'Deutreronomy," 948; and *The Pentateuch*, 58–86.

42. Thomas B. Doseman and Konrad Schmid eds., *A Farewell to the Yahwist? The Composition of the Pentateuch in Recent European Interpretation* (Atlanta: Society of Biblical Literature, 2006).

43. Konrad Schmid, "The So-Called Yahwist and the Literary Gap between Genesis and Exodus," in *A Farewell to the Yahwist? The Composition of the Pentateuch in Recent European Interpretation*, ed., Christopher R. Matthews, no. 34, Society of Biblical Literature Symposium Series, (Atlanta: Society of Biblical Literature, 2006), 48.

44. Van Seters, Report of the Yahwist Demise. Van Seters argues that the connection connected the promises of the patriarchs with the exodus and covenant traditions came from J not P.

Chapter Seven

Form Criticism

Form criticism is perhaps the most useful historical method primarily because of its applicability to every part of the Bible. Form criticism is based on the observation that certain types of literature share certain patterns of language and structures. The type either consciously or unconsciously guides one's understanding. When readers encounter a letter, for instance, they have certain expectations about what is in it. A letter is just one type of literature. Another common biblical example is a parable. But even with letters we know there is more than one type. Under the broad classification of the letter, there are personal and business letters. While ancient letters would be similar in some ways to modern ones, they would also differ. Consequently, one must consider its particular historical and social settings.

The differences between a letter and a poem, for instance, matters. For Paul's letters, it means that his communications are to a church or individuals at a particular place and time. They sometimes contain communications of a personal nature and on other occasions they encourage or command actions. The letters may serve as instructions for the recipients. Letters contain materials of a moral and theological nature. When we read these letters, we must realize we are reading someone else's mail. Modern readers must try to understand and apply these communications in their own modern settings.

Certain types of literature use specific kinds of language and structures. Consider fairy tales. The phrase "Once upon a time" is a clear marker of a particular type of literature. The ending is also identifiable in the phrase "they lived happily ever after!" In other words, certain phrases, structures, and conventions lead to reader expectations. Letters, for instance, begin and end in ways that allow the reader to recognize them as letters. Once recognized, the reader expects certain elements to be present. The absence of these elements, changes in the normal structure or the presence of unusual elements may surprise the recipient.

Fixed phrases and structures can be associated with certain types of literature. The expression "thus says the Lord" is a fixed phrase, which one often finds in prophetic texts associated with oracles. An oracle is a word from the divine. It typically comes through a "priest, prophet, seer, or diviner. It may be solicited by the intermediary on behalf of himself or a third party, or it may come unsolicited."[1]

Types may also contain other types. A letter may contain a poem that one wants to send to his or her friend. Or one may tell the recipient a story in the letter. Elizabeth Schüssller Fiorenza argues that in Paul's letter to the Galatians, there is a pre-Pauline baptismal formula (Gal 3:28).[2] If correct, imagine the implications. The connection with a baptismal formula shapes the meaning and importance of this text for the newly formed Christian communities. It is a statement that both males and females will become full and equal members of the Christian community through the act of baptism.[3]

Within broad types such as Gospels or Psalms, one can find many other types. Gospels contain miracle stories, controversy dialogues, parables, aphorisms just to name a few types. Psalms can be further categorized as lament psalms, praise psalms, creation psalms, or wisdom psalms.

Types may often display a certain amount of flexibility. Not every letter in the New Testament is identical nor is every praise psalm in the book of Psalms. Creation stories may differ even though they may share common themes and ideas. Within the ordered and predictable elements of a type, there may be things one could not have foreseen. This unforeseen aspect may function to call attention to something, or it may alert the reader to something significant.

The method for doing form criticism is fairly straight forward. For the moment, we can identify four basics steps. First, one needs to define the boundaries and structures of the text (identifying where a passage begins and ends). Second, one should determine the type or types of literature in the text. Third, one needs to determine the *Sitz im Leben* or social setting of the text. And finally, one has to ascertain the purpose of the text.

BOUNDARY AND STRUCTURE OF THE TEXT

The first step is to identify a beginning and ending point for the study. The resulting text may be large or small depending on the study. It could be as large as several chapters or as small as a few verses. The unit could be the Gospel of Luke or a parable within the Gospel of Luke. The larger the unit, the more likely one will encounter more than one type in it. If one selects the

Gospel of Luke as the unit of study, he or she will find several types and sub-types in it.

Still there should be reasons why one begins in one place and ends in another. Perhaps, the structure of a text clearly indicates its beginning and ending. Certain formulaic language such as "Thus says the Lord" and "says the Lord" may mark a beginning or end of a unit (e.g., Amos 1:3–4). In Amos 1:3–2:6, a series of oracles against the nations including Judah and Israel begin with the phrase "Thus says the Lord" and ends with "says the Lord."

Other times there may not be clear markers of the beginning and ending. One may have to look for structural markers or shifts in context and theme. Looking for transitional indicators is often helpful. The word "Now" or "Next," for instance, may indicate the beginning of a new section separate from what came before. It may be that one story is concluding while another is beginning.

There has been a tendency in early form-critical studies to focus on short, self-contained oral units of speech. German scholar Hermann Gunkel (1862–1932) was instrumental in the development of form criticism. He focused on short independent units. Gunkel states that:

> Many of the stories of Genesis extend over scarcely more than ten verses. ... [T]he older legends are absolutely abrupt to modern taste. Now, of course, the brief compass of the old legends is at the same time an index of their character. They deal with very simple occurrences which can be adequately described in a few words. . . . The earliest story-tellers were not capable of constructing artistic works of any considerable extent; neither could they expect their hearers to follow them with undiminished interest for days and even weeks continuously. On the contrary, primitive times were satisfied with quite brief productions which required not much over half an hour.[4]

Gunkel sees the expansion of the compositions developed at a later date. So in Genesis, Gunkel focused on legends or sagas,[5] which are short, poetic stories originally oral in nature. In Gunkel's view, a "class of professional storytellers, familiar with old songs and legends, wandered about the country, and were probably to be found regularly at the popular festivals"[6] The sagas may have begun as independent units, but they eventually were combined into saga cycles focusing on different topics and themes.

Form critics in the New Testament also tended to focus on the short individual units. The Gospel writers were in possession of a number of short pericopes or units of traditions. These individual short units were important either for what they could tell us about the early Church or about the historical Jesus. Some limited collections of these units may have existed before becoming part of "written tradition."[7] The Gospel writer brought these short units together into a larger narrative framework. Early form critics focused on these short units.

Marvin A. Sweeney pushes for a form-critical analysis that focuses more on larger units of texts. He studies "literary and linguistic structures and modes of expression of the much larger textual compositions in which smaller units function."[8] Likewise, Gene M. Tucker does not limit form criticism to the study of short units.[9] For Sweeny, form criticism can examine the texts as we now have them. He would extend the analysis to shorter units within the larger whole. Sweeney and Tucker are saying that form criticism can examine the larger whole as well as the shorter units.

TYPE OR GENRE

Once the beginning and ending of the text are defined, one is ready to address the issue of classification. A unit may be classified as one type or as a collection of types. 2 Samuel 9–20 and 1 Kings 1–2 has been classified as a Succession Narrative. Hugo Gressmann has argued that this so-called Succession Narrative actually contains four independent short novels: 2 Samuel 10–12, 13–14, 15–20 and 1 Kings 1–2. W. Caspari also sees smaller independent novels making up this larger whole.[10]

To identify the type, one should begin with a close reading of the text. In this close reading, one looks for special language, conventional speech patterns, formulas, structures, and themes that can help one make a classification. Besides reading the text carefully, reading commentaries on the text can be rather useful. Some commentaries focus on form-critical analysis such as *The Forms of the Old Testament Literature* published by William B. Eerdmans and *Hermeneia—A Critical and Historical Commentary on the Bible* published by Fortress Press. Many other works can serve the interpreter as well. A close reading coupled with adequate research can yield a well-informed classification of the text.

SITZ IM LEBEN

Sitz im Leben is a German phrase commonly used in form criticism. It means situation in life. It refers to the "sociological situation which produced and maintained the various genres."[11] *Sitz im Leben* refers to the social setting in which a type functioned. Laws would clearly belong to a legal setting and hymns of praise to a private or public worship setting. Wisdom types such as proverbs may derive in large part from a family setting. The settings provide insight to the message of the text.

A text such as Hosea 4:1–3 draws upon legal language in the form of prophetic judgment speech. Here both legal and prophetic settings are important. The legal setting shapes a person's understanding of this brief oracle. This oracle contains a call for the people to hear the charge being made by Yahweh. The charge is followed by a description. Finally, the judgment is announced followed by a description of the punishment.

> Introduction: Hear the word of the LORD, O people of Israel; for the LORD has a controversy (rîb) with the inhabitants of the land."
>
> Charge: There is no faithfulness or kindness, and no knowledge of God in the land; there is swearing, lying, killing, stealing, and committing adultery; they break all bounds and murder follows murder.
>
> Punishment: Therefore the land mourns, and all who dwell in it languish, and also the beasts of the field, and the birds of the air; and even the fish of the sea are taken away. (RSV)

The legal setting might reflect cases brought to the "court assembly at the city gate."[12] Disputes were often heard and settled there. This setting provides one with a framework for understanding the text. The setting for prophetic speech comes from a context where the prophet receives an oracle from God. The prophet then communicates this message to the people. Such communication could take place in a formal or informal public gathering.

Sweeney expands the task of identifying the social setting to include the historical and literary settings. The historical and social settings are similar. While the historical setting may be concerned with a description of the date and location of certain events, the social setting provides a broader social context. The social setting of the rules of royal succession, for example, relates to the royal court. It may also have a tie to the family where the eldest surviving son has the right to his father's possessions.[13] The social setting is not, therefore, tied to a particular place, event, or date. It is a larger context from which one gains a better appreciation of the text.

By considering the historical and literary settings, Sweeney has enlarged the scope of form criticism. The historical aspect focuses on locating events in their proper historical context. It also entails determining the causes for those events. The context of the so-called Succession Narrative would reflect the time of David's reign. It would focus on the years at the end of his reign and the struggle for the throne.

The literary setting looks at the context of this unit in the larger literary perspective. What is the role of the Succession Narrative, for example, in relation to the larger DH? It would focus on how themes in this text relate to the larger narrative framework. The whole question of Yahweh's covenant with David in 2 Samuel 7 along with succession plays a significant role in 2 Samuel through 2 Kings. Issues relating to David's heirs and the loss of the united monarchy along with the later loss of both northern and southern kingdoms tie the Succession Narrative to larger Deuteronomistic concerns.

PURPOSE OR INTENTION OF GENRES/TYPES

The focus on the intent of a type raises questions and objections from some scholars today. Knowing the mind or thoughts of an author living over a thousand years ago is problematic. Even if one gets it right, one cannot confirm it since the writer is long dead. The writer's text is all we possess. All one can do is to assume a connection between a text's meaning and the author's intentions. When one says what the author had in mind, that is only a general approximation based on a historical reading. It can only be judged on the basis of textual and historical information.

Form criticism is not so much asking about the intent of the writer as the purpose of a particular genre. As Tucker puts it, a type of literature "arises in order to fulfill a particular purpose."[14] A letter, for instance, serves a particular purpose. Analyzing the structure, language, and setting of a letter may help one determine the letter's purpose. In the case of a letter, it might be a call for support, an attempt to offer instruction, or a situation where the sender is making a demand.

ILLUSTRATION OF THE METHOD

To demonstrate this method, I have selected two passages. Both passages focus on a fairly short self-contained unit. One could, however, concentrate on larger text such as Genesis 1–11. Even with larger blocks one can concentrate on the small units within them. The following discussion is short. A full form critical study would go into more detail.

GENESIS 22

Step One: Establishing the Boundaries of the Text

Genesis 22:1–19 tells the story about God testing Abraham's faith. These verses do appear to constitute a complete unit. It is, of course, part of a larger narrative that extends throughout the Book of Genesis and beyond. Genesis 22 represents a threat to the promise made to Abraham in Genesis 12. God promised Abraham that the world would be blessed through his seed (Gn 12:1–3). By taking a quick look at commentaries, one can see that source critics identify Genesis 22 as mainly the product of E. It is likely, however, that Genesis 22 contains a rather small contribution from either a redactor or from J found in Genesis 22:17. The chapter on a larger scale belongs to a cycle of stories about Abraham.

Genesis 22:1 begins a new story. It is not a continuation of Genesis 21. It contains a clear transition. The phrase "after these things" clearly separates this section from what comes before it. The content of Genesis 22 confirms this division as well. Genesis 21 is about a covenant Abraham made with Abimelech leading to the founding of Beersheba whereas Genesis 22 is a story about God testing Abraham by asking him to offer his only son as a burnt offering. The two stories are connected, however, in that the end of the story (Gn 22:19) has Abraham returning back to Beersheba.

The ending is also clearly visible. Verse 19 concludes the account with Abraham returning "to his young men, and they arose and went together to Beersheba; and Abraham dwelt at Beersheba" (RSV). The next verse begins a new unit with the phrase "after these things", which the reader encountered in verse 1. Verses 20 and following begin a new story. So we can define the unit of study as Genesis 22:1–19.

The structure or form of this passage begins with an opening statement that informs the audience that what follows is a test of Abraham. This statement is followed by an address and a command. It seems clear throughout that Abraham will obey God. What follows is perhaps horrifying for modern audiences. God tells Abraham to take his only son whom he loves and go to the land of Moriah. There he is to offer him as a burnt offering on one of the mountains (Gn 22:2). The structure of the unit focuses on Abraham. The structure of the story depicts him as a righteous person who never wavers in his faithfulness and obedience to God even when asked to give up his only son, a son he loves. This individual story, apart from the larger Abrahamic cycles of stories, never suggests that Abraham might hesitate to follow God's command; he is never in danger of failing the test. The structure of the unit emphasizes his unquestioning faithfulness.[15]

Following upon the announcement of the test, the second major part of the text discusses Abraham's virtue. It includes a dialogue between God and Abraham, Abraham's implementation of God's commands, the angel's intervention and declaration of Abraham's willingness to go through with the sacrifice. Genesis 22:17 concerns the promise and ties this event to the promises made to Abraham in Genesis 12:3 and Genesis 15.[16] Either E has knowledge of such a promise, or we have an editor augmenting E with the J material. The final verse brings the section to a conclusion with Abraham's return to Beersheba.

Step Two: Genre

Gunkel identifies Genesis 22 as a saga or legend. He notes that sagas have a clear beginning and ending,[17] which is certainly true of Genesis 22. Taken as a whole, much of Genesis reflects the structure and characteristics of a saga or legend. A legend, according to George W. Coats, has the following features. "Its structure does not represent a plot based on a narration of tension, increasing to a point of resolution. . . . It employs a relatively static narration."[18] Legend puts weight on a particular aspect of the hero. A legend is not defined by any specific content but by its typical structure. It is generally about a person or a place (i.e., it could be associated with a holy person, cultic site, or sacred place). The legend is part of a storyteller's "repertoire"; it may be told in "cultic shrines, at the royal court, [or in a] . . . family setting."[19] It may serve as a model for behavior[20] by encouraging people to follow the example of the hero. Legends may also inspire and bolster pride in family, tribe, or nation.[21]

It does not take much work to see how this fits Genesis 22. Based on Coats description, Genesis 22 clearly fits these characteristics. Overall, the text focuses on the hero's virtue, and the structure of the text does emphasize the virtue of Abraham. The promise reiterated in the text from Genesis 12:3 underscores Abraham's faithfulness. His example provides the model for others to follow. Through him, God's promise extends to Israel and beyond. There is no plot leading to tension in the E material because there is no indication that Abraham ever falters in his resolve to do God's will.

Gunkel identifies Genesis 22 specifically as a cultic legend. He reconstructs the name of the cultic site, which has not survived in the present form of the text. He identifies the site as Jeruel in the Judean wilderness. He concludes that Genesis 22 was "originally the legend of child sacrifice at Jeruel."[22] Interestingly, he speculates that the original legend points back to an earlier time when child sacrifice was required but was later replaced by a substitute. In this passage, the goat becomes the substitute for the child.[23]

Step Three: *Sitz im Leben*

After genre, the next focus is *Sitz im Leben*. As stated above there are three settings of importance: the social, historical and literary settings. In relation to the social setting, a legend is the product of a society's collective stories that typically extol particular virtues. Often legends are about individuals who have the status of heroes. As part of the shared lore of a people, they carry some measure of authority. So legends can legitimate certain actions and views within a culture or society.

Unlike modern people who may often think of legends as made-up stories, ancient peoples would have viewed them differently. They may not have considered every legend as having equal weight, but they would have seen legends as conveying real information. In fact, legends may contain a blend of real and mythical information. Anthropologist William A. Haviland describes them as "semi-historical narratives that account for the deeds of heroes, the movements of peoples, and the establishment of local customs."[24]

The hero of Genesis 22 is clearly Abraham. He is a model for the behavior of others. The story continues to have a significant impact on readers. For some readers, the emphasis on Abraham's faithfulness is paramount. He is a hero of the faith. He simply trusted in God and was willing to do whatever God told him to do. For others, the story is quite disturbing. His character for some may be highly questionable; he is one who seems to be blindly obedient. A secondary effect of this story may be to delegitimize human sacrifice in favor of animal sacrifice.

The historical setting for this story is difficult to determine. Most critics assign Genesis 22 to the E source, but the appearance of Yahweh and the reference to J's account of Yahweh's promise to Abraham in Genesis 22:17 calls this identification into question. It is likely as E.A. Speiser argues that "J was either appended to E [by a redactor], or that E was superimposed upon J. There was admittedly some fusion"[25] of the two sources.

A redactor who would have integrated J into this story is connecting the Davidic dynasty to the promises of Abraham as discussed in both in Genesis 12:1–3 and Genesis 22:15–18. The monarchy is an extension of the promise made to Abraham. This text would add legitimacy to the Davidic dynasty and its ultimate role as a means of blessing. For E, the story centers on the "fear of God." The historical setting for E's account would have reflected the conditions of the Northern Kingdom during the eighth century. According to certain biblical texts, this setting is characterized as a time and place where the people are often unfaithful.[26] For biblical writers, faithfulness to God and the rejection of foreign gods were key concerns.

A redactor has employed elements of J to emphasize the promise, and E is about obedience and faithfulness. In Genesis 22, it is the obedience of Abraham that leads to the promise. Does this mean that the promise in Genesis 12:1–3 is conditional on Abraham's obedience? As stated in Genesis 12:1–3, the promise is not conditional, but here it appears to be. "Because you have done this, and have not withheld your son, your only son, I will indeed bless you" (Gn 22:17b). It could be the conditional aspect arose in the editing of the two sources. The language "not withheld your son, your only son" is the language of E. It ties this part of the text to Genesis 22:1–14. Genesis 22:17b adds to what is found in Genesis 12:1–3 by stating that Abraham's "offspring shall possess the gate of their enemies." Also, the conditional aspect is consistent with the notion of a test, which Abraham passes. Perhaps, it is possible that E like J has an account of a promise made to Abraham, and E's promise is conditional. If so, the entire passage could derive from E.

The literary setting moves the interpreter to look at the larger picture. Genesis 22 is part of the Abrahamic cycle that relates to the Primeval stories of Genesis 1–11 and moves forward to an ongoing history where the promise made to Abraham plays itself out. Genesis 22, then, is a threat to that larger divine plan. Thomas W. Mann situates the place of the Abraham cycle in the Torah.

> In relation to the Primeval cycle [Genesis 1–11] these stories represent the new reality God intends for the world; at the same time, the stories point beyond themselves to the central event of the Torah—the redemption from Egyptian bondage and the formation of the covenant community. In the end, the great-great grandchildren of Abraham and Sarah, who were summoned from the 'old world' of Mesopotamia to the 'new world' of Canaan, find themselves as resident aliens (albeit highly favored) in the strange land of Egypt, and *their* descendants (highly unfavored) will have to be 'brought out' of Egypt 'with an outstretched arm and with great acts of judgment (Ex 6:6).[27]

While Mann connects the Abraham narratives to the Exodus event, Wolff connects J's account of Yahweh's promise to Abraham to David, who would never be without an heir on his throne (Gn 12). So the Abrahamic literature has larger connections in the ongoing relationship of Israel to her God. The promise in Geneses 12:1–3 is a gift from God. In the larger narrative, there is a tension between God's favor directed toward Abraham and his descendants and the testing of Abraham's faithfulness in Genesis 22.

In the larger narrative, Abraham's faithfulness may not be so certain. Coat argued that a legend does not contain ambiguity—everyone knows Abraham will be obedient. Not necessarily true when reading the larger Abrahamic cycle. In earlier stories, Abraham was not always a model character (cf., Gn 12:10–20; 16; 20). According to Mann, the test in Genesis 22 is a real test because God wants to know if Abraham will be faithful.[28]

With this brief look at different possible settings, one can enlarge one's understanding and appreciation of this biblical text. It can focus on the smallest unit and see it in relation to the whole. It can also understand what is going on in a social context as well as historical. Socially, the text functions to legitimate unquestioning obedience to God. It is a form of national pride and an example for others. Historically, the text speaks in a particular historical context where obedience to God alone is demanded. Obedience derives from a proper respect or "fear of God," and the promise serves to legitimate the monarchy as the vehicle of God's blessing for ancient Israel. His character for some may be highly questionable; he is one who seems to be blindly obedient.

Step Four: Purpose of Genesis 22:1–19

Legend or saga is a type of communication that describes the actions of a hero figure. This figure serves as a model for other people to follow. The story of Abraham's complete and unwavering obedience to God holds him up as a model for other people to follow. His devotion to God was tested, and he proves himself to be faithful. This story then is to challenge the audience. They are to strive to follow Abraham's example and exhibit the same type of faith.

MARK 2:23–3:6

New Testament scholars have identified the overall structure of Mark in different ways. Mark 1–3 contains a number of small units dealing with the calling of disciples, healings or cleansings, casting out unclean spirits, and a number of conflicts. These early short units describe the growing crowds and the growing resistance of the Jewish authorities toward Jesus. The two situations are connected. Growing crowds indicate an increasing threat to the status quo where Jewish leaders have enjoyed a certain privileged position of respect.

Step One: Establishing the Boundaries of the Text

In Mark 1–3, some texts are a little odd. Jesus instructs those he healed not to tell others (Mk 1:43–44, 5:43; 7:36; 8:26). Jesus commands demons who know his name not to reveal it (Mk 1:25, 34, 3:12). What is the reason for this secrecy? F. T. France suggests that it is Jesus' role as the Messiah that is the secret at this stage in the Gospel. [29]

Conflict is common in the first three chapters of Mark. Jesus is regularly being questioned by Jewish religious leaders. The tension grows and eventually reveals the intent of the Pharisees to destroy Jesus. Mark 3:6 says that "the Pharisees went out and immediately conspired with the Herodians against him, how to destroy him." The conflicts seem to center around the issues of authority and Jesus' behavior. They charge Jesus with doing what is unlawful on the Sabbath in 3:1–6. These elements tie the stories in the first three chapters together.

For the sake of this illustration, I will focus on the latter part of Mark 2. The last short unit in Mark 2 appears to begin with verse 23. Mark 2:23 follows upon Jesus' encounter with the Pharisees on the issue of fasting. Like many of the stories before and after, Mark casts the Pharisees as Jesus' adversaries. Mark 2:23 begins with Jesus and his disciples "going through the grainfields; and as they made their way his disciples began to pluck heads of grain" (RSV). Oddly, a field would be a place where one might expect privacy, but the Pharisees are right there to confront them. Jesus responds to their charge of working on the Sabbath by citing an example from the Hebrew Bible and then stating a principle for how one should understand and treat the Sabbath. Verse 28 brings this brief account to a conclusion.

Mark 3:1 marks a transition to yet another short unit. It begins with "And again" indicating another short episode in the life of Jesus during his activities in Galilee. Still, verses 1–6 tell about a healing on the Sabbath, which again brings up the question: What is lawful on the Sabbath? Jesus had just defended his disciples who had plucked some heads of grain on the Sabbath. He then laid down a principle condemning an overly legalistic attitude about the Sabbath. Jesus declares that the Sabbath is intended for the benefit of humanity. The Pharisees did not accept this view, which is evident in Mark 3:6.

The Pharisees are looking for something to use against Jesus, and the issue of the Sabbath provides them with what they want. Jesus poses the question: "'Is it lawful to do good on the Sabbath, to save life or to kill?'" (Mk 3:4) The Pharisees are silent. Jesus responds with anger and grief at their silence, and then he heals the man with the withered hand. Jesus' words and actions push the Pharisees to make their intentions known—they intend to destroy him.

In short, Mark 1–3 contains many short units with common themes and elements. Within these chapters, the following discussion has singled out two of these short units beginning with Mark 2:23. That unit ends in verse 28 and Mark 3:1 begins another episode in Jesus' ministry. It ends with verse 6, which brings this second short unit to a conclusion by pointing to danger ahead for Jesus and his followers. These two short units (i.e., Mark 2:23–28 and Mark 3:1–6) are closely related as shown above. Both focus on the Sabbath and on a principle that Jesus applies to human relations. On the whole, Mark 1–3 has many small units, and they are all knitted together by common themes.

Step Two: Genre

The Synoptic Gospels contain a number of genres. Some of the types are as follows: pronouncement stories, controversy stories, scholastic dialogue, biographical sayings, dominical sayings, proverbs, prophetic and apocalyptic sayings, laws, parables, miracle stories, and legends. Different scholars use different terms for some of these types. New Testament form critic, Rudolph Bultmann, classifies Mark 2:23–3:6 as "apophthegms." Apophthegms are "short pithy and instructive sayings."[30]

Bultmann identifies three types of apophthegms and their settings. The first type is a controversy dialogue. It results from some sort of conflict. The conflict may relate to the healings or the actions of Jesus and the disciples. A second type is a scholastic dialogue. It too may reflect conflict, but the type is designed to instruct. It contains questions asked to a master or teacher by someone truly seeking knowledge. The third type is biographical apophthegms, and they appear in the "form of historical reports"[31] telling about a particular individual.

Both stories below fit the description of apophthegms. The next question is which one of the three types are they? Since both stories report a conflict, the controversy dialogue is a prime candidate. Yet, both stories also have opponents asking questions, which raise the possibility of scholastic dialogue. The form critic must analyze the text closely to determine which is correct.

Scholastic dialogues and controversy dialogues are similar in that both can contain conflict. According to Edgar McKnight, the most important distinction depends upon the "starting point."[32] Does the story begin and focus on a genuine question or is it focused on a particular controversy? This is not an easy call. From the larger group of stories, the reader knows trouble is brewing since there is a malicious intent behind the question. But from a form critical perspective, we should not allow the issue of the genre to be determined solely by the larger narrative framework and its content.

One might make a case for Mark 2:23–28 being a scholastic dialogue because the Pharisees ask Jesus a question: "Look, why are they [referring to Jesus' disciples] doing what is unlawful on the Sabbath?" Yet the language seems more indicative of a charge being leveled than a legitimate question. Unlawful implies something other than a mere desire for knowledge. Still it could be construed that way.

Moreover, it is a legitimate question since there is no definitive definition of work in the Hebrew Bible. What constitutes work on the Sabbath? The Book of Jubilees, the Damascus Document of Qumran, and "halakhic case law, ultimately codified in the Mishnah"[33] all demonstrate the importance of this question for religious authorities. These texts not only listed things unlawful, but they also discussed particular situations where actions may be lawful or unlawful. Work, therefore, constituted a serious discussion within Judaism. What may have frustrated the Pharisees is not that Jesus addressed the question. His response, however, seems a little too cavalier for them.[34]

It is clear in both of these stories (Mk 2:23–28 and 3:1–6) that Jesus' actions are not directed toward saving a life or averting a harmful situation on the Sabbath. In other words, there is no emergency or ox in the ditch. The disciples are not described as facing starvation; it does not even say they are hungry, although Jesus' reference to David and his companions may imply that is the case. Neither is the man with the withered hand in 3:1–6 in a life or death situation.

Plucking ears of grain would have been considered as reaping by the Pharisees and would have been regarded as an unlawful activity according to Exodus 34:21.[35] If this is how the Pharisees really understood the disciples' actions, then Jesus' citing of David as an example highlights their misunderstanding of the situation. The overall context seems to indicate that Jesus' opponents are not seeking the truth about work, but they are looking to strengthen their case against Jesus and his disciples.

Therefore, both stories seem to be controversy dialogues. In the first story, unlawful appears to function as a charge, not a real question. For the Pharisees, it is a matter of breaking the letter of the law for no legitimate reason. What the disciples are doing is work. In their minds, Jesus' response is unacceptable.

The next story in Mark 3:1–6 seems to raise the same issue. The real question that weaves its way through many of these stories concerns the issue of authority. Where does Jesus get his authority to make such pronouncements? The authority is implied in 2:28—"The Son of Man is lord even of the Sabbath" (NRSV). The following story demonstrates this authority when Jesus is able to heal the man with the withered hand.[36] Both stories, therefore, may be understood as controversy dialogues.

Step Three: *Sitz Im Leben*

There are several possible social settings for the controversy dialogue. It can occur in legal matters, disputes between friends or groups, or any number of other social settings where there is human interaction. Bultmann sees this type emerging out of the ongoing conflicts between the early Christian communities and their opponents concerning issues related to the law. For Mark's Gospel, these stories show the "mounting hostility of the Jewish authorities toward Jesus and his disciples."[37] The stories function to define the attitudes of Jesus and his followers in Galilee. They provide instruction for the Christian communities, and they offer legitimacy for their beliefs and practices.

The socio-historical setting for these two stories relates to events occurring in Galilee. The population of Galilee is ethnically mixed. As a result, Jews in this region are exposed to Greek culture and influence. These stories reflect real confrontations between Jesus and his opponents. The opponents in Mark 1–3 are mostly identified as scribes and Pharisees. Scribes were "middle-level officials" serving the central government in bureaucratic roles. They would have some power and influence. In Galilee, however, they would be dependent upon Herod Antipas.[38]

According to Burton Mack, evidence for a significant presence of Pharisees in Galilee before the Roman-Jew war is lacking.[39] Anthony J. Saldarini's study of Pharisee accepts their presence in Galilee. Still, he does not believe they are "leading political, social or religious forces" in that area.[40]

Mark's Gospel has the Pharisees active in Galilee.[41] Saldarini notes that the Pharisees in Mark "act like a well-connected political interest group." The so-called "scribes of the Pharisees" referred to in Mark 2:16 might actually be "Jerusalem representatives."[42] The Pharisees attempt to preserve a community of people in Galilee who live by purity rituals. Such purity rituals establish boundaries for the Jewish community there. Jesus' teachings function to broaden the "community boundaries and loosen the norms of the membership in this community."[43] The depiction of the growing popularity of Jesus might indicate his views are winning the day putting the Pharisees on the defensive.

The literary setting focuses on how these two units fit into the larger narrative of Mark. In this narrative, several short units are brought together to illustrate a growing conflict over the issue of authority. The seeds of this growing conflict begin in Mark 1:21. It begins with Jesus teaching in the synagogue at Capernaum. The people there are astonished. Why? Because Jesus teaches as "one having authority, and not as the scribes." Jesus then casts an unclean spirit out of a man thus effectively demonstrating his power. The act amazes the crowd. From this point on, Jesus popularity grows, and the scribes and Pharisees become increasingly upset. Interestingly, his popularity grows in spite of his effort to keep some of his acts a secret.

Mark 2:23–28 and Mark 3:1–6 bring the larger narrative tension to a high point. Still, the tension is not resolved in Mark 3:6. That verse points to future conflict for Jesus and his followers. In Mark 3:6, the intent of Jesus' opponents is clear. They now plan to destroy him.

Step Four: Purpose of Mark 2:23–28 and Mark 3:1–6

The last step concerns the purpose. Controversy dialogues function in different ways. They represent a struggle for influence, authority, and power. A major issue in Mark 1–3 relates to authority. Jesus' opponents assume a position of power and authority. Jesus' words and activities call this power and authority into question. These two stories depict Jesus' growing popularity as a threat to his opponents. Jesus' ability to heal and cast out demons provides him with a claim to authority that his opponents do not possess.

The Sabbath is the subject of both units. The Pharisees define what Jesus and his disciples do as unlawful. The so-called experts charge Jesus' disciples with working on the Sabbath. For them, the picking and eating grain constitutes working (i.e., reaping) on the Sabbath. Jesus, however, does not see his actions this way. Jesus sees their response as legalism. Jesus' reference to David's action in 1 Samuel 21:1–6 shows the Pharisees that the Sabbath was not intended to stand in the way of human welfare.

In 1 Samuel 21:1–6, David and his companions "were hungry and in need of food." David went into the "house of God" and Ahimelech, the high priest, allowed David and his companions to eat the "bread of Presence." This act is considered unlawful because only the priests are allowed to eat this bread. From this story, Jesus formulates the following principle: "The sabbath was made for humankind, and not humankind for the sabbath; so the Son of Man is lord even of the sabbath" (Mk 2:25–28, NRSV).

Mark 3:5 reveals something about Jesus' emotional state. Jesus genuinely tried to redeem his opponents. "He looked around at them in anger and, deeply distressed at their stubborn hearts" (NRSV). Jesus' anger reveals disappointment. His opponents refuse to respond to him with any degree of good will. It is clear that they are set upon his demise. The stories demonstrate the intentions of Jesus' opponents, and they show Jesus as the one who really understands both the meaning and the spirit of the law. These stories underscore the principle that doing good on the Sabbath should govern one's behavior.[44]

The purpose of these two units, therefore, is to provide legitimacy for the early Christian communities. Even though it is not a scholastic dialogue, it does instruct early Christian communities about the actual meaning of the Sabbath. Still, the Sabbath is not the real issue. These encounters are an excuse to attack Jesus. The conflict, therefore, is misplaced. The so-called heart of the matter is mistrust, jealousy, and envy. The Jewish religious leaders are portrayed as being afraid of losing their privileged status. The real purpose or function of these conflict stories, therefore, is to provide legitimacy for these early Christian communities. When conflict emerges, these Christians can appeal to Jesus' words and deeds recounted in these short stories.

CONCLUSION

Form criticism is a useful tool for understanding biblical texts. It can focus on small or larger units of material. It allows one to examine many different aspects of the text. It provides valuable information for a better appreciation and understanding of biblical texts. Form critical approaches that look at larger blocks also help one see the smaller units of material as part of the larger whole. Such an approach provides a broader context for understanding the smaller units.

NOTES

1. Gene M. Tucker, "Prophetic Speech," in *Interpreting the Prophets* ed. James Luther Mays and Paul J. Achtemeier (Philadelphia: Fortress Press, 1987), 30.
2. Elizabeth Schüssller Fiorenza, *In Memory of Her: A Feminist Theological Reconstruction of Christian Origins* (New York: Crossroads, 1983), 205–241.
3. Ibid., 211.
4. Hermann Gunkel, *The Legends of Genesis: The Biblical Saga and History* (New York: Schocken Books, 1964), 46–47.
5. The English translator has translated the German noun Sage into the English legend. On page 3, Gunkel notes that calling a unit a legend/saga is not the same thing as calling it a "lie."
6. Gunkel, 41.
7. Edgar V. McKnight, *What is Form Criticism of the New Testament*. Guides to Biblical Scholarship New Testament Series ed., Dan O. Via Jr., (Philadelphia: Fortress Press, 1969), 18.
8. Marvin A. Sweeney, "Form Criticism," in *To Each Its Own Meaning: An Introduction to Biblical Criticisms and Their Application*, ed. Stephen R. Haynes and Steven L. McKenzie (Louisville: The Westminster Press, 1999), 60.
9. Tucker, Form Criticism, 12.

10. W. Caspari, *Die Samuelbücher mit Sacherklärungen*, Kommentar zum Alten Testament, 7 (Leipzig: Deichter, 1926), 18–19, 504–505, 509–519; Hugo Gressmann, "The Oldest History Writing in Israel," in *Narrative and Novella*, trans. David E. Orton and ed. David Gunn, Historic Texts and Interpreters in Biblical Scholarship, 9 (Sheffield: Almond Press, 1991), 22–58.

11. Tucker, 15.

12. Hans Walter Wolff, *Hosea*, ed., Paul D. Hanson, Hermeneia: A Critical Historical Commentary on the Bible, (Philadelphia: Fortress Press, 1974), 66.

13. Claus Westermann, Claus, "Zum Geschichtsverständnis des Alten Testaments," in *Probleme biblischer Theologie: Gerhard von Rad zum Geburtstag*, ed. H. W. Wolff, München: Chr. Kaiser, 1971. 611–619.

14. Tucker, 16.

15. George W. Coats, *Genesis: with an Introduction to Narrative Literature, The Forms of the Old Testament Literature*, eds., Rolf Knierim and Gene M. Tucker, vol. 1 (Grand Rapids: William B Eerdmans Publishing Company 1983), 157–161.

16. Ibid; von Rad, *Genesis* 242.

17. Gunkel, 43.

18. Coats 8.

19. Ibid., 9.

20. Ibid.

21. William A. Haviland, *Anthropology*, (New York: Holt, Rinehart and Winston, Inc, 1974), 526.

22. Hermann Gunkel, *Genesis*, Mercer Library of Biblical Studies Translated by Mark E. Biddle (Macon: Mercer University Press 1997), 237–238.

23. Ibid., 239.

24. Haviland, 526.

25. E. A. Speiser, 166. Also see von Rad, *Genesis*, 242. Von Rad sees the E account concluding with verse 14; Hermann Gunkel, *Genesis*, 233, 236–240.

26. Wolff, 42–59, 70–75.

27. Thomas W. Mann, *The Book of the Torah: The Narrative Integrity of the Pentateuch*, (Atlanta: John Knox Press, 1988), 30.

28. Ibid., 45.

29. R. T. France, *The Gospel of Mark*, The New International Greek Testament Commentary (Grand Rapids: William B. Eerdmans Publishing Company, 2002), 31.

30. Edgar V. McKnight, *What is Form Criticism?* New Testament Series: Guides to Biblical Scholarship, ed., Dan O. Via, Jr., (Philadelphia: Fortress Press, 1969), 26.

31. Ibid., 26–27.

32. Ibid., 26.

33. France, 143.

34. France.

35. Hugh Anderson, *The Gospel of Mark*, The New Century Bible Commentary ed., Matthew Black (Grand Rapids: Wm B. Eerdmans Publ. Co., 1976), 109.

36. Pheme Perkins, *Mark*, New Interpreter's Bible Commentary, ed., Leander E. Keck, vol. 8, (Nashville: Abingdon Press, 1995), 558.

37. Anderson, 98–99.

38. Anthony J. Saldarini, *Pharisees, Scribes, and Sadducees in Palestinian Society*, The Biblical Resource Series (Grand Rapids: William B. Eerdmans Publishing Company 1988), 274.

39. Mack, 60.

40. Saldarini, 292–295.

41. Ibid., 149, 291–293.

42. Saldarini, 149–150.

43. Ibid., 150.

44. Perkins, 556–557.

Chapter Eight

Redaction Criticism

Redaction means editing. Redaction criticism is a study of how texts are edited and what the editing tells us about the purpose of the editor. Historical critics traditionally placed a limited value on the editor's contribution since they desired to focus on the earliest form of the text prior to any editing. The editor's work was seen as secondary. Redaction criticism, however, values the editor's contribution; the editor is often regarded as a theologian or author in some cases. A redactor takes earlier work and fashions it in a creative manner. The key components of this approach can be demonstrated with a couple of examples.

The first example comes from common experience. Most of us have written a letter or an email only to edit it before sending it to the recipient. Often we go back and edit these communications not because there are mistakes but because we may have second thoughts about what we wrote. Perhaps, it is too direct, too harsh, or not direct enough. If another party could look at the changes we made, he or she might be able to understand why we made them. Redaction criticism, therefore, may involve making this kind of comparison. If one can isolate and identify the changes (i.e., edits), then he or she can draw conclusions about what they mean.

For a second example consider a text produced by the third president of the United States, Thomas Jefferson (1743–1826). Jefferson sought to recover the actual words of Jesus and separate them from the words of others found in the four Gospels. The resulting work is known as *The Jefferson Bible: The Life and Morals of Jesus of Nazareth*. Jefferson created this Bible by editing all four Gospels. So what could one learn by comparing the *Jefferson Bible* to the other Gospels?

In reading the *Jefferson Bible*, one would be struck by the lack of miracles. One might compare a familiar passage from one of the Gospels with

Jefferson's version. Matthew 3:13–17, Mark 1:9–11, and Luke 3:21–22 all recount Jesus' baptism. All three passages recount the voice from heaven in almost the same words. In Matthew 3:17 we have "This is my son, the Beloved, with whom I am well pleased." Jefferson's Bible only says, "Then cometh Jesus from Galilee to Jordan unto John, to be baptized of him."[1] There is no mention of a voice from heaven. Reading further one might be struck by the complete lack of miracles in Jefferson's Bible. One may wonder why Jefferson never mentions the virgin birth.

Even without knowing anything about Jefferson, this lack of anything supernatural may lead one to wonder why he has omitted these stories. If one reads the introduction to *The Jefferson Bible* by Forrest Church,[2] it becomes clear why he has omitted them. He omits everything except for the moral teachings of Jesus, and he does not accept the miracles. He has a low opinion of the disciples and believes that much of what is in the Gospels did not come from Jesus. Comparing *The Jefferson Bible* to the Gospels provides one with an insight into Jefferson's thinking about Jesus and the Gospels.

Both examples demonstrate a simple idea. Seeing how an editor changes a text provides insights into the intentions of that editor. But how one proceeds depends on the nature of the editing. Only biblical texts that exhibit signs of intentional editing can benefit from this study. Many texts have been edited but do not provide enough information for one to draw any definite conclusions about the redactor's intent. Clearly, there was editing in the Pentateuch. An editor likely combined J and E and later JE and P. That editing is present, however, is not enough. One must be able to identify the edits and be able to draw meaningful conclusions about why the changes were made. The editor's own contributions must be evident and significant. In some cases, editors may have tried to keep their contributions hidden.

So how can one know if a text is open to this type of analysis? Just to say that a redactor made modifications in combining J and E does not necessarily mean we can study how this editor worked. For a redactional study, there must be significant and identifiable editorial activity. An editor making minor changes or putting stories together does not provide the critic with enough information to draw firm conclusions about why one made changes.

At a minimum, a redaction critic needs the following to make any study fruitful. He or she must first be able to locate the editorial material. This discovery would also require convincing proof of such activity. Second, the editorial activity would need to reveal a particular pattern, plan, structure, point of view, and purpose. If both are present, there may be fertile soil for this kind of approach.

Making comparisons is another crucial way redaction critics work. This approach is the one taken in the study of the Synoptic Gospels. It entails identifying changes by comparing the writer's work to the source he or she used. If Luke used Mark as a source, then we can compare Luke's recounting to Mark. Does Luke reproduce Mark or does he modify it in some ways? Does Luke add anything or delete anything from Mark's account? And if Luke does modify Mark why does he do so?

This particular kind of redactional application requires at least four things: (1) there must be a literary connection between sources, (2) one source must be dependent upon another, (3) the comparison must show how one writer used, modified, and added to the original, and (4) the comparison must provide sufficient results that allows a redactional critic to draw meaningful conclusions about the overall composition and nature of the editor's work.

We find texts in the Synoptic Gospels and the Hebrew Bible that meet all four requirements. One can compare the Chronicler's work with 1 and 2 Samuel and 1 and 2 Kings since the Chronicler probably used these writings in the construction of his or her own work. Knowing that the Chronicler had access to these works establishes a connection and dependency. It allows one to see how the Chronicler used them and to draw conclusions about his or her thoughts and goals. Without being able to make these comparisons, the critic's observations about the editor are limited. [3]

To apply this method, one first needs to select a passage that shows ample evidence of editing. Second, he or she must analyze the writer's work and identify literary connections to other texts. In this part of the study, the goal would be to locate the editorial activity and see what it can tell us about the intentions of the editor or writer. Next, one needs to analyze the editorial changes to determine if they are significant for a proper understanding of the work. If they are significant, they can help one understand the theological or ideological views of the editor.

Once editorial changes have been located and studied, it is important to pay attention to the specific language. Attention to words or phrases is rather important. Certain writers may be fond of particular words or terms to convey their ideas. One should also consider style and structure. There may be certain patterns of thought and speech that would be helpful as well. Consideration of the larger narrative structure can help one discover patterns that may explain aspects of the editor's work. Comparing the outline and plot of Mark with Luke, for instance, provides clues as to how the two are similar and different.

If possible, it is best to look at the texts in their original languages. If, however, one does not know Hebrew or Greek, it is important to read a text in different translations. I would recommend the Revised Standard Version (RSV) be one of the translations. Some translations are much more like free interpretations or paraphrases than translations. All translations of the Bible are partly interpretation, but some translations try to minimize this aspect by sticking close to the wording of the text.

Consider the following example. Comparing Mark 1:22 to Luke 4:32, one can see that the King James Version (KJV) of Luke 4:32 is translated as follows: "And they were astonished at his doctrine: for his word was with power." The RSV translates the same verse as "And they were astonished at his teaching, for his word was with authority." In this case, the KJV is more of an interpretation. The Greek noun "*didchē*" means teaching although the verbal form in the passive tense could mean doctrine. In this particular instance, the RSV leaves the interpretation to the reader whereas the KJV has provided an interpretation. Likewise, the primary meaning of the Greek word "*exousian*" is authority, but it has a secondary meaning of power. The KJV has taken it to mean "power." Consulting a very literal translation such as Young's Literal Translation (YLT) may be helpful because it sticks to the wording of the original as closely as possible. YLT has "and they were astonished at his teaching, because his word was with authority," which is basically the same as the RSV in this case. So Luke focuses on Jesus' teachings as being authoritative. One who does not read Greek should consult different translations and useful commentaries.

Moving on now to illustrate this method, I build on the work of others who have used this approach. The goal is to allow the reader to see how others have employed the principles of redaction criticism on biblical texts. The first reading below identifies redactional activity in the Book of Judges to determine what it can tell us about the editor's work.

REDACTION OF THE BOOK OF JUDGES 2:6–16:31

There is a strong consensus that the Book of Judges reflects the theological views of Deuteronomy. The book itself contains old material arranged and supplemented by the work of later editors. While some may see this as the work of one editor, it is more likely the work of a group of redactors. These editors have made several key contributions to Judges. They gathered material, arranged it in its present order, and added their own theological perspectives into the very framework of Judges 2:16–16:31. Their work, therefore, is not random or piecemeal; it reflects a purpose. These editors developed a theological perspective directed to a seventh century audience. The resulting message concerns the promise of God's help for those who obey God and a threat of punishment for those who disobey.

Judges 2:6:–16:31 expresses a particular theology most closely identifiable with the book of Deuteronomy. The prevailing theory about the book's composition views it as part of a larger work called the DH. Beginning with Judges 1:1–36, the conquest of the land is still incomplete. Judges 1:1–36 tells how the ancient Israelites continue fighting, but they are unable to take the land completely. Some scholars think that the unitary picture of a complete conquest found in Joshua 1–12 (especially Jo 3–5) originated in the sanctuary at Gilgal.[4] This picture would view Joshua as the leader of all Israel. However, the book of Judges begins with the incomplete conquest. This situation leads to a theological interpretation by the Deuteronomistic redactors who shaped Judges 2:6–16:31.

The hand of the Deuteronomistic editors is evident beginning with Judges 1:1 extending through chapter 16. Most scholars agree that non-Deuteronomistic redactors appended chapters 17–21 to Judges later.[5] Based on the two edition theory of Frank Moore Cross and Richard Nel son, Judges 1:1–2:5 and 6:7–10 are probably the product of a second Deuteronomistic edition done during the Babylonian Exile.[6] So these verses will not be part of this analysis. I am focusing on Judges 2:6–16:31. Most all of this material belongs to the original edition completed around the time of King Josiah.

This first edition contains older, pre-Deuteronomistic material. Deuteronomistic editors worked with this older material applying it to their contemporary audience. Redaction critics can identify stereotypical language associated with the Deuteronomistic editing. They can also identify a consistent structure or framework for these stories. This framework is the product of the editors. Being able to identify these elements also allows one to identify older, pre-Deuteronomistic materials. As a result, the historical critic can focus on this early material and ignore the editorial changes. Redaction critics, however, analyze the editorial additions and modifications to reveal the theological outlook of these editors.

One finds the fullest expression of the Deuteronomistic redactor's theology in two areas. First, this theology occurs in Judges 2:6–3:6. This introduction provides the authoritative voice for the chapters to follow.[7] After the death of Joshua and the generation who followed him, the next generation proves to be unfaithful. As a result, Yahweh leaves the other nations in the land as a test for these people. The second theological element concerns the interpretative passages in Judges 3:7–16:31. In these chapters, a distinctive pattern plays out. This pattern puts historical events or traditions into an interpretative framework. The pattern involves ancient Israel's disobedience resulting in their suffering at the hands of their enemies. Next, the people cry out to God for help, and God raises a savior figure to deliver them from their enemies. The pre-Deuteronomistic material, then, is arranged and given a definite theological shape and meaning within this larger interpretive framework.

This unit can be divided into four sections: (1) Judges 2:6–3:6, (2) 3:7–5:31, (3) 6:1–10:5, (4) 10:6–16:31. The first section, Judges 2:6–3:6, functions as a Deuteronomistic introduction to the whole (i.e., Jgs 2:6–16:31). Joshua and his generation, according to the Deuteronomistic redactors, are faithful to Yahweh. This faithfulness is in contrast to the former generation who died in the wilderness (Nm 14:26–35) and who did not trust Yahweh to give them the land. Consequently, the contrast between faithfulness and unfaithfulness is important for the editors. This new generation after Joshua's death is found lacking in two respects. First, they go after other gods (e.g., Jgs 2:11, 12, and 13), and second they have abandoned their own God (Jgs 2:12 and 13).[8] They have done "what was evil in the sight of the Lord and served the Baals" (Jgs 2:11).

The redactors' work in this section is based on the distinctive Deuteronomistic principal of divine retribution. This principle is conditional. If one's actions are good in the sight of Yahweh, a person or community shall be blessed. If, on the other hand, the person or community does evil punishment shall follow. In Judges 2:6–16:31, ancient Israel does evil and receives punishment for her actions. After this punishment, Yahweh delivers her, and the land is at rest.

After an introductory statement in Judges 2:6–10, the Deuteronomistic redactors make a charge against the people. They have been disobedient breaking the commandment in Exodus 20:3 about putting others gods before God (Ex 20:3). As a result, God becomes angry and allows them to be punished by "plunderers." The text says the people are in "great distress" so God raises up judges to deliver them from their enemy. The exception to this pattern occurs in Judges 2:11–21 where the text does not mention the people crying out for help. In this passage, the people are in distress, but God raises judges before the people cry for help. Also, the names of the judges referred to in this passage are not given.

This passage serves two purposes for the redactors. First, it serves as a general introduction to the pattern that emerges in the following chapters. This pattern is usually described as apostasy, oppression, repentance, and deliverance. Second, it provides an explanation. Why did God not allow the ancient Israelites to complete the conquest of Canaan? The conquest had been less than successful. So why are the people of the land left? They are left to test the ancient Israelites (Jgs 2:22, 3:1, 4). They function as instruments of divine retribution against the disobedient Israelites.

In the accounts that follow, the editors provide the names of the judges. The Deuteronomistic redactors probably possessed old stories about these judges. The redactors incorporated the older material into their own theological perspective. The stories are no longer independent stories of ancient Israel's problems with their neighbors; they are given a specific theological interpretation.

Judges 3:7–5:31 begins the stories of specific judges. The cycle, starting with Othniel, repeats itself throughout much of Judges 3:7–16:31. Abimelech and Samson are two figures who do not fit into this cycle. The cycle repeats itself three complete times in Judges 3:7–5:31 with Othniel, Ehud, and Deborah. In some cases, the number of years given for a judge's activities is only an approximation. The "forty years" found more than once should not be taken literally. In some places, it is possible that the Deuteronomistic redactors made use of information in the pre-Deuteronomistic traditions about the duration of a judge's actions.[9] The time frame is mostly part of the Deuteronomistic plan for the book.

The third section, Judges 6:1–10:5, tells of a hero, Gideon, from the tribe of Manasseh. With Gideon, the Deuteronomistic contributions are less extensive, which indicates that they possess more details about him. After the death of Gideon, the Deuteronomistic redactors end this part of the story with the statement that "the people of Israel turned again and played the harlot after the Baals, and made Baal-berith their god" (Jgs 8:33).

The Abimelech story in Judges 9 represents a departure from the Deuteronomistic pattern. Abimelech was Gideon's son. Abimelech's mother was Gideon's concubine. Abimelech becomes an oppressor. He appears to be ancient Israel's punishment for not treating the family of Gideon kindly "for all the good he had done to Israel" (Jgs 8:35). Eventually, Abimelech is killed by a woman at Thebez (Jgs 9:50–57). Afterward, a minor judge named Tola rules for 23 years. Jair follows Tola, and he rules for 22 years. There is no mention of the people's disobedience or their crying out to God for help although Tola is said to have delivered Israel. Jair's claim to fame is that he had "thirty sons who rode on thirty donkeys; and they had thirty towns, which are in the land of Gilead ...." (Jgs 10:3–4). The unit ends with these two minor judges.

The final section, Judges 10:6–16:31, tells of Jephthah, three minor judges, and Samson. Judges 10:6 resumes the Deuteronomistic cycle of disobedience, punishment, and the crying out for help. At this point, however, the cycle is interrupted. Judges 10:10–16 is a pivotal point in Judges. Yahweh, for the first time, responds negatively to the people's cry for help (Jgs 10:13). God is tired of their behavior. Ancient Israel can no longer take God's graciousness for granted. At this point, we have the first sign of real repentance. Whether this repentance is genuine is questionable. One may certainly be suspicious of their sincerity. To this point, the Deuteronomistic redactors have not given any indications that ancient Israel felt any real remorse for their sins. Nor does the text say that the people actually turned away from their sins until now.

Yahweh responds to ancient Israel's call for help in Judges 10:10 with sarcasm. Yahweh tells them to "cry to the gods whom you have chosen; let them deliver you in the time of your distress" (Jgs 10:14). Here is a comparison between the gods of the Canaanites who could not deliver with the God of Israel who can. The people, seeing that Yahweh will no longer deliver them, try putting away their foreign gods and serving Yahweh alone. They hope Yahweh will reconsider. Consequently, Yahweh in his graciousness can no longer bear to see them suffer (Jgs 10:16). Still, he does not raise up a savior as he had earlier. This time, the people take the initiative. Judges 11 indicates that God accepts their choice. They selected "Jephthah, a Gileadite, the son of a prostitute, [who] was a mighty warrior" (Jgs 11:1). Yahweh uses Jephthah as a means of delivering the people from the hands of the Ammonites.

The narratives of Jephthah and also Samson are relatively free from their theological frame work. Jephthah delivers the people from the Ammonites at a high personal price. Like Genesis 22, the story raises the issue of human sacrifice. Jephthah makes a vow to God. If God allows him to defeat the Ammonites, he pledges to offer the first one who comes out of the doors of his house as a burnt offering to Yahweh (Jgs 11:30–31). Unfortunately, it is his daughter who comes out first. Eventually, he makes good on this horrific vow.

After Jephthah's death, we have three minor judges introduced in Judges 12:8–15. Chapter 13 begins again with the familiar phrase, "The Israelites again did what was evil in the sight of the LORD, and the LORD gave them into the hand of the Philistines forty years." This verse introduces the entrance of the next major figure in the story, Samson. This story is familiar to many, and it continues to the end of chapter 16. The Deuteronomistic editors must have had considerable material about Samson who is a hero, but who also has human weaknesses. In the end, he too is successful although at the cost of his own life. We are not told that he ended the Philistine threat altogether. In spite of his uniqueness as a judge, the passage ends with a note that he had judged Israel for 20 years.

In summary, the Deuteronomistic redactors present their message to a seventh century B.C.E. audience. They take stories with their historical settings in the pre-monarchic period interpreting them in a way that relates to their own day. One can conclude three things about their work: (1) they gathered older materials, (2) they arranged them in their present order, and (3) they added their own theological perspectives. These editors, writers and theologians address a people and leaders who have not been faithful to Yahweh. The stories highlight what happens to unfaithful people. The stories also reveal a loving God, who stands ready to intervene on the people's behalf. The message is one of threat and promise. The threat is addressed to disobedient children and the promise to those same children. The redactors want to urge people to choose obedience and life leading to God's blessings, which consist of a full life in relationship with Yahweh.

REDACTION OF LUKE 4:31–44

The illustration from the New Testament focuses on a short passage from Luke's Gospel. I begin with a comment on the whole of Luke's work. Hans Conzelmann's study of Luke's Gospel describes the writer as a theologian instead of a historian. This conclusion resulted from his identification of Luke's editorial activity. Once he identified Luke's contributions to the Gospel, he examined them to determine their significance for Luke's theology. He identified key passages indicating the writer's theological purpose. Luke 13:35 and Luke 16:16 were key passages "for understanding the totality of the Lucan theological enterprise."[10] His detailed study of the changes Luke made to his sources throughout the Gospel supported his interpretation of these key passages.[11] He concluded that Luke developed a *Heilsgeschichte* (i.e., salvation history) in three stages. The first phase includes the content of the Hebrew Bible through John the Baptist. The next period covers the ministry of Jesus (i.e., the center of time), and the final period is the time of the church.

These three stages represent Luke's answer to the main theological problem of his day—the delay of the second coming (i.e., the *parousia*). His theology stresses the necessity for the church to continue her mission in the world. The time left for the church in this world is unknown. It is the church's task to proclaim the good news to everyone, Jews and Gentiles alike.

This approach builds upon the results of source criticism, which dates Mark's Gospel earlier than Matthew and Luke. Here, Luke uses Mark as a source for his own theological composition. Redaction criticism looks at how the writer of Luke modified Mark's account and what the modifications tell us about Luke's theology. One could do the same with the Gospel of Matthew.

Some of the modifications Luke makes to his sources, Mark and Q, are stylistic and do not reflect anything significant. Other changes may give a glimpse into key aspects of Luke's thought. Developing an understanding of the structure and flow of the two narratives independently of each other helps to orient the reader and identify key points. The Gospel of Mark in the first three chapters centers on authority. It depicts Jesus' growing popularity as a source of conflict with Jewish religious leaders such as the scribes and Pharisees.

Luke 1:1–4 begins with a dedication to Theophilus. Luke 1:5–38 foretells the births of John the Baptist and Jesus. Luke 2:22–4:15 relates Jesus' visit to the temple at age 12, the proclamation of John the Baptist, the baptism of Jesus, and his temptation. Luke 4:14 begins the description of Jesus' ministry in Galilee.

Luke 4:14–15 refers to events not recounted in Mark 6:1–6a. These verses indicate that news about Jesus had "spread through all the surrounding country. He began to teach in their synagogues and was praised by everyone" (Lk 4:15). This statement sets the stage for Luke 4:16–29. This unit turns the tables, and instead of praise, Jesus experiences rejection. The reason seems to be related to his view of the Gentiles.[12]

This passage is important for understanding the Gospel. It initiates Jesus' ministry and informs the reader what that ministry is all about. In Luke 4:16, Jesus goes to the synagogue and reads a passage from Isaiah. His reading contains portions of Isaiah 61:1–2 and 58:6. He says, "The Spirit of the Lord is upon me, because he has anointed me to bring good news to the poor. He has sent me to proclaim release to the captives and recovery of sight to the blind, to let the oppressed go free, to proclaim the year of the Lord's favor" (Lk 4:18–19). Following his reading, Jesus offers a bold interpretation; he identifies himself as the one anointed, as the fulfillment of Isaiah's prophecy.

Gail P. C. Streete has performed a redactional reading of Luke 4:16–30. She provides a number of helpful insights that can provide a larger context for the study of Luke 4:31–44. One key point is the presence of reversals. Those excluded will be included which is good news for them. In fact, this reversal is the key to understanding the sudden shift at the end of this unit. At first, the people hold Jesus in high regard, but suddenly this esteem disintegrates into violence. They seek to throw Jesus off a cliff (Lk 4:29). Why is there such a sudden shift in people's reactions? Streete's study provides a cogent explanation. Luke maintains that "God had always intended the inclusion of the excluded, especially Gentiles, but also that his activity is specifically directed to them. Luke's Gentile Christians may thus consider themselves rather than the Jews to be God's elect."[13] This conclusion explains the abrupt change in verses 16–30. Consequently, Luke's account is rather different from Mark's account in Mark 6:1–6a.

After a consideration of background information, a redactional approach calls for one to read the text closely and compare it to its counterpart in one or more of the Synoptic Gospels. This study considers Luke's use of Mark 1:21–45 in relation to Luke 4:31–44. It entails placing Mark 1:21–45 and Luke 4:31–44 side by side and comparing the two accounts noting any modifications or changes. It assumes that Luke uses Mark in composing his own account of Jesus' ministry. The story in Luke contains most of the same elements as the one in Mark. Nevertheless, these elements do not always have the same meaning or significance. The reading below focuses on some of the most significant differences.

Both Mark and Luke deal with the issue of authority but in different ways. Luke 4:31 provides a setting for this event. The incident takes place in Capernaum, a city in Galilee. There Jesus begins teaching those in attendance on the Sabbath. The people "were astounded, because he spoke with authority" (NRSV). Mark 1:21–28 reflects the same setting. It takes place in Capernaum on the Sabbath in the synagogue. Comparing Mark 1:22 with Luke 4:32 is informative. The first half of Mark 1:22 is identical to Luke 4:32, but the second half of Mark differs from the latter part of verse 32 in Luke. Mark says, "for he [Jesus] taught them as one having authority, and not as the scribes" (NRSV). Here the text is setting the stage for a continuing conflict between Jesus, the scribes, and Pharisees. The text is all about the issue of Jesus' authority. Where does it come from? For Luke, however, the focus is on Jesus' teaching. The latter part of Luke 4:32 says "he spoke with authority" (NRSV) with no mention of the scribes. In Luke, there is no immediate context of conflict between the scribes and Jesus.

As noted above, the King James translation of Luke 4:32 translates *exousian* as power. There is a significant difference between authority and power. Authority implies legitimacy of something, which gives it authority. Power itself, however, can refer to brute force. Anytime one can impose his or her will on another, he or she may be described as exercising power. Both senses are present in Greek. Which reading is most likely implied in Mark and Luke? In Mark, authority and legitimacy are clearly the issue. In Luke, the people of Capernaum "were astonished at his teaching because he spoke with authority." Jesus' legitimacy is not in question here. In Mark, Jesus' teaching is distinguished from the scribes because of its authority. The people are astonished in both Mark and Luke at Jesus' teaching. In Mark, however, it is not merely the teachings themselves that is the point of amazement, but the manner of his teaching. He taught them "as one who had authority, and not as the scribes." The emphasis in Mark is on the ongoing and growing conflict between Jesus and his opponents—the scribes and Pharisees. Jesus stands as a challenge to their authority. This is not a concern for Luke. Luke adds the notion of power in 4:36, which is only implied in Mark 1:27.

The story in Luke is also about authority but with a difference. The first mention of authority in Luke occurs in 4:6 where the devil offers it to Jesus in return for his worship. The next mention is in this passage (Lk 4:32). The people are "astonished at his teaching, because his word was with authority" (RSV). The exorcism below shows that Jesus' power and authority come from his words and deeds. The words are made known in his extraordinary works. There is a "contest of spirits" portrayed here. Jesus is able to do what he did because the "Spirit of the Lord" is upon him (Lk 4:18) and the spirit of an unclean demon is no match (Lk 4:33–36).[14] Herein rests the source of the conflict in Luke; it is not between Jesus, the scribes and Pharisees as in Mark, but between Jesus and demonic forces.[15]

An additional similarity and difference concern Jesus' command for the demons to be silent. Both texts make this point but for different reasons. Mark does not reveal Jesus' true nature early on. He attempts to keep his messianic identity secret, which is reflected in Mark 1:25, 1:34, and 3:12. He also commands silence in many other places concerning miracles or when "he commanded silence after Peter's confession (Mk 8:30) and after the transfiguration."[16] Luke, on the other hand, has no interest in hiding Jesus' identify as the Messiah since he announces it in Luke 4:16–21. Jesus' command to the demon to be silent in Luke 4:35 may relate to the notion that allowing Jesus' opponent to use his name may give the demon control.[17] Or more simply, it could just reflect Jesus' irritation. He did not want to hear what the demon had to say; he just wanted the demon to exit the man. The command is certainly not about keeping his anointed status secret.

Luke 4:31–37 focuses on "the word". Luke replaces Mark's "new Teaching" in verse 27 with "word". The word has power and can accomplish its goal. The power and authority of this word are demonstrated in the exorcism. In both Gospels, the results of Jesus actions and teachings are amazement and in Mark it also leads to the spread of his fame. Luke just notes that reports about Jesus went out to the surrounding areas. Luke does not specify the nature of the reports nor does he mention Jesus' growing popularity.

There are also several minor differences. Luke deletes certain names from Mark's account such as Andrew, James, and John since they have not yet been introduced in Luke's Gospel. Luke rewords some of Mark 1:29–39 and deletes the phrase "And the whole city was gathered together about the door" (Mk 33). Luke also deletes the statement "and there he prayed" after the mention of a lonely place in verse 35. In verse 36, Mark says that Simon and those who are with him went after Jesus whereas Luke simply says the people went after him. Luke deletes Mark's "Everyone is searching for you" (Mk 1:37). Luke replaces this comment with the statement that the people "wanted to prevent him from leaving them" (Lk 4:42). None of these changes seems especially important in relation to Luke's message.

There are four significant modifications in style and wording between Mark 1:29–39 and Luke 4:38–44. These differences relate to changes and additions made by Luke. First, the curing of Peter's mother-in-law plays a unique role in Luke's account (Lk 4:38–39). For Luke, it "demonstrates the fulfillment of Jesus' prophetic announcement in Nazareth and it dramatizes the power of Jesus' word."[18] In Mark, the story is another example of Jesus' activities that attracts good and bad attention and eventually leads to a declaration of open hostility by his opponents in Mark 3:6.

The next significant difference involves an addition. In Luke 4:41, the writer says that Jesus' healings and exorcisms are the activities of the Messiah (Lk 4:41). Mark, however, does not make such an open claim. Luke retains Mark's restriction about the demons being silent. This limitation makes sense in Mark since the writer is attempting to conceal Jesus' true identity as the Messiah. In Luke, however, one wonders why the demons are commanded to be silent?

It is possible that this call for silence is present in the information Mark possesses, and it is not a creation of Mark. However, the silence serves a particular function for Mark. Jesus wants people to discover his true identity for themselves, which Peter does in Mark 8:29. Peter's statement in Mark 8:29 that "You are the Christ," is followed by "tell no one." Perhaps, he does not want to attract followers by miracles or great works. The way he is going results in suffering and death (Mk 8:31) and following him is dangerous.[19]

So why does Luke maintain this element of Mark? Luke 4:41 explicitly rebukes the demons and does not "allow them to speak, because they knew he was the Messiah." Nevertheless, Luke clearly identifies Jesus as the Messiah in Luke 4:18. Therefore, Luke is not trying to keep it a secret as is the case in Mark. Alan Culpepper believes that the command may reflect a particular magical notion possibly relating to the realm of satanic activity.[20] Luke may share the assumptions of "'ancient magicians [that] words backed up with sufficient authority could wreak terrible damage.'"[21] To use Jesus' name might allow misuse of it, which could have bad effects. Or Luke may have chosen to retain this aspect of Mark's telling as it stood.

The third difference between Mark and Luke comes in Luke's addition in Luke 4:43. Mark in the corresponding verse makes no mention of the kingdom of God (Mk 1:38). Luke adds this phrase to Mark's comment about Jesus preaching in the "neighboring towns." Luke's mention of the kingdom of God is a crucial concept in the Gospel as a whole.[22] Jesus was sent to "proclaim the good news of the kingdom of God to the other cities" (Lk 4:43). To "proclaim the good news of the Kingdom of God" is part of his divine mission.

One last difference worth noting concerns Luke 4:44. After the mention of his purpose, verse 44 says that Jesus went to the synagogues in Judea proclaiming his message. Mark 1:39, on the other hand, reports what the reader would expect. Mark says Jesus went "throughout Galilee." According to Culpepper, the "reference is not to mark the end of Jesus's ministry in Galilee but to drive home the point of its spread throughout all the region of Palestine."[23]

CONCLUSION

Redaction criticism views the editor as a creative writer or theologian. This approach works with the final form of the text, and it views the author/editor as a creative individual or group. It focuses on significant edits including deletions, modifications, and additions. The approach then seeks to spell out the significance of such changes. This chapter demonstrates this approach in Judges and Luke. In Judges, the contributions of Deuteronomistic editors and their resulting theology become evident when studying the additions and arranging of the materials. In Luke 4:31–44, we see how Luke's work differs in some important ways from Mark 1:21–28. The results of such studies lead to a richer understanding of the texts being studied. In Judges 2:6–16:31, the emphasis is on obedience and faithfulness to Yahweh alone. In Luke 4:31–44, Jesus is able to do the things he does because the Spirit of the Lord is upon him (Lk 4:18). He casts out demons and heals the sick. These activities are associated with the Messiah, the anointed one (Lk 4:18).

NOTES

1. Thomas Jefferson, *The Jefferson Bible: The Life and Morals of Jesus of Nazareth* (Boston: Beacon Press, 1989), 39.

2. Forrest Church, "The Gospel According To Thomas Jefferson," in *The Jefferson's Bible: The Life and Morals of Jesus of Nazareth* (Boston: Beacon Press, 1989), 1–31.

3. John Barton, *Reading the Old Testament: Methods in Biblical Studies*, (Philadelphia: The Westminster Press, 1984), 52–58.

4. For example, see J. Alberto Soggin, *Joshua*, Old Testament Library, ed. Peter Ackroyd (Philadelphia: The Westminster Press, 1972), 9–11; Cross, 103–105.

5. Gale A. Yee, "Ideological Criticism," in *Judges and Method: New Approaches in Biblical Studies*, ed. Gale A. Yee (Minneapolis: Augsburg Fortress 1995), 152; Jacob M. Meyers, *The Book of Judges*, The Interpreters Bible, ed. George Author Buttrick, Vol. 2. (Nashville: Abingdon, 1980), 680.

6. Frank Moore Cross, *Canaanite Myth and Hebrew Epic*, (Cambridge: Harvard University Press, 1973), 274–289; Richard Nelson, *The Double Redaction of the Deuteronomistic History*. Journal for the Study of the Old Testament Supplement Series, ed. David J. A. Clines, 18 (Sheffield: JSOT Press, 1981).

7. Susanne Gillmayr-Bucher, "Framework and Discourse in the Book of Judges," *Journal of Biblical Literature* 128, n.4 (2009):687–691, 701–702.

8. Gillmayr-Bucher, 689.

9. J. Alberto Soggin, *Introduction To The Old Testament*, Old Testament Library, ed. Peter Ackroyd. Philadelphia: The Westminster Press, 1980), 177.

10. Norman Perrin, *What is Redaction Criticism?*, ed. Dan O. Via Jr., New Testament Series (Philadelphia: Fortress Press, 1969), 31.

11. Ibid.

12. Gail P. C. Streete, "Redaction Criticism," in *To Each Its Own Meaning: An Introduction to Biblical Criticisms and Their Application*, ed. Stephen R. Haynes and Steven L. McKenzie (Louisville: The Westminster Press, 1999), 110–116.

13. Ibid., 115.

14. Alan Culpepper, *Luke*, New Interpreter's Bible Commentary, ed., Leander E. Keck, vol. 98 (Nashville: Abingdon Press, 1995), 110.

15. Susan R. Garrett, *The Demise of the Devil: Magic and the Demonic in Luke's Writings*, (Minneapolis: Fortress Press, 1989), 101–109.

16. Perrin, 10. Perrin here is discussing the work of Wilhelm Wrede.

17. Culpepper, 110.

18. Ibid., 111.

19. Hugh Anderson, *The Gospel of Mark*, The New Century Bible Commentary, ed. Matthew Black, (Grand Rapids: Wm. B. Eerdmans Publishing Company, 1976), 93–95.

20. Garrett, 102–104.

21. Ibid., 86.

22. Culpepper, 112.

23. Ibid.

Chapter Nine

Sociological Studies of Biblical Texts

The use of sociology for studying biblical texts has become quite influential in biblical research since the 1960s. This approach has been applied in many ways. This diversity makes it impossible to lay down one simple set of guidelines for implementing the approach. For that reason, it is best for the beginner to learn about some basic sociological tools and concepts that can help provide a better understanding of the biblical texts. In this case, the societies in question are ancient Israelite or Roman. The Roman society provides the social context for early Christianity.

Sociological models and theories provide important ways of reading and analyzing biblical texts. They can help fill in gaps where historical information is lacking. Caution is in order in this endeavor. Models and theories can be suggestive but cannot take the place of real evidence. Scholars use models and theories to provide a broader picture of social life in a given society by describing the dynamics of social life. Among other things, it pays close attention to social stratification in relation to class, gender, and ethnicity.

In sociology, there are macro-sociological and micro-sociological approaches. Macro approaches focus on the larger picture by looking at the large scale social forces and how they shape society. It focuses on social institutions and how they function in society. It focuses on how societal order is maintained. It can also focus on societal conflict in terms of competing groups or institutions.

Micro-sociological approaches look at how individuals experience the social world and how this world imposes itself on the individual. It is not at odds with a functional or conflict approach mentioned above, but it focuses more on the individual level. Human activities occur within a "common-taken-for-granted-world."[1] Sociologist Peter Berger notes that we are born into a world that is not of our own making. Over time, however, this world is absorbed by individuals. The norms and values of this world become the standards and values of both the individual and the group. In time, they may become second nature or taken-for-granted by the individual. In the extreme, people can be prisoners of society; they are bound by common practices and views. However, Berger also claims that they can make changes to this social world. [2]

In biblical studies, a sociological approach draws upon biblical and other literary sources, as well as the material remains of people. Historians and archeology can provide essential information that helps to fill in gaps. Reliance on a written text alone may provide little useful information about the daily life of people whereas archeology can often offer a glimpse into that past showing how the poor lived as well as elites.

Archeological data is crucial. It can reveal how people lived in the past by studying the materials they left behind. William G. Dever considers this data "superior" to written texts. Without recounting all his reasons for this conclusion, he is correct to point out that artifacts have a more direct connection to the past. A text, for example, has come down to us by more than one hand. Typically, biblical texts have a history of being interpreted and edited for years before they come down to modern readers. This ongoing process is why they did not perish or why we did not dig them up; they are and have always been living texts. These written texts are not unfiltered or raw looks at the past. They present an ideal look at the past that leaves out information necessary for understanding the whole picture. [3] The biblical text may not tell us how the common people in ancient Israel raised their food, but the discovery of cisterns and terraces along with farming implements can provide information about those practices. The archeologist must interpret artifacts as well, but they do not build their interpretation on layers of earlier interpretation. Consequently, archeology is an important tool for understanding the past.

Rather than trying to provide a specific method, the following discussion has three goals. First, it provides some background by introducing important aspects of the sociological study. The discussion offers a basic definition of sociology and an understanding of functional, conflict, and phenomenological theories in the social sciences. Second, the discussion provides examples of how biblical scholars have used these sociological approaches to the Bible. Finally, it demonstrates the use of a sociological perspective in a study of two biblical texts.

Sociological models and theories are merely tools that can provide insights into the texts. There is not a four-step way of doing it. This approach is not a science as some might see it. [4] This tool allows the interpreter to have a better and more complete understanding of the realities behind the texts as well as providing insight into the text. It does not offer a mere description of a historical event; it produces an understanding of the social world of these texts.

DEFINITION AND BACKGROUND
OF SOCIAL SCIENTIFIC STUDY OF BIBLICAL TEXTS

One could look at most any sociology textbook to find a definition of sociology. It is a field of study that focuses on social phenomena. It examines how society functions along with its organization. It looks at the roles individuals and institutions play in society. It identifies who has power and authority, and it examines how people use and maintain that power and authority.

Berger in his book *Invitation to Sociology* defines sociology as a "form of consciousness."[5] It is a way of looking at the world that is different from the way a lawyer or school teacher typically looks at the world. This perspective provides insights that other perspectives cannot provide. The social perspective allows one to see the world in relation to social phenomena. This simple definition can suffice for the discussion below.

There are three main approaches used in biblical studies. The first type is functionalism. This approach analyzes the role that institutions, groups, and people play in the ongoing existence of any social system. To understand this approach, one may think of society as a machine. Institutions, groups of people, or individuals are the cogs in the machine that make it work. The parts of the machine allow the whole to achieve its designed purpose. Such an analysis does have pragmatic value. If there is a problem in society, such an analysis may explain what is wrong and suggest ways to fix it.

The work of sociologist Robert K. Merton provides a useful way of examining biblical texts. For Merton, functions are those contributions or consequences that "'make for the adaptation or adjustment of a given system.'"[6] Functions refer to the consequences of an act. Dysfunction refers to something that has "'consequences which lessen the adaptation or adjustment of the system.'"[7] Ruth A. Wallace and Alison Wolf observe that this move takes conflict seriously, but it is not conflict theory. Unlike conflict theory, Merton does not focus on power and authority or on who benefits from certain actions.[8]

A second major sociological approach deals with conflict. Conflict theory focuses on power, authority, and interests. Karl Marx associated conflict primarily with class struggle. However, it occurs due to many other reasons as well. Max Weber broadened this approach by examining other areas in which conflict arises such as economics and politics. Other specific areas of consideration relate to gender and race.

The third major approach focuses on the interaction between individual and society. Symbolic interactionism, sociology of knowledge, and phenomenological sociology are three different areas of this approach. Scholars have used all three in biblical studies. The individual has "common-taken-for-granted views" about the world. These common-taken-for-granted views are not universal but relate to particular times and places. The view of people in one area may differ from those in another. Societal views shape an individual's understanding of the world. Socialization imposes the existing worldview on individuals as they develop.

Symbolic interaction explains how people learn the rules and norms of society. People learn the proper roles associated with certain activities. Children form an idea of what others do, and they can mimic those actions. The game of cops and robbers is possible because children have an idea of what cops and robbers do.

These approaches see everyone as operating from a particular perspective, which they share with other members of society. Human perspectives belong to a common stock of knowledge. People are socialized to act in accordance with these perspectives; they internalize them to the point that they take them for granted. According to Berger, "society is a dialectic phenomenon in that it is a human product and nothing but a human product that yet continuously acts back upon its producer."[9] Dialectic simply means there are two sides to our material existence: Society and the individual. In biblical studies, one might seek to reconstruct the worldview of ancient Israelites and their neighbors from the materials available. This reconstruction provides a framework for understanding texts that come from that time and place.

SHORT EXAMPLES OF DIFFERENT SOCIAL APPLICATIONS

Functionalism

One might want to begin a functionalist reading by asking a simple question: What does it do, or what is its function? The example below begins by identifying and describing the "it" in this question. The pronoun, it, refers to ancient Israelite society. So what is the society in question like? What are the constituent parts of this society? Once we have an adequate description, we can move on to answer the question about the social function of these parts.

Before the ancient Israelite state, most peoples who identified themselves as Israelites were poor peasants. The structure of that society revolved around three basic units: the bêt 'āb (i.e., the father's house), the mišpāḥâ (i.e., family/clan/village), and the maṭṭeh/šēbeṭ (i.e., tribe). The *bêt 'āb* or extended family represents the primary social unit.[10] It contains the nuclear family averaging around 4.1 to 4.3 persons.[11] Clusters of dwellings housed the extended families in a particular geographical area. This group of families makes up a clan or village. These families could represent up to three generations and at most thirty individuals.[12] Stager bases these population estimates on an equation relating to the size of the "roofed" area of the house. The mišpāḥâ was likely a combination of several extended families living in close proximity.

So what is the function of the mišpāḥâ? It provided protection,[13] and it became the means of pooling key resources. Protection and agricultural cooperation[14] are essential for their subsistence livelihood. This family and the social unit would cooperate on joint projects beneficial to everyone such as building terraces or cisterns.

Several *mišpāḥōt* (i.e., villages) in a particular region combined to form a tribe. While the primary purpose of the *mišpāḥâ* is protection, there are times when the outside threat may require more than the individual *mišpāḥâ*. In that case, a tribe may be needed. Robert Wilson says that the tribe is unified by several different factors such as "geographical proximity, common religious and cultural experience, and the need for more military protection than could be provided by an individual mišpāḥâ.[15]

Villages depend upon the family units for their survival. Their livelihood rests upon agriculture. Individual families would probably cooperate with others in the village on a regular basis. Their existence would have been at a subsistence level. Rarely would they be able to produce a surplus.

The functionalist approach can also help us understand slow developmental changes in society. Functionalism often describes how societies adjust and adapt to new situations. This aspect can be seen in the development of ancient Israel from a segmented society as described above, to a chiefdom society and finally becoming a state under David. A segmented society is "egalitarian" in a sense. Segmented here indicates that pre-monarchic Israel lacked three things: a clearly defined social stratification, a hierarchal order, and a centralized form of government.[16] Nevertheless, it consists of individual segments that are both equal and independent.[17] As this society evolves, it becomes more complex with increasing heterogeneity contributing to an adjustment or the rise of a chiefdom society. While segmented societies maintain boundaries,[18] chiefdom societies become more stratified.[19]

According to James W. Flanagan, a chiefdom society is a middle point between a segmented society and state.[20] Competition is one defining characteristic of chiefdom societies.[21] Competition increases in a chiefdom society and becomes high with the state. David lives through the transition between a chiefdom society and a monarchic one.[22] The causes of this transformation include the external threat from the Philistines and the rise of a prospering agrarian class[23] leading to increasing societal stratification.

Conflict

The growth and adaptation in functionalism are gradual. Conflict theory looks at changes that are more abrupt and related to factors such as class, race, gender, or status. Norman K. Gottwald, in his book *The Tribes of Yahweh*, puts forth a thesis based on a conflict approach. He draws on a proposal made by George E. Mendenhall.[24] Mendenhall rejects the old view that ancient Israel conquered the land of Canaan. He also rejects the peaceful infiltration view that says nomadic Semites infiltrated and settled the land from the outside. Both views have been around for some time. Mendenhall proposed a different model known as the peasant revolt theory, and Gottwald builds upon it.[25]

The basic theory is that ancient Israelites are largely made up of native Canaanite peasants within Palestine who rebelled against the Canaanite city-state rulers. Moreover, these Israelites joined forces with other groups such as pastoral nomads and social outsiders known as the *'apiru*. They resisted the oppressive forces of the "city-state hierarchies of aristocratic warriors and bureaucrats."[26] This resistance leads to an outright revolt.

For Gottwald, the revolt consists of an armed conflict. The exodus event is the work of a group of Israelites in Egypt who escaped. This group brings with them the belief in Yahweh. Yahweh is a militant God, who liberates his people from Egyptian servitude. This idea becomes central in Israelite religious belief. This group is the "final catalyst" that brought about a break between the marginalized Canaanites and the city-state rulers.[27] The marginalized Canaanites join the group escaping Egypt, and they settle in the central highlands.

The oppressive practices of the Canaanite elite's against the peasants lead to the rebellion. These elites take the agricultural surplus of the villages where most of the people live. This situation placed a heavy burden on the peasants. These peasants are also subject to "forced labor and military service."[28] He finds evidence of discontent among the peasants in the fourteenth and thirteenth centuries. These peasants joined to resist the control of the city-states. Gottwald suggests that the exodus group might have benefited from this unrest.

After the joining of these groups, there is a "conceptual shift." This linking represents the point where ancient Israel comes together as a people. Here, the liberated people cease to view themselves as Canaanites. They are now Israelites and followers of Yahweh who delivered them from Egyptian bondage.[29]

This theory today is still viewed as questionable, but scholars widely accept two points. Most people who came to make up ancient Israel were indigenous to Palestine. They were not outsiders or culturally distinct from the Canaanites. Second, the biblical traditions emphasizing liberation are sometimes at odds with other texts celebrating creation and order. These texts often represent the interests of two opposing groups. Liberation texts support the values of an agrarian peasant class who often feel oppressed by the wealthy and upper classes. Creation texts are more supportive of a royal ideology.[30] It supports and legitimates the positions of those who have power and influence in society. Creation texts value order and may gloss over the oppression of the poor. Prophetic literature often picks up on the liberation traditions criticizing the present oppressive order.

Phenomenological Approaches

The third area described above involves sociological approaches that deal with both the social world at large and the individual as a part of that larger world. In biblical societies, individuals feel the pressure to abide by certain norms. In all societies past and present, there is a view of what constitutes honorable actions and what is shameful. What is honorable depends upon the conventional wisdom of a group. It is internalized during a person's primary and secondary socialization. The honor system does not have to be written down as a set of rules and guidelines. It is part of the stock of knowledge or the common-taken-for-granted world of people. Typically everyone in a given society knows what is honorable and shameful. The concept of honor and shame, however, differs from society to society.

Every society has boundaries. These boundaries shape one's identity. They determine how people see themselves and others. The social dynamics that go into making these boundaries shape the individual's sense of worthiness or unworthiness. The social world in which the Hebrew and Christian Scripture took shape is no exception. The Bible contains a code of what is honorable and shameful. Conventional wisdom represents what most people in society think and believe; it is the dominant view. Alternative wisdom may refer to a counter view that is at odds with the conventional.[31]

The concept of honor and shame is present in the biblical literature. One needs to be careful not to impose our modern views of honor and shame on the past.[32] The notion of honor and shame is common in the wisdom literature of the Hebrew Bible. The wise person has honor, but the foolish person acts shamefully. Also, words like clean and unclean in Hebrew are used to distinguish between those who keep the law and those who disobey it.

Based upon this understanding, we can see there is a basis in all societies for legalism to develop. It is a human temptation to judge ourselves and others in reference to a generalized or significant other.[33] One judges his or her actions by what this generalized or significant other would expect, and we use that view to judge ourselves and others. Often this projection creates a mental checklist. To measure up one must do what is expected, which leads to legalism. Pharisees have often been singled out as legalists,[34] but, in fact, this approach shows that legalism is not the possession of one group. It infects most everyone.

Many of Jesus' opponents live by the concepts of holiness and purity. They emphasize two concepts, which involve separation from anything impure or unclean. For them, living holy lives in accordance with Leviticus 19:2 and 20:26 require separation. This separation includes keeping one's distance from "women after childbirth, lepers, women and men with bodily discharges . . . [and] the dead."[35] In some cases, they would separate themselves from other Jews who are uneducated or from the *am ha-arez* (i.e., common people) who may be a little lax in keeping the commandments.[36]

Borg's description of the historical Jesus provides an excellent and simple portrayal of this mindset. Conventional wisdom contains the kind of thought and behavior that characterizes what is honorable and shameful in a society. From this context, he paints Jesus as one who proclaims a counter or alternative wisdom. Within the purity system, women remain subordinate to men, certain peoples are not allowed to interact with other people, and divisions between good and bad are clearly marked. The result of the "purity system was to create a world with sharp social boundaries: between pure and impure, righteous and sinner, whole and not whole, male and female, rich and the poor, Jew and Gentile."[37] Jesus overturned these boundaries. This observation provides a valuable insight into his life and teachings.

Now that I have discussed three types of approaches and their relationship to the study of biblical texts, I will now demonstrate a social reading of Leviticus 1–7 and I Peter 2:11–3:22. These demonstrations incorporate parts of all three approaches just discussed. They pay attention to both functional and conflict analysis of these texts. They also consider the individual's perspectives and how these perspectives shape their thoughts and actions.

METHOD DEMONSTRATED

Leviticus 1–7

Leviticus 1–7 in its final form dates to the post-exilic community.[38] The literary setting for this book, however, comes from the time of Moses after the exodus. The sacrifices discussed in chapters 1–7 likely took place over many years in ancient Israel. Consequently, the ideas and concepts expressed in these chapters had a life before the Babylonian Exile in 587 BCE. These chapters discuss animal sacrifices performed by priests. Priests are "full-time religious specialists who are typically found in socially stratified agricultural societies with complex political systems."[39]

A functionalist approach begins with an analysis of the social function of animal sacrifice for ancient Israelite society. In other words, what are the consequences of this practice for ancient Israel? Such a social reading can also draw attention to the ideology of the priests and the Israelites. The conditions and views expressed in the text relate to those Israelites living during or just after the monarchy.

There were three types of animal sacrifice in ancient Israel: (1) whole burnt offerings, (2) offerings partly burned and offerings partly consumed by the priests, and (3) offerings meant to atone for the unintentional sins of the people and priests.[40] Interestingly, we can infer from the description of burnt offerings in chapter one that the society is stratified. The sacrifice of the oxen relates to the wealthier landowners. The other two sacrifices are burned offerings of birds, which are fitting for the poorer people.

All three types played a significant role in the priestly ritual. The priestly writers set these sacrifices in the wilderness prior to the settling of the land. It is fairly safe to assume that initially these sacrifices took place in sacred places throughout the land of ancient Israel. With the reforms of King Josiah in the seventh century B.C.E., however, these practices may have been limited to Jerusalem.

Leviticus 1–7 constitutes the first section of Leviticus. Leviticus 1:1–6:7 contains directions for the people while 6:8–7:36 is a manual for the priests.[41] This manual for the priest is idealistic. It contains a priestly worldview, and it discusses ways in which the priests and the people ought to carry out sacrificial rituals.

In reading the priestly material, especially Leviticus 1–7, it is evident that sacrifice is crucial to the faith community. Equally evident is the attention to detail and repetition in these priestly writings. The detail and repetition indicate the seriousness with which the priestly officials took their task of teaching the community. The reason the priests took their task so seriously is to avoid wrong "procedure," which ensures disastrous results.[42] Following right procedure (e.g., Lv 10:1–20) is necessary for an orderly life. Priestly materials make it clear that adherence to the law is the only way to secure Yahweh's blessings and protection. Maintaining boundaries between clean and unclean or holy and unholy is a prerequisite for an orderly existence.[43] Correct ritual or sacrifice allows people to remain clean and holy. As a result, Yahweh can remain in the presence of the people.

Additionally, the proper procedure is important because it protects one from mishandling holy things. For instance, Yahweh gives specific orders that no one is to eat either the fat or the blood of a sacrificial animal (Lv 3:17 and 7:22–27). Both of these portions belong to Yahweh alone. A violator "shall be cut off from his people." Exclusion from the community puts one outside God's presence. To allow the violator to remain in the community contaminates and endangers the entire community since God cannot remain in the presence of an unclean people.

The remedy for the violator is a sacrifice. Sacrifice provides the necessary means for reentry into the community undoing the consequences of disobedience. Each animal sacrifice has a different focus, but all sacrifices work toward the same goal. They help maintain order in society by allowing individuals a way to repent and return to the community so they can again engage in a meaningful life having the renewed status of being clean and holy.

Repetition of sacrifices underscores the importance of correct ritual. Berger describes rituals as reminders. The rituals remind ancient Israelites about the importance of obedience. The sacrificial system along with its function and meaning are part of ancient Israel's world (i.e., the worldview that is taken-for-granted).[44] If the priestly worldview is integrated into the larger Israelite perspective, a sacrifice will function to reinforce the norms and expectations of that society. Therefore, this priestly ideology would justify and legitimate the role and social status of the priests in society. They would play their part in keeping society safe and orderly. In return, they would enjoy the privilege of high social status.

Still, it is hard to know the extent to which these ideas influenced ordinary people in ancient Israel. Looking at Josiah's reforms in 2 Kings 23:1–20, one does not get the impression that worship in ancient Israel was pure and faithful to Yahweh alone. In this passage, not even the priest measure up. The "idolatrous priests" connected to the high places in 2 Kings 23:5 are probably involved in fertility rites. The passage views the priests of the high places in a negative fashion in this passage. Yet, most people may regard them as legitimate priests whose practices are acceptable. Their practices are far from what Leviticus 1–7 requires. So the view painted by this text is highly idealistic. The priestly ideology in Leviticus probably has some influence on elites living in or around Jerusalem, but for the rural populations of common or peasant peoples this view may have been lacking.

Nevertheless, these chapters do serve a purpose. As an expression of the priestly ideal, they instruct and motivate the priests and the people to obey the law. If they fail whether intentionally or unintentionally, they have a way of redemption. They must make the proper sacrifice. While this priestly ideal may have had limited appeal during the monarchy, it still advocates actions that would maintain the relationship between God and the people. The ideal may have carried more weight after the fall of Jerusalem. The priest then can tell the people that God's absence is due to their sins, which likely fueled a renewed emphasis on the law and obedience to it.

Animal sacrifices also functioned on a political level since the official religion helped maintain the state. The tithe in the Canaanite world, as well as ancient Israel, constituted a part of the revenues of the state. Therefore, the state benefited from the operation of the official religious order. Even if Leviticus in its present state dates to the Babylonian Exile or later, it promotes priestly practices and views present during the monarchy. These views supported the creation of the state and its continued existence. The ideas of the priest would become even more influential in the post-exilic period.

One could see this through conflict theory as well by focusing on power, control, and self-interests. Priests are rather conservative since it is in their best interest to maintain the status quo. However, their high status and trust-worthy behavior is not taken for granted by everyone. As we have seen, certain biblical texts are critical of the priests. In the prophetic literature, there are some clashes between the priest and prophets where the priests are described as enemies of Yahweh since they comfort the people rather than causing them discomfort as they should.

As long as the structures upholding this priestly world-view remain intact, the order continues. However, in times of crisis, these structures may lose their legitimacy. In this instance, the individual or community may question and reevaluate the existing order. Prophets attack the priestly views and actions at times. The result may be a rejection of the existing order or a re-appropriation or modifications of that order.

Conflict theory in sociology might be interested in priests not for their functional value but for their influence. The priests as leaders of the official religion have a great deal of power. Corruption is always possible when power is at play. They may sometimes use their favored status in an abusive fashion or simply to benefit themselves and their fellow elites. Because the priests benefited by the existing order, they are motivated to maintain it even when it is oppressive. Often the prophets speak against the standard religious practice for its inability to bring about justice (e.g., Am 5:21–24).

1 Peter 2:11–3:22.

This passage contains the household code. The household code defines the basic structure of family life in ancient Greece and Rome. According to Jewish writers Philo and Josephus, this is also true of Palestine as well. Some scholars maintain that the household code either came into Christian litera-ture through Stoic influence or from Hellenistic Judaism, which "developed this code out of the Decalogue" (Ex 20:12).[45] David L. Balch, however, has cogently traced the household code back to its roots in the Greek political ethics of Plato and Aristotle.[46] In Aristotle, for instance, there is a relation-ship between the city and house concerning the matter of those who rule (the superior member) and those who are ruled (the inferior member). This code is characterized by assigning certain obligations to pairs so that "one member of the pair is to be subordinate to the other."[47] In the case of the household, the husband is to rule the wife, the parents the children, and the master the slaves. Balch says these ideas are popular in the Roman period,[48] and he also traces them to Bithynia near the time of 1 Peter's composition.[49]

It is true that the topic of household is present in Philo, a Hellenistic Jewish writer, and certain Jewish Christian writers.[50] Balch says this code served an apologetic function for Philo and Josephus both Jewish writers. The need for an apologetic or defense derives from the fact that the Romans are critical of foreign, eastern cults such as Dionysius and Isis. The Romans feel that such cults "produced immorality (especially among Roman women) and sedition." The apologetic of Josephus clearly defends the Jews from this type of criticism.[51] Balch also thinks that the household code in 1 Peter functions the same way. This topic is active in the Asia Minor province of Bithynia. Bithynia is one of the provinces named in 1 Peter 1.

Keeping the discussion brief, one can say that the letter dates to a time between 70–93 C.E. The author is an anonymous Christian. Writing under a pseudonym, in this case, Peter is a relatively common practice at that time. The letter is addressed to the exiles. They seem to feel threatened with the possibility of persecution. Evidence from the letter does not indicate that the state is at odds or hostile to this Christian community. There are indications in the text that real tensions exist between Christians and their neighbors. The author and most of the addressees appear to be Hellenistic Jews while some are Gentiles.

The household code seems to function as a defense. It assures the Romans that the Christian community is not a threat to Roman authority. They too share the views of the code accepted by the larger Roman society. The author's message appears to encourage Asia Minor Christians to conform to Roman laws and avoid unnecessary conflict with Romans. The message is that Christians have no reason to fear the state, and they have no reason not to be good citizens (1 Pt 2:11–17).

It is clear that the Christians are experiencing problems with their Gentile neighbors, but one should not see these conflicts as a conflict between the Christian community and the Romans. There does not seem to be any place where the author is setting the Romans up in opposition to the Christian communities in Asia Minor. The author expects there could be trouble (1 Pt 4:12–15). Consequently, if one must choose either God or the state, a Christian must obey God alone. However, the writer does not seem to think it will come to that. In any event, one should be a model citizen, and if Christians suffer it should not be because they have done wrong (1 Pt 4:15).

The code begins in 1 Peter 2:11 and continues through 3:12. 1 Peter 2:11–3:12 belongs to the larger unit of 2:11–4:11. The main focus of this analysis is on the passage concerning slaves and wives (1 Pt 2:18–3:6). It addresses two of the usual three pairs found in the household code. Normally, the household code covers master/slave, husband/wife, and parent/child. 1 Peter addresses master/slave and husband/wife. In both cases, the writer shows the Christian community to be in line with Roman expectations for the home. In these pairs, the husband and master are in a place of authority. Servants are to be submissive to their masters and wives to their husbands.

As the Romans saw it, such a structure was necessary for the peace and security of the state. Romans looked upon innovation with suspicion. The household code was part of this stable society. The family in the Greco-Roman society was inextricably tied to the city in that there must be a ruler and those ruled in both relationships.[52] This order of family life represented the ordinary function of family and city governance in Rome at this time.

The situation in 1 Peter suggests that Gentiles in the area felt that Christians are disturbing the peace of their community. From the content of the letter, one can infer that the sources of the complaints stem from what the non-Christians perceive to be a deviation from the normal function of the household. If slaves and women are converted to Christianity from a pagan household, one can easily see where the tension is located. If a slave converts to Christianity with its notion of freedom and equality in Christ, does that mean submission to his or her master is in any way compromised? Alternatively, what if a wife converts to Christianity, and her husband is upset by the conversion? The resulting conflict could spread beyond the domestic arena. Any change to the household structure would tend to upset that society and lead to questions and close scrutiny. Such attention could invite trouble.

As a result, the writer is trying to calm the situation. The letter is a defense of Christian activities in Asia Minor. The writer shows that Christians abide by the same norms as their Gentile neighbors. However, the writer is not attempting to avoid conflict at all cost. Rather this letter encourages and instructs Christians to be faithful to the state, the legitimate Roman authorities, and to God. One might call the author a realist. He calls for a process of accommodation. The author of 1 Peter is not offering the Asian Christians a way to avoid conflict, but a way to reason with the people outside the Christian community as well as with the Roman authorities. The author wants the Christians to be able to give a "defense to anyone who calls you to account for the hope that is within you" (Pt 3:15). The author of 1 Peter, like Paul, does not see the Roman Empire as an evil entity that Christians must resist. The writer feels that if the Asian Christians follow the advice given in the letter, they might avoid persecution.

Based on this information, one might ask: What is the function or consequences of the household code for the Roman society and the Christian community in Asia Minor? For Roman society, the code's demand for adherence to certain family and state structures produces a stable societal structure. This structure supports traditional views of authority. It defines who has legitimate power in the domestic realm. For the Christian community, it defends and protects the Christian community there from possible suspicion and hostility of the Gentile population.

There is another side. While this code has a particular function in Roman society and the Christian communities, it could be perceived as dysfunctional for slaves and wives. A conflict approach would focus on who has the power and authority to define what the family should be in the first place. Some Christians could appeal to Paul's comments in Galatians 3:28 as a way of countering this code espousing freedom and equality for all Christians. The issues of slavery and gender could cause problems for Christians who might desire to abolish slavery and gender discrimination.

Above, I have tried to provide some background information about the sociological approach and show several examples of how it can be used to interpret biblical texts. This discussion brings the historical section of this book to a conclusion. Now the discussion turns to literary and ideological approaches.

NOTES

1. Alfred Schutz. Alfred Schutz, "Common-sense and Scientific Interpretation of Human Action," in *Collected Papers I: The Problem of Social Reality*, ed. Maurice Natanson (The Hauge: Martinus Nijhoff, 1967); and Alfred Schutz and Thomas Luckmann, *The Structures of the Life-World*, Northwestern University Studies in Phenomenology & Existential Philosophy, ed. John Wild and trans. Richard M. Zaner and H. Tristram Engelhardt, Jr. (Evanston, Ill.: Northwestern University Press, 1973).

2. Peter L. Berger, *Invitation to Sociology: A Humanistic Perspective*, (New York: Anchor Books, 1963), 120-121.

3. William G. Dever, *The Lives of Ordinary People in Ancient Israel: Where Archaeology and the Bible Intersect*, (Grand Rapids: William B. Eerdmans Publishing Company, 2012), 4-6.

4. Dale B. Martin, "Social Scientific Criticism," in To Each Its Own Meaning: An Introduction to Biblical Criticisms and Their Application, ed. Stephen R. Haynes and Steven L. McKenzie (Louisville: The Westminster Press, 1999), 129-132.

5. Berger, *Invitation to Sociology*, 25-53.

6. Ruth A. Wallace and Alison Wolf, *Contemporary Sociological Theory: Continuing the Classical* Tradition, 2d ed. (Englewood Cliffs, New Jersey: Prentice Hall Inc., 1980), 48-49.

7. Ibid., 49.

8. Ibid., 50.

9. Peter Berger, *The Sacred Canopy: Elements of a Sociology of Religion*, (New York: Anchor Press Book, 1969), 3.

10. K. W. Whitelam, *The Just King: Monarchical Judicial Authority in Ancient Israel*, Journal for the Study of the Old Testament Supplement Series, ed. David J. A. Clines, 12 (Sheffield: JSOT Press, 1979), 39.

11. Lawrence Stager, "The Archaeology of the Family in Ancient Israel," *Bulletin of the American Schools of Oriental Research* 260 (1985): 18.

12. Ibid., 18-20.

13. Norman K. Gottwald, *The Tribes of Yahweh: A Sociology of the Religion of Liberated Israel 1250-1050 B.C.E.* (Maryknoll, N.Y.: Orbis Books, 1979), 257-274.

14. David C. Hopkins, "The Dynamics of Agriculture in Monarchical Israel," in *Society of Biblical Literature 1983 Seminar Papers*, ed. Kent Harold Richards (Atlanta: Scholars Press, 1983), 183, 192.

15. Robert R. Wilson, "Enforcing the Covenant: The Mechanisms of Judicial Authority in Early Israel," in *The Quest For the Kingdom of God: Studies in Honor of George E. Mendenhall*, ed. H. B. Huffmon, F. A. Spina, and A. R. W. Green (Winona Lake, IN.: Eisenbrauns, 1983), 63.

16. Frank S. Frick, *The Formation of the State in Ancient Israel*, The Social World of Biblical Antiquity Series, ed. James W. Flanagan, 4 (Sheffield: Almond Press, 1985), 52.

17. Elizabeth Bellefontaine, Customary Law and Chieftainship: Judicial Aspects of 2 Samuel 14:4-21," *Journal for the Study of the Old Testament* 38 (1987): 49.

18. Frick, Formation of the State, 68-69.

19. Ibid., 76.

20. James W. Flanagan, "Chiefs in Israel," *Journal of Biblical Literature* 20 (1981): 55-58.

21. James W. Flanagan, *David's Social Drama: A Hologram of Early Israel's Iron Age*, The Social World of Biblical Antiquity Series, ed. James W. Flanagan, 7 (Sheffield: Almond Press, 1988), 57-58; and Frick, *Formation of the State*, 42.

22. Flanagan, "Chiefs," 67-69.

23. Marvin L. Chaney, "Systematic Study of the Israelite Monarchy," *Semeia* 37 (1986): 60-74.

24. George E. Mendenhall, "The Hebrew Conquest of Palestine," *The Biblical Archaeologist Reader* 3 (1970): 100-120.

25. Mendenhall does, however, disagree with Gottwald's approach. See George E. Mendenhall, "Ancient Israel's Hyphenated History in *Palestine in Transition: The Emergence of Ancient Israel*, ed. David Noel Freedman and David Frank Graf. The Social World of Biblical Antiquity Series vol. 2 (Sheffield: The Almond Press, 1983), 91-103.

26. Norman K. Gottwald, *The Hebrew Bible: A Socio-Literary Introduction*, (Philadelphia: Fortress Press, 1985), 272.

27. Ibid., 272.

28. Ibid., 272-273.

29. Ibid., 275.

30. Walter Brueggemann, "Trajectories in Old Testament Literature and the Sociology of Ancient Israel," *Journal of Biblical Literature* 98 (1979): 161-185.

31. Marcus J. Borg, *Meeting Jesus Again for the First Time: The Historical Jesus & the Heart of the Contemporary Faith*, San Francisco: HarperSanFrancisco, 1994).

32. Victor H. Matthews and Don C. Benjamine, "Introduction: Social Sciences and Biblical Studies," *Semeia* 68 (1994): 10-11.

33. Generalized other and significant other are terms drawn from George Herbert Meade and symbolic interactionism.

34. For a positive view of the Pharisees see Daniel Patte, *Paul's Faith and the Power of the Gospel: A Structural Introduction to the Pauline Letters* (Philadelphia, Fortress Press, 1983), 87-121; and Patte, Early Hermeneutics in Palestine (Chico, Calif.: Scholars Press, 1975), 11-127. Daniel Patte says that the heart of Pharisaic faith is election, which is not earned but a gift from God. Observing the laws is the proper response to this gift.

35. John E. Stambaugh and David L. Balch, *The New Testament in Its Social Environment*, Library of Early Christianity, ed., Wayne A. Meeks (Philadelphia: The Westminster Press, 1986), 100.

36. Ibid., 101.

37. Borg, 52.

38. Erhard S. Gerstenberger, *Leviticus*, ed., James L. May The Old Testament Library (Louisville: Westminster John Knox Press, 1996), 10-14, 24-26.

39. McNutt, 177-178.

40. Norman K. Gottwald, *The Hebrew Bible: A Socio-Literary Introduction*. (Philadelphia: Fortress Press, 1985): 214-215.

41. N. H. Snaith, *Leviticus and Numbers*. New Century Bible ed. R. E. Clements (Greenwood, S. C.: the Attic Press Inc., 1969), 2-3; Frank Gorman, *Ideology Of Ritual: Space, Time and Status in the Priestly*, Journal for Testament Supplement Series, ed. David J. A. Clines, 91 (Sheffield: Journal for the Study of the Old Testament Press, 1990), 46; D. W. Baker, "Leviticus 1-7 and the Punic Tariffs," *Zeitschrift für die alttestamentliche Wissenschaft* 99 no. 2 (1987): 197.

42. Gorman, 52-53. See, for example, Leviticus 10:1-20.

43. Ibid., 59. This idea of separation from impurity is also found in the Holiness Code in Leviticus 17-26.

44. Peter Berger and Thomas Luckmann, *The Social Construction of Reality: A Treatise in the Sociology of Knowledge* (New York: Doubleday & Company, Inc., 1966), 19.

45. David L. Balch, "Household Codes," in Greco-Ronan Literature And The New Testament. ed. David E. Aune *SBL Sources For Biblical Study* 21 (Atlanta: Scholars Press, 1988), 25.

46. David Lee Balch, "'Let Wives Be Submissive. . .' The Origin, Form And Apologetic function of the Household Duty Code (Haustafel) In I Peter" (Ph.D. diss., Yale University, 1974), 33-60.

47. Balch, "Household Code," 25.

48. Balch, "Let Wives Be Submissive...," 35-36 and 48-57.

49. Ibid., 44-47.

50. Ibid., 114.

51. Ibid., 179 and 134-138.

52. Balch, "Let Wives Be Submissive . . . ," 112.

Chapter Ten

Historical Versus Literary Readings

This chapter forms a bridge between historical and literary approaches. History deals with the fundamental historical questions such as authorship, date, and audience to discover the text's meaning. One might recognize a story as historical but also appreciate artistic talents of the storyteller. In contemporary literary readings, however, history plays little or no role. A literary approach does not attempt to place a text within a historical or social setting. Instead, it is not interested in sources or editing. Literary critics read Genesis or Matthew as they now exist. They often focus on the study of fiction. Consequently, many feel uneasy about applying literary approaches to the Bible.

GENRE: HISTORY OR FICTION?

An important issue facing biblical critics who use literary criticism is the nature of biblical texts. Is a method designed to analyze fiction suitable for reading the Bible? Even those who use the literary approach do not agree on the nature of biblical narratives. Robert Alter describes the biblical narratives as "historicized prose fiction" or "fictionalized history."[1] By historical prose fiction, Alter allows for elements of fiction and history. The two are mixed in biblical narratives. In this way, the Bible can be studied as literature.

Meir Sternberg, on the other hand, takes issue with Alter's classification. Sternberg views biblical narratives as historical, which for him does not exclude them from a literary analysis.[2] The difference between their views is not that great. Alter recognizes that the biblical narratives contain history while Sternberg acknowledges that historical narratives contain fiction. Sternberg says, "history writing is not a record of fact-of 'what really happened'—but a discourse that claims to be a record of fact. Nor is fiction writing a tissue of free inventions but a discourse that claims freedom of invention. The antithesis lies not in the presence or absence of truth but of the commitment to truth."[3]

For Sternberg, there is a significant difference between "truth value" (reporting what actually happened) and "truth claim." It seems he is arguing that a person who tells a story believing it to be the truth is writing history. If a text has to be historically correct to be history, then the status of a text depends upon its historical accuracy. Sternberg is correct to question "truth value" as a measure of the historical nature of a work. As he says, what happens when a text is found to be historically inaccurate? Does it cease to be history writing? But is there a way to distinguish history writing from fiction?

Perhaps, it might be better to say a writer intended his or her work to be a historical account, but it falls short. The writer intends to tell what actually happened. On this view, a writer's intent becomes the determining factor. Still, there are problems. I might intend to write a history, and I believe I am correct when I say that "aliens" built the Egyptian pyramids. Historians would be completely justified in saying my history is a bad one or that it does not conform to the rules of good history writing at all and, therefore, is not really history. So is it really about one's intent? Who is to say that one text is history and another fiction without falling back on Sternberg's notion of truth claim?

Maybe the best solution is to ask if a work follows the established rules for writing about the past. Is it following the established practices of the academic discipline of history? This view seems best, but it too has limitations. If the rules of history writing are primarily modern constructs, how can we allow them to judge works developed in ancient or pre-modern times? Is what passes for history today the only possible way of writing history? Is history a modern invention? Can we recognize ancient writings as history? As one may recall, John Van Seters made such an argument. Ancient histories use the past to explain the present. These type histories may contain myths, legends, and supernatural causality, but this is not necessarily a problem for their being identified as history.[4]

So where does this leave us? I do not think it is wise to categorize a biblical text as either history or fiction. Most texts have both elements. Using Van Seter's definition, one could describe many biblical texts as history. The problem is the mindset that views history and fiction as binary oppositions. Such a mindset gives the wrong impression. To follow Sternberg's approach and call these texts history plays into the hands of fundamentalists, and it misleads people into thinking that the Bible is a history book. To call it fiction plays to the other extreme. Some people point to this characterization and say it is merely a book of fiction and of little importance.

On the side of fiction, Sternberg says that fictional writings may contain real historical facts, but this does not make it history. He then identifies a key difference between the two: "What opposes fiction to historiography is not the writer's breach or avoidance but his independence of factuality."[5] In other words, fiction writers feel free to create a story about events and people. Nevertheless, how do we know that the biblical writers are not exercising this kind of creativity in many places? So why call biblical narratives history?

In fact, biblical narratives are a mixture of history and artistic storytelling containing historical and fictional elements. In short, seeing the texts as storytelling or narratives leaves room for both history and fiction. Labeling it according to the genres of history or fiction seems unnecessary and misleading. The two bleed over into one another.

There is another point to be made here. If literary methods focus on the artistic and not the historical, then does it matter whether something is history or fiction? R. Alan Culpepper addresses this issue in relation to a literary reading of the gospels.[6] For him, "truth and history are neither synonymous nor antithetical. As narratives, the gospels tell true stories."[7] However, it does not necessarily follow that they are literally true. What does Culpepper mean by saying they are true if he is not basing this statement on a historical notion of truth? Wolfgang Iser says that fiction in literature is a "means of telling something about reality."[8] Stories, myths and legends may convey truths although not necessarily historical truth.

In this vein, Culpepper talks about "encountering" Jesus in the gospel texts. Reading the text properly and identifying the power the text has on its reader is key to any proper interpretation. A correct reading derives from a reader making proper connections allowing him or her to "read correctly." Reading the gospels in this fashion "requires the suspension of critical probing. . . . It requires . . . 'a willing suspension of disbelief.' That means we must read without asking whether such events are possible or plausible. ... Only when we assume the role of the implied reader . . . can we enter the narrative world of the gospels and experience their regional power."[9] His approach requires a proper reading and response with texts guiding this response.

In conclusion, I differ with Alter and Sternberg in trying to describe biblical texts as history or fiction. Moreover, literary analysis is possible even with literature that reports historical information. The biblical narratives exhibit imagination and artistic creativeness. I agree with Iser and Culpepper that truth is not solely tied to historical reliability. Alter, Sternberg, and Culpepper have all provided valuable readings of biblical narratives.

KEY DIFFERENCE BETWEEN
HISTORICAL AND LITERARY APPROACHES

Some historical and literary critics value one perspective at the expense of the other. Historical critics may feel that literary approaches are not focusing on the real source of meaning (i.e., the author's intentions). Some literary critics have viewed historical approaches as limited and unnecessary. For the literary critic, meaning is located not in the author's intentions but in the text. Such either/or approaches are in my view unjustifiably limited. Both types of readings are helpful; they provide richness to our understandings.

Initially, the literary approach refers to a close reading that examines the text as a whole. It tries to understand the world within the text not the world behind the text. The text is not a window to the past. One should read the text on its own terms. Literary readings view the text as an end in itself. We read the text as it is without historical reconstructions. The historical background has little or no role to play. The reader is primarily passive. The various elements of the text guide the reader and determine the text's meaning.

Literary critics would need to consider issues related to textual criticism. When variations in different manuscripts of a given text occur or when the text seems to have something wrong with it, textual criticism seeks to determine the original words of the text. If the text is so important, one needs to have the most reliable text possible for literary analysis. How can one do an in-depth literary analysis when the text under consideration has problems that affect the interpretation?

One key issue that has defined the debate between historical and literary critics goes back to an article published in 1946. W. K. Wimsatt and Monroe Beardsley rejected the historical emphasis on the author's intention. The now well-known article[10] undermined the entire basis for historical studies. Before the 1940's, secular literary criticism like historical biblical studies attempted to understand the historical background of a writing and its author to discover the author's intentions. With the emergence of New Criticism, this focus came under fire.

Wimsatt and Beardsley reject the historical focus on the author's intent since it is "neither available nor desirable as a standard for judging the success of a work of literary art."[11] Wimsatt and Beardsley's statement contains two parts. It is neither "available nor desirable." It is the first part that is of concern for a literary approach to the Bible. Literary approaches to biblical texts are not really trying to judge the "success of a literary work of art." The debate is over the notion of availability. Is the author's intent available?

Consequently, the claim that the author's intention is unavailable could be construed as saying that historical approaches are impossible and a waste of time. For these literary critics, it is a fallacy to consider a text's meaning as identical with the author's intentions.[12] Many literary critics, therefore, find the legitimate meaning in a proper reading of the final form of the text rather than in the author's intentions.

Literary critic, E. D. Hirsch, is a notable exception to this dismissal of authorial intention. For Hirsch, focus on the author's intent is necessary since it steers the interpreter away from a relativistic viewpoint where the text can have almost unlimited meanings.[13] Meaning is "absolute and immutable, wholly resistant to change."[14] Hirsch distinguishes between meaning and significance. A text has one meaning, but the significance of the text can change as times change. Literary critic, Terry Eagleton, sees Hirsch's work as an attempt to police the text and protect private property (i.e., the property of the author). Eagleton describes Hirsch's view as follows: "the author's meaning is his own, and should not be stolen or trespassed upon by the reader."[15]

Therefore, Eagleton rejects Hirsch's notion that one should privilege the author's intent. The author's intent is not in fact a private matter. The author is part of a community and uses language intimately connected to the social world. As Eagleton points out, "there is a real sense in which language belongs to my society before it belongs to me."[16] So for Eagleton, the author's intentions alone are not completely sufficient to determine a text's meaning.

Much of the above discussion points to a literary approach known as New Criticism, also known as formalism. In secular literary circles, it is mostly applied to poetry. Regarding poetry, it rejects a simple description or paraphrase of a work,[17] and it tends to devalue any connection to the real world. It favors the world represented or constructed by the text over actual historical reality. According to David M. Gunn, "meaning is to be found by [a] close reading that identifies formal and conventional structures of the narrative, determines plot, develops characterization, distinguishes point of view, exposes language play, and relates all to some overarching, encapsulating theme."[18] This perspective has influenced Narrative Criticism of the Bible. This approach has at least one commonality with historical criticism. Both are part of modern worldviews that set out to establish the legitimate meaning. Both assume a unity of thought and view the interpreter as an objective professional in the pursuit of truth.

For these literary critics, texts ultimately provide unity. The text may contain complexity and ambiguity, but a close reading by qualified critics reveals its unity.[19] Sternberg pays close attention to complexity in the text where tension is created and resolved through the art of the storyteller.[20] Sternberg also describes the interpretive process as "foolproof composition" by which he asserts that the meaning of biblical narratives is so plain that one cannot fail to understand it.[21] Again, there is unity in the text. Tensions exist, but in the end they are resolved.

More recently, there is growing interest in the reader as playing an active role in the process. This tendency moves away from the notion that meaning is located solely in the text. Now there is recognition by some that meaning is the product of the reader and not the text. At most, it is created in the interaction between the text and reader. When meaning becomes tied to the reader in any significant manner, it would appear one is moving toward some level of relativism. With recognition of this subjective aspect of interpretation, other approaches have emerged such as rhetorical criticism, deconstruction, and ideological approaches. I discuss these in later chapters. Before moving on to narrative criticism, however, I do need to discuss an approach that could be pursued from either a literary or historical perspective, and that is canonical criticism.

CANONICAL CRITICISM

The word canon often refers to a list of authoritative writings whose words define the norms for the believing community.[22] These lists developed over time before becoming finalized. The biblical canon is a product of ancient Jewish and Christian communities. The decisions and work of these communities lead to an established set of authoritative books. These decisions have had a long reach since they still exert control over modern faith communities.

Like the literary approaches, canonical criticism is not about getting back to an earlier form of the text. It focuses largely on the final, canonical shape of the text.[23] Still, a critical look at how certain religious communities shape texts into the canon is instructive. Such an approach looks at how the overall canon is arranged and put together.

Brevard Childs and James Sanders, two of the most important practitioners of this approach, consider how faith communities "shape" the canon by bringing books together into a larger collection. Childs acknowledges that "particular editors, religious groups, and even political parties were involved"[24] in this canonical process. He also says that the canonical approach studies biblical texts "as historically and theologically conditioned writings which were accorded a normative function in the life of this community."[25] The notion of religious community in Childs, however, does not seem to have any specific historical referent. While he refers to political parties or religious groups, he does not pursue their identities in a way that would lend itself to a socio-historical study of the process. According to Childs, "those responsible for the actual editing of the text did their best to obscure their identity."[26]

Without a clear group of people in mind, the notion of the community who shaped the canon is vague. A more concrete description of the community in relation to historical concerns would shed light on the reasons and motives behind the shaping of the texts. This approach could give one a glimpse into the final stages of the process in which traditions and texts are fixed in the canon.[27] However, this is not part of Childs' concern.

For Sanders and Childs, the canon is not tied to the past. For Sanders, the canon is both adaptable and stable.[28] Adaptability means that later communities adapt texts to a new context. In effect, this means that canonical texts speak to different communities in meaningful ways and in new situations. However, the meaning is stable. The text does not have different meanings at different times. Childs uses the term "actualization" to refer to a process whereby the canon is not tied to the past but is free to speak to the present. This actualization is built into the canonization process itself, and it makes "the text religiously accessible."[29]

The canonical approach can recognize diversity. Mary C. Callaway says that this approach locates authority in the full canon. There are competing voices in the Bible, and none of them has the final word; "no position is absolute." The canonical approach views the Bible as a "lively discussion in which theological ideas are constantly being reformulated in response to new data."[30] Nevertheless, the diversity is held in check. Callaway says that the "most significant theological contribution of canonical criticism is the axiom that no voice of the canon should be privileged over others; there is no text by which all other texts must be interpreted. Biblical texts become the Word of God in their full canonical context."[31] This view appears to mean that the interpreter has to live with the tension.

To provide a brief example of this approach, I have selected the Book of Ecclesiastes. The book of Ecclesiastes contains viewpoints that seem inconsistent with each other. In some places, it appears to say that good actions are rewarded and evil ones punished. In other instances, this view is reversed. Older scholars sought to explain these discrepancies as the result of different editions or sources. While one source says that the author hated life, the other said he or she valued it. Canonical criticism, however, views the book as a whole including the epilog.

Childs says that the book's "authoritative role lies in its function within a larger context. The editorial shaping of the book did not consist of a heavy-handed reworking of the original sayings of Koheleth. His words are left basically in their original form without being blurred or softened. Instead, a new and larger context is provided in which the book is to be interpreted."[32] For Childs, the epilog (Eccl 12:9–14) plays a significant role in the book's interpretation. In effect, it does soften and redirect the author's viewpoints. From a canonical context, the book closes with a meaning that is in tension with the book as a whole. Childs sees the writers' sayings as having no independent status of their own, but they become part of ancient Israel's body of wisdom literature and "function as a critical corrective."[33]

While this interpretation is valid from a canonical perspective, it does not follow that it becomes the final normative meaning for the book. If I understand Callaway's position correctly, the editor does not have the last word; the tension between the epilog and the book as a whole is maintained. Neither the editor nor the writer has the final say. Childs' position here, however, would not be a real concern if it were not for the fact that he does not recognize the legitimacy of other critical approaches. The canonical meaning is the normative meaning of a text. So the epilogue in Ecclesiastes has the final say even over the words of the author. The editor responsible for the epilog provides the normative meaning of the book, and it takes some force away from the writer's words.

On a positive note, the process of canonization is dynamic. Studying that process is a worthy endeavor. As one way of reading the text, it is an important addition to critical studies of the Bible. Since the notion of canon sets the boundaries and provides readings that many find normative for faith, it is important to pursue it with historical awareness. As practiced by Childs, canon criticism privileges the final form of the text as produced by the canonizing communities. As a result, elements of control, power, and authority are bound up in this canonization process. In my judgment, it is important to consider the power dynamics behind the process, which requires a more historical or social look at these so-called canonizing communities.

NOTES

1. Robert Alter, *The Art of Biblical Narrative* (New York: Basic Books, Inc., Publishers 1981), 23–46.
2. Meir Sternberg, Meir. *The Poetics of Biblical Narrative: Ideological Literature* (Bloomington, IN: Indiana University Press, 1985), 23–35.
3. Ibid., 25.
4. Van Seters, "The Pentateuch."22.
5. Ibid., 26.
6. R. Alan Culpepper, "Story and History in the Gospels," *Review and Expositor* 81 1984: 473–476.
7. Ibid., 475.
8. Wolfgang Iser, "The Reality of Fiction: A Functionalist Approach to Literature," *New Literary History* 7 (1975/76): 7.
9. Culpepper, 475.
10. W. K. Wimsatt and Monroe C. Beardsley, "The Intentional Fallacy," *Sewanee Review* 54 (1946): 468–488.
11. John Barton, *Reading the Old Testament: Method in Biblical Study* (Philadelphia: The Westminster Press, 1984) 149.
12. Ibid., 149.
13. E. D. Hirsch, Validity in Interpretation (New Haven: Yale University Press, 1967).
14. Terry Eagleton, *Literary Theory: An Introduction*, 2 ed. (Minneapolis: The University of Minnesota Press 1996), 58.
15. Ibid., 59.
16. Ibid., 61.
17. Baldick, 160–161.

18. David M. Gunn, "Narrative Criticism" in *To Each Its Own Meaning: An Introduction to Biblical Criticisms and Their Application*, ed. Stephen R. Haynes and Steven L. McKenzie (Louisville: The Westminster Press, 1999), 201.

19. Steven Lynn, *Texts and Contexts: Writing About Literature with Critical Theory*, 4th ed (New York: University of South Carolina Pearson Longman, 2005), 14–17.

20. Meir Sternberg, *The Poetics of Biblical Narrative: Ideological Literature and the Drama of Reading* (Bloomington, IN: Indiana University Press, 1985), 446–481.

21. Ibid., 48–56, 230–235.

22. See Brevard S. Childs, *Introduction to the Old Testament as Scripture* (Philadelphia: Fortress Press, 1979), 41–45, 49–68.

23. Ibid., 73.

24. Ibid., 78.

25. Ibid., 73. These observations allow ample room for a canonical approach among the historical approaches. Childs, however, makes it abundantly clear that he does not view his approach as another historical method that can be added to the list (pp. 82–82).

26. Ibid., 78.

27. Mary C. Callaway, "Canonical Criticism, in *To Each Its Own Meaning* eds., Steven L. McKenzie and Stephen R. Haynes Rev and expanded (Louisville: John Knox Press, 1999), 144.

28. James Sanders, *Canon and Community: A Guide to Canonical Criticism*, Guides to Biblical Scholarship Old Testament Series, ed. Gene M. Tucker (Philadelphia: Fortress Press 1984), 22.

29. Childs, *Introduction to the Old Testament*, 79.

30. Callaway, 147.

31. Ibid., 150.

32. Childs, *Introduction to the Old Testament*, 588.

33. Ibid., 588.

Chapter Eleven

The Basic Literary Approach

This chapter presents a brief discussion of the basic aspects of a literary approach. One of the first steps in such an approach is to determine the literary context. A literary reading could entail a reading of one chapter, but that chapter would fall within a larger literary context. A literary context could be the entire Book of Genesis. However, it could also be the Pentateuch or the Old Testament. For example, a literary critic could focus on Genesis 1–11 or on the Torah as a whole. One would need to explain why he or she begins in one place and ends in another. A literary approach would typically examine the final form of the text. A notable exception is Harold Bloom's book, *The Book of J.* Typical literary approaches would not strip away editorial layers trying to recover an older form of the text. It would read it as we now have it.

After deciding upon the literary context, one can focus on the literary aspects of a text such as a theme, plot, symbols, repetitions, and characterization. A theme is the main idea of a work. A work may have a central theme and also minor ones. Plot refers to the context in which the action takes place. It is, according to David Gunn, the "organizing force or design, which we see connecting event into some comprehensive pattern."[1] "Plots may be conceived on a simple model of exposition, conflict, climax, and resolution."[2] Gunn relates plot to desire. Identifying the character's desire helps one discover the plot.[3] Their desires push the action forward. Looking at characters, their motives, and their individual perspectives can also produce positive results.

These and other elements make the texts come alive. It allows the reader to enter into the narrative world. One no longer has to know all the history of the text. One simply has to use his or her imagination. Still, for several literary approaches, the text is the controlling feature, not the reader. The meaning is located in the text. The various elements of the text guide the reader allowing him or her to discover its meaning.

Culpepper expresses a slightly different view. According to Culpepper, "meaning is produced only as the reader follows the signals and directions of the text itself. The text does not contain a meaning; it produces its meaning in the reader."[4] The text is a "strategy" for "producing a given response, insight, or emotion."[5] Culpepper also rejects Stendahl's division between what a text meant versus what it means. He feels it "robs the experience of interaction with the text of most of its native power."[6] Finding meaning comes from the text's stimulation of the reader.

Culpepper's notion of the text as a strategy for producing meaning without any recognition of the author's intent is odd. Strategy implies a conscious motive, which requires a real author. It does not make sense to assign a strategy or design to an inanimate object such as a text. Still his main point has value; texts affect readers, and strategy implies a goal. Often the success of any strategy depends upon the rhetoric employed in the text. Rhetoric, therefore, is something else we can add to the list of items covered by a literary analysis.

I have selected two passages to show how one might apply a literary approach. Like the chapter on basic historical approaches (chapter four), it discusses modern application. The first passage is Psalm 6, which is a Hebrew poem. It expresses the psalmist anguish in a time of great distress. The second example is from the Gospel of Mark. Mark 1:21–28 focuses on the issue of authority.

PSALM 6

Hebrew poems tell stories in poetic language. They have a plot. The plot of this poem is about one who wants God's help. Its language is in part rhetorical because it means to persuade God to intervene. This poem has a narrative quality.[7] Hebrew poetry has some other literary qualities as well.

Parallelism is a key characteristic of Hebrew poetry. Typically, this aspect takes one of three forms: antithetical parallelism, synonymous parallelism, and stair-step parallelism. Antithetical parallelism occurs when the second line is a contrast to the first one. Proverbs 10:1–13 provides several examples of this type. Synonymous parallelism occurs when the first line says the same things as the second one only using different words (e.g., Ps 19:1). Stair step or progressive parallelism occurs when the second line advances the thought of the first line to some degree (Ps 95:3). Several other literary features enhance the art of biblical poetry as well. These include the use of metaphor, simile, imagery, repetition, wordplay, ambiguity, and figures of speech.

The reader should pay close attention to how the psalmist employs the literary features listed above to accomplish a goal. Psalms are not merely poems that express emotions and feelings. They are poems created to persuade the community of faith to believe or do something. Therefore, they have a rhetorical quality. Many psalmists direct their words at God. W. H. Bellinger notes that psalms often engage in an "honest dialogue of faith."[8] The Psalmist often does not hesitate to express his or her honest feelings even if they address them at God. They often ask God why and press God for an answer. Lament psalms often attempt to persuade God to act on the petitioner's behalf.

Psalm 6 is short. This Psalm begins with synonymous parallelism. "LORD, do not rebuke me in your anger, or discipline me in your wrath." Rebuke/discipline, anger/wrath highlights the urgency of the language. Clearly, the language of this psalm expresses great concern. It is a cry for help. The psalmist directs the rhetoric of the psalm toward God. What does the psalmist want from God? This gets at the plot. What does the psalmist desire? What is the tension going on in this text? How can this tension be resolved?

The second verse moves from an appeal for God's grace to a call for God's healing. It is clear from the Psalm that only God can help. The distress of the psalmist is punctuated by the words "how long?" The words "how long" are words spoken in hope. The psalmist hopes the words will move God to action. Other keywords directed to God are "save my life" and "deliver me." The psalmist feels his or her life is in danger.

Why should God save the psalmist? Given the poet, God should hear his or her cry and respond because of God's steadfast love. The Hebrew word *ḥesed* translated "steadfast love" is an important word for ancient Israel's faith. The word indicates a loyalty or kindness shown by one person in a superior position to another person in a lesser position such as a king to his subjects. It is associated with the notion of covenant or contract such as the covenant God makes with the people. The psalmist appeals to covenant language to persuade God to respond.

Verse 5 adds another reason for God to respond. The words death and Sheol are synonymous. Sheol is also synonymous with the pit or grave. Sheol is an image of death. The psalmist says "for in death, there is no remembrance of you; in Sheol who can give you praise?" The psalmist feels his or her very life is at risk and tries to persuade God to intervene.

Verses 6–7 continue to describe the psalmist's pain. The turning point comes in verse 8, "The Lord has heard." Hearing implies that God is going to respond favorably not that he just heard his or her words. It implies hearing accompanied by action. In these verses, the psalmist talks about his or her enemies and how God will defeat them. The psalmist, in short, moves from the crisis at hand to the positive resolution. One could say much more from a literary perspective, but this brief discussion illustrates some basic concerns of the text.

This text can easily speak across the ages. Most people can identify with the intense language of verses 6–7: "I am weary with my moaning; every night I flood my bed with tears; I drench my couch with my weeping. My eyes waste away because of grief; they grow weak because of all my foes." We can experience pain, ill health, or the sting of our enemy's words. Consequently, we may also be able to understand and empathize with the psalmist's situation.

MARK 1:14–28

The literary context of this passage is the Gospel of Mark. One would begin by asking about the major theme or themes in the Gospel of Mark as well as the plot. Then, one can see the themes and plot in relation to the larger whole. The discussion below focuses only on these two elements: theme and plot.

To quote Mark 1:2–3 about the messenger who will prepare the way introduces the role of John the Baptist that begins in verse 4. John prepares the way for Jesus' ministry and the coming kingdom of God that is drawing near (Mk 1:15). This statement is an announcement of Jesus' activity, and it informs the reader that Jesus' words and deeds are part of a larger and unfolding plan. The mention of *kairos* or time refers to the appointed time or the right time for Jesus' work, which has now arrived.

Mark 1:14 begins by saying that Jesus is the Son of God. This statement does not detract from his humanity at all. People in the Greco-Roman and Jewish worlds would understand "Son of God" as a reference to divinely inspired teachers or rulers. People believed that these individuals might sometimes perform "miraculous deeds" to help others. In the Jewish world, such extraordinary people do exist. Many Jewish people of the day believe that these individuals possess divine powers allowing them to perform miracles and to communicate "inspired teachings."[9]

Mark 1:14 begins the account of Jesus' activities in Galilee. The Kingdom or rule of God is near. As a result, Jesus calls the people to repent and believe in the good news. These verses introduce the first stage of God's rule. The second stage occurs in the second half of Mark's Gospel with the establishment of that rule.[10]

Some time ago, Wilhelm Wrede identified the main idea or theme of Mark as the messianic secret.[11] Bart D. Ehrman notes that only God, Jesus, and the demons understand Jesus' true identity. Even when Peter comes to proclaim Jesus as the Messiah, he misunderstands what that means.[12] For him, the Messiah is a military or political ruler that delivers Israel from Roman domination, not a suffering servant.

This misunderstanding relates to another theme. Jesus and his followers must suffer. Their suffering is difficult for the disciples to accept. That Jesus must suffer on behalf of others runs counter to their own expectations.[13] The good news, therefore, has a dark side. Nevertheless, the suffering leads to the establishment of God's kingdom. Therefore, the disciples are slow to understand who Jesus is and what his mission is really all about.

Jesus' ministry moves from Galilee to Jerusalem in chapters 11 and following. In Mark 1:14–28, the conflict between Jesus and the Jewish religious leaders in Galilee is intense. Authority is the key issue in these verses. This passage is first in a chain of stories that extend through Mark 3:6. These stories raise the issue of authority and highlight an ongoing and increasingly dangerous conflict between Jesus and certain Jewish leaders.

The story begins with Jesus coming to Capernaum (a town on the Sea of Galilee) where he enters the Jewish synagogue on the Sabbath and teaches those present. The text does not tell the reader what Jesus teaches. The Gospel focuses on the activity of Jesus. Mark uses the word "immediately" quite often indicating a sense of urgency. The reader only learns about the people's response to Jesus' teachings, and they are astounded.

The source for this reaction is not clear. At this point, the reader learns that Jesus teaches "as one having authority and not as the scribes" (Mk 1:22). This statement may prompt the reader to wonder: how exactly is Jesus' teaching different from the scribes who are professional interpreters of the law?

Authority is a source of conflict in the stories that follow. Jesus' authority is a threat to the religious leaders. Do the teachings of the scribe have any authority? Certainly, they have some authority because they have roots in established Jewish tradition. How does the authority of Jesus' teachings differ from the scribes? Jesus' authority may be closer to a charismatic authority than traditional.[14] Charismatic in this context means that Jesus may have had a special quality that draws people to him.

The second mention of authority in this passage helps the reader understand the distinction better. Jesus confronts a man with an unclean spirit. The unclean spirit cries out to Jesus "'what have you to do with us, Jesus of Nazareth? Have you come to destroy us? I know who you are, the Holy one of God'" (Mk 1:23).[15] Jesus responds, "'Be silent, and come out of him!'" The unclean spirit obeys although not silently. Again, the text says the people are amazed. While talking among themselves, they ask: "What is this?" The answer is "A new teaching—with authority!"[16] Jesus' ability to command and rid the man of this unclean spirit lends authority to what he says and does.

In the short stories that begin in Mark 1:21 and continue through Mark 3:6, it appears that what threatens the leaders is not traditional teachings but Jesus' activities of healing the sick, forgiving sins, and casting out demons.

Because of these actions, news spread about Jesus' activities. It spreads despite Jesus' instructions to keep it all silent. In Mark 1:44–45, Jesus tells the man to keep quiet. The ironic result of Jesus' attempts to avoid sensationalism is that his fame spreads.

The Jewish religious and political leaders of that day, therefore, rule the Jewish people in matters of Jewish law and religion. These leaders believe that God gives them authority and the right to rule the people. They hold "trials in the synagogue and in the temple; violators were punished, often severely."[17] The conflict between these leaders and Jesus continue throughout the Gospel. The theme of this story and much of Mark relate to an ongoing conflict between Jesus and his enemies.

Concerning plot of this short story, Jesus desires to proclaim the good news and call the people to repent. His ministry involves casting out a demon or unclean spirit. That Jesus does these things sets him apart from the traditional Jewish religious leaders. His authority comes from God; he does not go through the scribes or priests, which is at the heart of the conflict. Consequently, this story sets the stage for ongoing conflicts that build throughout the Gospel awaiting a final resolution. While the above discussion was limited to plot and theme, one could have also focused on characterization, rhetoric and the use of language. This brief discussion, however, shows that literary readings concentrate on the story told in the text. Whether the story is historically accurate or theologically accurate is not at issue. It is all about the perspective in the story and how the elements of the text guide the reader to understand the message.

CONCLUSION

The next chapter introduces narrative criticism, which focuses on biblical narratives. The literary approach could also focus on biblical poetry as we did with Psalm 6. As stated above, biblical poetry often has a narrative quality; it tells or recounts a story in poetic language. Robert Alter has written a book on narrative and poetry: *The Art of Biblical Poetry* and *The Art of Biblical Narrative*.[18] The narrative approach helps the reader enter the world of the narrative and experience its power and beauty. It encourages a close and detailed reading of the text.

NOTES

1. David M. Gunn, "Narrative Criticism," in *To Each Its Own Meaning: An Introduction to Biblical Criticisms and Their Application*, ed. Stephen R. Haynes and Steven L. McKenzie (Louisville: The Westminster Press, 1999), 213.
2. Ibid., 214.
3. Ibid., 214–224.

4. Culpepper, 471.

5. Ibid.

6. Ibid., 470.

7. W. H. Bellinger, *Psalms: Reading and Studying the Book of Praises* (Peabody: Hendrickson Publishers, 1990), 36.

8. Ibid., 44–73.

9. Bart D. Ehrman, *The New Testament: A Historical Introduction to the Early Christian Writings* 3d ed., (Oxford: Oxford University Press, 2004), 69. Note the textual note in the NRSV that some ancient manuscripts lack Son of God.

10. David Rhodes and Donald Michie, *Mark As Story: An Introduction to the Narrative of a Gospel*, (Philadelphia: Fortress Press, 1982), 74–77.

11. Wilhelm Wrede, *The Messianic Secret*, translated J. C. G. Greig, (Cambridge, 1971).

12. Ehrman, 74–75.

13. Ibid., 76.

14. Concerning traditional and charismatic authority, I am drawing on concepts of sociologists Max Weber.

15. Hugh Anderson, *The Gospel of Mark*, The New Century Bible Commentary, ed. Matthew Black, (Grand Rapids: Wm. B. Eerdmans Publishing Company, 1976), 91. Anderson notes that the shift to the plural pronoun "us suggests either that the demonic is the spokesman for the whole world of demons or that he is split in himself."

16. Graham N. Stanton, *The Gospels and Jesus* (New York: Oxford University Press Inc., 1989), 184.

17. Rhodes and Michie, 79.

18. Robert Alter. *The Art of Biblical Narrative* (New York: Basic Books, Inc., Publishers 1981); and Art of Biblical Poetry, (New York: Basic Books, Inc., Publishers 1985).

Chapter Twelve

Narrative Criticism

Narrative criticism does not exist in secular literary criticism. It does use literary theory to read biblical narratives.[1] A narrative is simply a story. A narrator tells a narrative or story about true or fictional characters and events. The narrative contains a point of view,[2] setting, and plot. The characters in the story keep the reader engaged. Careful readers are wondering and asking themselves: Why are they [the characters] doing that? What do they want? How do they view their actions? Is there something more to this character than meets the eye? The character's motives and worldviews are important to the reader because they help him, or her make sense of the story. By looking at the clues in the text, the reader can build up a mental picture of the different characters and world in which they operate.

Narratives also contain various literary devices for telling the story. A narrative consists "of a set of events (the story) recounted in a process of narration (or discourse) in which the events are selected and arranged in a particular order.[3] The narrator tells us about the narrative world of the text using various literary techniques. The narrative provides the reader with the essential information needed to understand the story. Some stories are more transparent than others. Some stories may contain more ambiguity making their meaning more challenging to discover.

The ancient audiences have an advantage over modern readers. Those living close in time to the events possess knowledge that modern readers lack. They breathe the air of that time, but we are foreigners and outsiders. We would not respond or experience it in the same way as earlier readers, but through our imagination we can make sense of it by following the cues in the text. For a literary reading, one has to suspend disbelief and skepticism. If the text assumes a person can literarily come back to life, the reader has to suspend his or her disbelief to be able to understand the text as it should be understood from a literary perspective. That is the reality for that narrative regardless of whether it fits into our own scientific or philosophical beliefs. The writer is telling the story through a narrator. The writer may omit certain information thus making it more challenging for the reader to find the meaning. Other times, the narrator may provide an explanation of particular events or practices. If we can understand the basic concepts of the story, we should be able to make sense of it. As long as we understand what is going on, the reader can take something away from the reading experience. Some readers, however, are much better at mining the riches of the stories than others.

Biblical narratives do differ in one important way from other short stories and novels. Consider a passage from Mark Twain's Huckleberry Finn:

> I got to feeling so mean and so miserable I most wished I was dead. I fidgeted up and down the raft, abusing myself to myself, and Jim was fidgeting up and down past me. We neither of us could keep still. Every time he danced around and says, "Dah's Cairo!" it went through me like a shot, and I thought if it WAS Cairo I reckoned I would die of miserableness.

In this passage, Huck Finn is having a problem with his conscience. He realizes that he is doing something that his friends and family would not understand; he is helping a slave gain his freedom. In biblical narratives, we rarely get significant insight into the mental or psychological state of the writer or narrator. With biblical narrative, the reader may guess or fill in the gaps, but we are not privy to one's inner thoughts and feelings. There are times where the reader would love to know what certain characters are thinking and feeling. For instance, what was Abraham thinking when he was preparing to offer his only son as a sacrifice in Genesis 22? That is not to say that inner thoughts are always missing.

One should also keep in mind that narrative critics work with the final form of the text, which exhibits a certain unity. Some literary critics such as formalists are primarily interested in texts that show complexity even though that complexity is eventually resolved. Many biblical narratives would not contain a significant amount of complexity. Like the formalists, narrative critics pay close attention to the formal structure and elements in the text. Formalists and narrative critics look for an ultimate resolution of ambiguity. For narrative critics, the meaning is not produced by the reader. It resides in the text, or the text generates it. A good or competent reading follows the cues of the text, which leads one to its meaning.

Narrative critic, Meir Sternberg, provides a rather helpful discussion of biblical narratives in the Hebrew Bible. His views can also be applied to New Testament narratives as well. He identifies some different aspects that one needs to consider when reading a text from a literary perspective. He is interested in the "communicative function" of the Hebrew Bible.[4] His book, *The Poetics of Biblical Narrative*, provides important insights and tools for reading biblical narratives. His treatment of the characters, their perspectives, motives, and the use of repetition are all quite helpful.

The literary approach has great potential; it can lead to significant insight, satisfaction, and enjoyment. Stories about forgiveness, love, relief from physical and mental anguish can be quite uplifting. I Corinthians 13 is a wonderful description of the gift of love. Other stories may leave one bothered and disturbed. Often the prophets challenge people to change their ways. The prophetic words may produce remorse and guilt. Other stories may produce confusion and resistance. What does a parent think when reading the account of Abraham's willingness to sacrifice his son at God's command? (Gn 22) Alternatively, how do modern people feel when reading a text where God commands the Israelites to kill "anything that breathes." They are to "annihilate them—the Hittites and the Amorites, the Canaanites and the Perizzites, the Hivites and the Jebusites" (Dt 20:16–17).

The discussion below provides descriptions of key concepts within the field of literary criticism. One can apply literary approaches to various biblical genres. It can offer a reading of biblical poetry as one would imagine, but it can also be extended to the study of letters or even apocalyptic texts. Letters, for instance, might not seem like literature to some people, but they are stories in a sense. Concerning the letters in the New Testament, David L. Barr says that "every letter implies a story that we can think of as having three levels: the explicit story about the occasion of the writing (the story of the audience), the implicit story of the life of the writer (the story of the author), and the underlying story on which the ideas and advice of the letter are based (the story of Jesus)."[5]

KEY TERMS OR ELEMENTS OF NARRATIVE CRITICISM

There are many different terms used in narrative criticism, and I have selected some of the most important ones for discussion. The first term is an author. Literary critics often focus on implied authors. The implied author differs from the real flesh and blood author. Simply put, the implied author refers to the picture one develops about the author when reading the story. As we read, we build up a mental image of the author. Whether our image matches the real author is not at issue. There is no need to worry about the historical or social influences on this hypothetical construct. All that is important is whether one has read the text correctly when forming this image. So it is our image and not the actual author that is of concern for literary critics. This implied author is conveyed through the story world and not through any biographical or autobiographical information.

The narrator is also important. Authors tell their stories partly through the narrator. A narrator is a tool that the author uses to tell the story. One may describe narrators speaking in the third person rather than the first person as omniscient; they know most everything. In the Genesis 1 creation story, for instance, the narrator knows what God is doing during the creation of the world prior to the creation of man and woman. The narrator can report on what God said and what happened as a result of the divine word. The narrator, therefore, appears to have all the knowledge necessary to tell the story.

Stories have themes, plots, and characters; they also use symbols, images, metaphors and some other elements to make the story compelling. Stories are often a thing of beauty, a form of artistic creation with words. Not all stories are interesting or artistic. Paying close attention to stories is the best way of getting more out of them. This kind of reading also requires one to enter into the story world. We may try to put ourselves into the story and imagine what the characters are like and what they desire. Images, metaphors, repetitions and many other literary aspects may add depth to the reading experience. Before engaging in the reading of two biblical narratives, a look at some of the key elements of a literary approach may be helpful.

Characterization is an important aspect of biblical narratives. The author "can reveal characters either by telling the reader about them or by showing the reader what the characters are like within the story itself."[6] Descriptions of characters vary. Some characters are surface characters while others have depth. A surface or flat character is one who makes all the obvious moves and says all the obvious things. This type character may not say anything, but he or she may simply function as a means of moving the story line forward. Abishag in 1 Kings 1–2 does not say anything, but her character is important because whoever possesses her has a stronger claim to David's throne. Characters with depth, on the other hand, possess aspects that are not so obvious. While characters may at times seem flat or surface, they may possess traits, motives, and perspectives that add depth. Certain aspects of the character's thoughts and behaviors may add mystery, uncertainty, complexity, mistrust, intrigue, conflict, or betrayal to the story.

The author sometimes offers clues to help the reader interpret the character. Clues such as a character's looks or age can provide an opportunity to create greater depth. For instance, old age can have a dual meaning. It may represent wisdom or senility. Younger versus older may be an indicator of seniority and wisdom versus youth that may imply rash and reckless behavior. Age may imply legitimacy. Youth could also mean vigor and energy while age could have a more negative connotation of being satisfied with a corrupt or unproductive status quo. In effect, images with dual meanings are particularly significant because they may introduce a certain complexity to the story and the characters in the story. 1 Kings 1–2 is a good example of a story where age is important in creating a sense of complexity.

Biblical writers do not develop their characters to the same extent modern writers do. In biblical texts, one must almost always infer psychological aspects of the character from what the narrator says or does not say. The narrator rarely tells us what is going on in the character's mind. One must take what is given to determine how a character might feel or think. The narratives are terse and to the point. One does not have to read through lengthy descriptions of what one is thinking or feeling.

Sternberg points out two areas of importance related to characterization.[7] The first concerns the character's perspective. How does the character see and perceive the world? Seeing things from the character's perspective is a key to getting more out of the reading experience. To enter into the story world, the reader may attempt to understand the different characters on their own terms. To appreciate the story, the reader may need to understand the perspective of villains as well as heroes. Doing so adds depth to the reading experience.

Looking at the different perspectives of the characters and seeing them as coinciding or diverging from each other is important. The viewpoints of the characters in a text may differ from the standpoint of the narrator, God, or the reader. There are multiple perspectives in a story. One might try to determine which perspective is consistent with the perspective of the narrator. These are all interesting questions that might move the reading experience to a deeper level. A narrative critic would tend to equate the normative perspective with the view of the narrator or God.

Tied to the character's perspective is motivation. Why do characters act as they do? Why does Abraham in Genesis 22 not resist the command to sacrifice his only son? Is it his faith in God that motivates his unquestioning obedience or something else? Why does the priest in the parable about the Good Samaritan pass on the other side of the road? What is his motivation for such an act? A close reading of the narratives may generate clues. One needs to read the story rather closely in search of these clues.

Gaps are also important. Readers frequently have to fill in gaps to make sense of a text. For instance, the reader may have to infer something about the story or its characters based on limited clues. According to Sternberg, "a gap is a lack of information about the world."[8] The absence of information may create ambiguity and uncertainty, or it may function to keep the reader's interest. The reader may wonder why something happened, and so he or she would have to fill in the gaps based on incomplete information. Sternberg also introduced the term "blanks". Blanks are gaps the narrator considers irrelevant. So-called blanks, however, may very well reflect the personal bias of the interpreter rather than the narrator.

Sternberg warns the reader against subjectively filling in the gaps. The closure comes when the gaps have been filled so that a complete understanding is possible. The text should guide the decisions about how to fill in the gap. Not everyone would agree that it is possible to remove the subjectivity from the interpretive process.

Repetition is another fertile area of interest in the study of biblical narratives. As we discussed earlier in source criticism, repetition may indicate the presence of different sources. In narrative criticism, repetition can also be important. It could be viewed as "redundancy or noise." However, the redundancy may often exist to produce a certain effect.[9] Sternberg identifies three kinds of repetition: verbatim, variant, and deliberate.

Verbatim repetition functions to stress or emphasize something (e.g., Gn 43:3, 5). Some verbatim repetition follows either a "forecast/enactment" pattern or an "enactment report" pattern.[10] Genesis 6:18; 7:17 is an example of the first pattern. The texts forecast that Noah is going into the ark and the second occurrence of the repetition says that he did so. Genesis 16 provides an example of the second type. The narrator says that Hagar "looked with contempt on her mistress" (Gn 16:4). In the next verse, Sarah reports to Abram that Hagar looked at her with contempt.[11]

Variant repetition is Sternberg's second type. In this form of repetition, one finds in the repeated material elaborations, deletions, changes in order, changes in grammatical construction, or substitution. Alter notes that repression and the omitting of words in a repetition serve to reverse "an initial impression."[12] This type of repetition may highlight something significant.

Variant repetition is similar to Sternberg's third type of repetition, which he calls deliberate repetition. Deliberate repetition goes back to motive. Why was the repetition altered? At times, the changes may be intended to manipulate one or more characters in the story, which I demonstrate later in the discussion of I Kings 1–2.

The plot is another important element of narrative criticism. In simple terms, the plot is the plan of a story. It consists of a sequence of events that move the storyline along coming to some sort of resolution. According to Chris Baldick, plot is a "pattern of events and situations in a narrative or dramatic work, as selected and arranged both to emphasize relationships—usually of cause and effect—between incidents and to elicit a particular kind of interest in the reader or audience, such as surprise and suspense."[13] The suspense is created by tension or conflict. An analysis of conflict may include the instigator, the concerns that fuel it, its intensity, its resolution, and the "consequences" of that resolution.[14]

David M. Gunn connects plot to characterization. He says we can only know characters through considering their actions and motivations. These actions and motivations constitute a plot. In order to identify the plot, it is helpful to consider the narration of the story for what it tells us about the character's actions, desires, and motives. The plot is an "organizing force or design" that connects "events into some kind of comprehensible pattern."[15] Gunn says one might ask when reading a story: what does this or that character desire? How are the desires of the different characters moving the story along and how are the desires satisfied? Considering plot in this way prevents it from being defined solely by the desire of the main character. Instead, each character may be "envisioned as having his or her own plot, distinct threads in a web of plots."[16]

OTHER CONSIDERATIONS

There are several other aspects of the literary approach that we could consider. The setting is an important consideration for a narrative approach. The setting has to do with the context of the story. It may relate to where the story takes place. A story takes place in a certain context, which may include a place, time, and particular situation. The setting is the backdrop for the story.

Other elements of the story include a look at the ideas or ideology found in the story and the rhetoric. A look at the ideology may focus on what the story is trying to communicate. What are the major ideas being expressed? How do the narrator and the characters relate to these ideas? Are they in favor or opposed to them? Authors, particularly biblical writers, and editors, frequently present views in a favorable or unfavorable light. Biblical stories often espouse some ideology.

Coupled with the ideology is rhetoric. Rhetoric is largely about persuasion. Rhetoric looks at how the narrators and characters express their thoughts and how they attempt to influence the audience. They do this through the language employed in the text. In some cases, one might view this attempt as a form of manipulation. Sociologist, Ervin Goffman, has described how people in their everyday life play roles, and in the course of playing these roles they try to manage the impression they make on others.[17] They attempt to make the best possible impressions because of the potential rewards. While Goffman is not discussing literature, his views can apply to stories that are rooted in reality. The narrator and the characters in the story try to manage the impressions of their audience for a reason. Managing impressions can have favorable outcomes. These outcomes result from the effective use of persuasive language.

Goffman's insights are helpful in studying different characters. He looks at social actions based on front and back stage. Front stage is where the actions are played out in social settings. The social setting could be large group settings or small private settings. The notion is that characters want to be perceived in a favorable light. In their public and semi-public interactions, they try to impress others. Backstage, however, they feel free to be themselves. They are not attempting to impress others. It is true, from a sociological perspective that there is a social force present even in our private moments.[18] Nevertheless, one may formulate ideas and plans in a backstage setting for implementation in a public setting. However, the character's true motives may remain secret leaving the reader to supply the motive.

The omniscient narrator is in the position of knowing everything whether backstage or not. The narrator may share this information with the audience through the different characters. When reading, one may want to consider how information is disclosed and in what setting it is disclosed.

Enough has been said to provide a starting point for a narrative analysis. One might pursue such a study in different ways, but I propose to consider plot, characterization, repetition, and gaps. At one point or another, the discussion will include most everything discussed above. I have selected two texts. The first one comes from 1 Kings 1–2. The focus in this reading is primarily on one character, Bathsheba. Other characters are discussed as they relate to her. The New Testament passage comes from Mark 7. Again, the focus is on characterization, but other elements are also considered.

NARRATIVE CRITICISM OF 1 KINGS 1–2

This text tells of the conflict between two rival parties. The central theme is succession. Who will take over the throne after David's death? The plot consists of a number of conflicts that create considerable suspense building to a climax. Even after the resolution of the conflict, Solomon feels insecure about his claim to the throne. The tension builds to the very end where we read the "kingdom was established in the hand of Solomon" (1 Kgs 2:46).

The basic story line begins with a portrait of an old king. David is old and sick. His servants decide to seek out a "young virgin" who can take care of him. They bring in a beautiful woman named Abishag for that purpose. Meantime, David's eldest son, Adonijah, seizes the opportunity to claim the throne for himself seeing that his father is incapacitated and perhaps near death. He gathers his supporters and prepares to take the throne. Nathan, the prophet, intervenes. Nathan approaches one of David's wives, Bathsheba, and advises her to confront David about Adonijah's actions. Nathan opposes them and hopes to reverse them with the help of Bathsheba. Bathsheba goes to David and informs him about the situation. David responds by making Solomon, his younger son, king.

Following this set of events, Adonijah and his supporters are viewed as enemies of Solomon. From this point on their lives are in danger. Adonijah flees to grab onto the horns of the altar, which under Hebrew law would afford him some protection. Chapter two begins with David instructing Solomon on how to proceed. After David dies, the remainder of the story deals with Solomon's securing the throne and removing his enemies. After eliminating his enemies one by one, the story ends with Solomon in firm control of the kingdom.

CHARACTER ANALYSIS OF BATHSHEBA

Bathsheba's performance in this narrative is the most important of all the characters. She is present in two backstage and two front stage scenes. The scenes alternate between backstage where private meetings take place and a front stage where she carries out her plans. Her character, more than any other, moves the action of the story forward. Traditionally, interpreters have viewed her as Nathan's puppet, but she more than anyone else helps Solomon succeed. A close reading of the story shows that she is not merely following the lead of Nathan. She is a pivotal character in this story.

The reader first encounters Bathsheba in a private meeting with Nathan. Nathan approaches her with a scheme to win the throne for Solomon. There are clear sides. Adonijah has his supporters who are important people such as Joab, the commander of David's regular army, and Abiathar, his priest. There is no indication from the narrative that Solomon is even aware of what is going on although it is hard to imagine that he was not at work behind the scenes. Throughout most of chapter one, he is merely mentioned. He remains in the background until he becomes king. Solomon too has important supporters. Nathan and Solomon's mother, Bathsheba, are the two key figures. In this private meeting, the audience learns that Nathan comes to Bathsheba with a plan to persuade David to make Solomon king.

Nathan advises Bathsheba to go to David and remind him of a promise. Nathan instructs Bathsheba to say the following: "'Did you not, my lord the king, swear to your servant, saying: Your son Solomon shall succeed me as king, and he shall sit on my throne? Why then is Adonijah king?'" (1 Kgs 1:11–13) Bathsheba agrees. She goes to David, and she repeats these words in verse 17 with one important addition: "My lord, you swore to your servant by the Lord your God, saying: Your son Solomon shall succeed me as king, and he shall sit on my throne." At this point, the repetition becomes important for understanding Bathsheba's role in this whole affair, and her addition to Nathan's words makes all the difference.

Notice what Bathsheba adds to Nathan's words. She says to David "you swore to your servant by the Lord your God."[19] By adding the words, "by the Lord your God," it is no mere promise. It is a promise made in all seriousness. The additional words add emphasis. Also, Nathan tells her to put it in the form of a rhetorical question, "Did you not say." But Bathsheba is direct, "My lord, you swore." She does not want to give David any room to waiver. The directness is a bold move in that she takes an aggressive tone. Notice too that Nathan poses the question: "Why then is Adonijah king?" Bathsheba turns the question into a statement followed by another addition that moves David to respond: "But now suddenly Adonijah has become king, though you, my lord the king, do not know it." (1 Kgs 1:18)

The words, "you, my lord the king, do not know it," must have had a substantial impact on David. They underscore David's unfamiliarity with current events, which implies criticism of the old king. Moreover, Bathsheba calls David's attention to the fact that the nation awaits his reaction. Perhaps, Bathsheba pressures David into accepting her statement concerning the oath. He feels now that he must act decisively, and he does. One is left to wonder if he ever made such an oath in the first place. Her assertiveness and his weakness raise this possibility since we are not ever told outside this passage that he made this promise. Perhaps, it is a ploy thought up by Nathan and executed by the both of them.

Then she tells David about Adonijah's guest list, which excludes Solomon among others. She informs David that the people eagerly await his response. This tactic is wise because it puts pressure on David to act quickly. She also relays her fear of what might happen to her and Solomon if Adonijah's plan is successful.[20] The part she plays reflects the conventional concern of a mother for her son, but if she is successful, she will also gain considerable power.[21]

While Bathsheba may play the part of a dutiful mother, a role society expected women to play she also has political insight and ambitions of her own. Her statement in 1:20 that "the eyes of all Israel are upon you" puts pressure on David to act on her behalf. The mention of Adonijah's mother who never makes an appearance calls attention to Bathsheba, who played an instrumental role in Solomon's success.

The narrative, therefore, portrays Bathsheba as having a leading role in the success of her son's rise to the throne. Many commentators portray her as a simple-minded tool. On this telling, Nathan merely uses her to help Solomon gain the throne and ensure his place among Solomon's supporters. She simply followed Nathan's lead. However, a close reading shows a different story. She is the leading figure. The writer depicts Nathan as taking the initiative, but overall he plays a supporting role in the narrative by simply reinforcing the words of Bathsheba in 1 Kings 1:22–27. Nathan adds to Bathsheba's words more information and presses David for a response.

The two of them are successful in getting David to act in their interests. Now David reverses the actions of Adonijah. With Solomon's success, Adonijah is in an extremely dangerous situation. Solomon moves from a topic of discussion to an acting king in 1 Kings 1:52. Now he looks for any excuse to take action against Adonijah, his elder brother. Again Bathsheba plays a central role in Adonijah's ultimate downfall. In a private scene between Adonijah and Bathsheba, Adonijah asks her to help him obtain Abishag as his wife. He says, "You know that the kingdom was mine, and that all Israel expected me to reign; however, the kingdom has turned about and become my brother's, for it was his from Lord" (1 Kgs 2:15). Bathsheba then agrees to bring his request to Solomon.

Did Bathsheba agree to approach Solomon out of sympathy for Adonijah? The writer leaves the audience with questions. What are Adonijah's motives? What are Bathsheba's motives? These are crucial questions. Bathsheba appears to be a puppet in Adonijah's hand. She will be undermining herself and her son if this request is honored. Obtaining Abishag from Solomon would give him claim to the throne. Perhaps, she thinks that if Solomon grants Adonijah's request he will not cause any more trouble. Alternatively, could she be thinking how this is an opportunity to rid herself and her son of a potential threat?

It is highly probable that Bathsheba knew how Solomon would react to Adonijah's request. She now has an opportunity to rid herself and Solomon of a dangerous adversary. Again, repetition is important. As Alter notes, repression and omitting of certain words in a repetition serve to reverse "an initial impression."[22] In this scene, Adonijah was careful to recognize Solomon as David's legitimate successor and as Yahweh's choice to rule over the people. He admits that Solomon is the legitimate king since he is Yahweh's choice.

Significantly, Bathsheba's repeating of the request is terse. She simply says: "'Let Abishag the Shunammite be given to your brother Adonijah as his wife.'" Is Bathsheba sincerely trying to help Adonijah? She could have been much more convincing. For instance, she does not expand on Adonijah's words. To the contrary, she omits his recognition of Solomon as the legitimate successor to David. She gave Solomon a good excuse to take deadly action. The confirmation of this interpretation comes in Solomon's response to his mother: "Why do you ask Abishag the Shunammite for Adonijah? Ask for him the kingdom as well! For he is my elder brother" (1 Kgs 2:22). The taking of Abishag, who had belonged to King David combined with the fact that he was the elder living son would have bolstered Adonijah's claims to the throne, a fact that Bathsheba would have well-known.[23]

1 Kings 1–2 portrays Bathsheba as a wise woman.[24] She used her limited means to gain as much power as permissible. She, more than any other figure, destroys Adonijah's aspirations of becoming David's successor. The variation of Adonijah's request is significant. Adonijah's fate may have been sealed due to the way she presents it to Solomon. Not only does it hint at Bathsheba's shrewdness but it also points to character flaws in Adonijah. Adonijah's actions and his request do not present him as a wise figure. Bathsheba and Solomon are at risk as long as Adonijah is alive, so why would Adonijah trust the mother of his enemy? Is it a miscalculation or worse the act of an impulsive person?

Adonijah's request for Abishag's hand in marriage is a little odd considering the statements in 1:49–52 about his fear of Solomon. Did he not know that Solomon might seize upon this opportunity to get rid of him? Or did he not realize that Solomon might interpret his request as a threat? In 2:17, the narrative clearly indicates that Adonijah saw Bathsheba as a means of gaining Abishag. Did he also see her as a means of gaining the throne?[25] Solomon certainly sees it that way.[26] Alternatively, did Adonijah simply desire Abishag as a concession for his future obedience? None of these questions receives a definite answer.

Bathsheba's meeting with Adonijah reinforces the view of Adonijah as one who acts rashly without consideration of the consequences. Adonijah's speech suggests that he thinks Solomon should grant this request as a concession to him since he is really David's rightful heir. His speech recognizes that Yahweh is free to choose, and he acknowledges that Yahweh selected Solomon as the rightful successor. These words are most likely meant to gain Bathsheba's aid and Solomon's consent. I doubt they are sincere. Adonijah's action costs him his life. On the whole, Adonijah has a legitimate claim to the throne, but the narrative as a whole presents him in a bad light.

Bathsheba does have depth as a character. A superficial reading might portray her as a mere tool. However, our reading shows her as a person of ability. She pursued her self-interest and the interests of her son. She was genuinely concerned about her future as well as her son's future. Adonijah would certainly have been concerned about Solomon if he had become king. Bathsheba confides to David that she feels her life and her son's life is in danger if Adonijah becomes king (1 Kgs 1:21). She seizes an opportunity to protect herself and her son. Her actions would also be motivated by the desire for power and influence. As a woman in a patriarchal society, this would afford her the most power and influence possible.

GAPS IN 1 KINGS 1–2

The writer of 1 Kings 1–2 does not have to spell everything out because the author assumes the reader understands the story in a certain way. In 1 Kings 1:13, 17, Nathan and Bathsheba indicate that David swore that Solomon would become king upon his death. Did David really make such a promise? David, in 1 Kings 1:30, says that he did make this promise. Does that settle the issue? However, these are the only three places where there is a mention of such a promise. Did it happen or did Nathan and Bathsheba orchestrate it? Since the writer portrays David as old and sickly, one wonders if he indeed remembers the promise or if he is caving into the pressure.

It is a gap because the reader does not know for sure. The reader would also have to consider the fact that this narrative may be connected to a larger narrative that extends back at least to 2 Samuel 9. So how would this affect one's reading of the text? The fact that the first we hear of the promise is with Nathan in verse 13 raises doubt. Therefore, it is possible that Nathan and Bathsheba manipulated David to reverse Adonijah's initiative.

These are just a few observations about this succession story. A close reading of the text can raise some other interesting questions. One question that remains open concerns the stance of the narrative. Is it supportive of Solomon? Most scholars agree that the narrative is pro-Solomonic in nature, but there is room for doubt. There remains some ambiguity. All things considered, I would conclude it favors Solomon over Adonijah, but the writer also shows Solomon's bad side. Perhaps, this is the mark of a good story. It leaves one with more questions than it answers.

NARRATIVE CRITICISM OF MARK 7

For the New Testament passage, I have selected Mark 7. This story is part of the larger whole, so I would begin with some observations about the Gospel of Mark. We can look at the setting, plot, and rhetoric of Mark. Fortunately, David Rhoades and Donald Michie have written a book on Mark as Story. The settings for the Gospel "provide the overall framework for the movement and for the development of the plot."[27] Much of the action takes place in Galilee. The story moves from Galilee to Jerusalem and with this movement comes mounting tension. Jesus' ministry takes place in a threatening environment both in Galilee and Jerusalem.[28]

The plot of Mark concerns God's reign (Mk 1:15), which forms the story's context. The approach of God's reign along with Jesus' acts and teachings leads to conflict. Conflict is a major part of Mark's plot.[29] The Gospel consists of a number of short stories that recount events in the life of Jesus and his disciples. It is "good news" that threatens the powers of this world. The good news proclaimed by Jesus is not seen as good news by certain Jewish groups such as the scribes and Pharisees. Confrontations between Jesus and his enemies move the action along where it ultimately leads to a tragic resolution.

Scholars have long noticed in Mark's Gospel an element of secrecy. Rhoades and Michie note that there is secrecy concerning the coming of God's rule and the secrecy of Jesus' true identity. Even when Jesus' identity is perceived, the rule of God may remain hidden. The "establishment of God's rule" dominates the second half of the Gospel. The hiddenness of God's rule and the establishment of God's rule lead to conflict.[30]

The story's ending is obscured by later additions to the text. If one takes the text as we now have it, one must consider Mark 16:9–20 as the ending. If not, however, the story ends at verse 8. Scholars largely agree that verse 8 marks the end of the original story. The other verses are added later and are not original to Mark. It is understandable that someone would add additional material to Mark because verse 8 provides an ending that may be somewhat unsatisfying.

The original ending has Mary Magdalene, Mary the mother of James, and Salome coming to the tomb of Jesus. They found the stone rolled away so they could enter the tomb. Upon entering the tomb, they encountered a "young man, dressed in a white robe, sitting on the right side" (Mk 16:5). They were distressed (*ekthaumbeomai*). The tomb is empty. The young man tells them not to be distressed. Jesus "has been raised." They are to go tell the other disciples that Jesus will see them in Galilee. The story, however, ends this way: "So they went out and fled from the tomb, for terror and amazement had seized them; and they said nothing to anyone, for they were afraid." Just imagine that as the ending. It is abrupt leaving the reader wanting more. It points the audience back to Galilee where Jesus' ministry began. In this case, one may read the story again with renewed understanding.

The narrator of Mark's Gospel is omniscient. The narrator has all the important details and insight to tell the story. As in 1 Kings 1–2, the narrator provides the audience with the knowledge that the characters may or may not possess. The audience in Mark's Gospel may perceive Jesus' role in the divine plan, but other characters in the story do not. As stated before, Jesus' true identity is hidden even from his disciples (Mk 9:30–32). The people do not know who Jesus really is, but Peter recognizes Jesus' true identity in Mark 8:29. He correctly identifies Jesus as the Messiah. Jesus then instructs Peter and the other disciples to keep it silent (Mk 8:30).

The following verses report that Jesus rebukes Peter. Just after Peter's correct response, he takes a step backward. When Jesus tells his disciples that suffering is in his future, Peter objects. Peter may understand that Jesus is the Messiah, but neither he nor the other disciples understand what that really means (Mk 8:31–38, 9:30–32). Peter presumably had a different view of what the Messiah would be.

Mark 7 takes place in Galilee. It immediately follows an event that takes place on the northern shore of the Sea of Galilee. From the first verse of Mark 7, the reader learns of the religious leaders coming from Jerusalem. The reader knows what this means. These leaders approach Jesus to find fault in him and his disciples. So, it is just another clash. Jerusalem is a place of special religious significance. In Mark's Gospel, it is a place of danger for Jesus. This event is just another example of the ongoing tension between Jesus and conventional religious authorities. The opponents are supposedly religious experts. Mark reverses this perspective. It is the experts that oppose God and err in their interpretation of Scripture.[31]

The point of view of this story is clear. Jesus tells the reader what God wants. God wants people to be clean on the inside for that will result in right thought and action. It speaks to one's motivation. One does the right thing because it is right not because it is part of a tradition. It is about authenticity. One should be pure on the inside and allow that to shape one's life. Therefore, the heart is the source of one's actions.

The Pharisees and scribes want people to follow proper rituals based on human traditions. These views do not represent what God desires or God's commandments. They merely reflect a human construction (i.e., the traditions of the elders) of what God expects from human behavior. It becomes a conflict over rituals. For the Pharisees and scribes, it is putting rituals above morality. Jesus rejects such a view. Washing or not washing one's hands is not of ultimate concern. It is not what goes in from the outside that is a problem. What is of concern is the heart, the place from which true moral actions originate.[32] Jesus turns the criticisms they make of him into criticism of their misguided fascination with ritual purity. They elevated ritual purity over morality. Jesus gives priority to moral concerns.[33]

How is one to understand Jesus' words about the traditions of the elders? Is it a reference to the Torah? Would Jesus refer to the Torah as a human institution (Mk 7:8)? It seems clear that Jesus contrasts the tradition of the elders with the Torah in verses 9–10. So Jesus is not rejecting the Torah or the dietary laws.[34] He is addressing human traditions.

The characters of this story, except Jesus, are not individuals but groups such as the disciples, Pharisees, and scribes. The narrator sets the scene up and provides the necessary background for understanding Jesus' interactions with his opponents and disciples. Jesus is confronted by the Pharisees and scribes because his disciples do not wash their hands before eating (Mk 7:1–5). This confrontation sets up Jesus' response in verse 6 when he goes on the offensive. He charges his opponents with abandoning God's law or commandment (Mk 7:8). Next, Jesus offers a specific example of their failure to follow God's commandment (Mk 7:9–13). This section is followed by Jesus addressing the crowd (Mk 7:14–15). The episode ends with Jesus responding to his own disciple's questions about the encounter (Mk 7:16–23).

The story clearly portrays Jesus as rightly understanding the meaning of the Torah and representing God's will. Jesus speaks with authority and confronts the views of the so-called religious experts. He draws upon the authority of the prophet Isaiah by quoting Isaiah 29:13.[35] The quote makes a clear distinction between the outward show and one's true inner nature. Because they fail to make this distinction, their worship is in vain. Their teachings derive not from God but from human tradition.

Jesus offers a particular example of their error. Jesus says to them, "You have a fine way of rejecting the commandment of God to keep your tradition!" (Mk 7:9) He then accuses them of breaking the commandment about "'honoring your father and mother'; and, 'Whoever speaks evil of father or mother must surely die'" (Mk 7:10). The next verse tells how they have broken this commandment. The support they were to give to their father and mother is "Corban," which means that is "an offering to God." While the term Corban may not be understood by many audiences, the brief description makes the meaning reasonably clear. They have found a way through human tradition to abrogate their responsibility to their parents. Therefore, they have invalidated "the word of God" by the traditions they have passed on to others (Mk 7:13).

Next Jesus calls to the crowd again. The "again" must be understood in the larger context of Mark's Gospel. This episode contains Jesus' address to the crowd. He tells them a short parable, which is a brief statement.[36] Jesus says: "There is nothing outside a person that by going in can defile, but the things that come out are what defile" (Mk 7:15). Moving then to a private setting in the house, the disciples express their lack of understanding. Jesus' response to them is terse. He is disappointed that they do not understand. Jesus explains the meaning of his statement. Jesus names various evils and declares that they come from the human heart. Jesus refers to the inner self, but he is not overly descriptive. Still, it is what is hidden from the outside world that defiles a person (Mk 7:20–23). The inner self then is what matters.

In short, Jesus sees the world correctly; his perspective matches the will of God. His motive is to do the will of God and show his opponents the errors of their ways. He also teaches the crowds, the disciples, and the audience what is important. The leaders' perspective seems to be concerned with authority, status, and human dogma. They see themselves as defenders of God. They view themselves as legitimate representatives of God's will. Their motives are to maintain their status and legitimacy over against Jesus.

The writer does not describe the crowd at all in this passage. The reader does not know whether they accept Jesus words or whether or not they understand them. The disciples are described as slow to comprehend. Jesus has to explain his words to them. The side effect of the disciple's lack of understanding is that the audience or reader should clearly understand Jesus' words. His explanation to the disciples is also a means to instruct his audience as well as future ones.

Mark 7 clearly depicts the Jewish religious leaders who should possess true knowledge misinterpreting Scripture. Powell sums it up well in the following observations:

> They (the leaders) think, for instance, that they have found justification for ignoring the command to honor one's parents (7:9–13). . . . Jesus, who is able to interpret Scripture in accord with God's evaluative point of view, denounces such interpretations and accuses them of forsaking God's commandment in favor of what is only human tradition (7:8). Two divergent views emerge in Mark, then, as to what it means to do the will of God. Jesus correctly identifies the doing of God's will with exercising love (12:28–31) but the leaders repeatedly define it in terms of their own legalistic prescriptions (2:24; 3:2; 7:1–5). Ironically, they failed to realize the extent to which the Scriptures they cite actually prophesy against them (7:6–7).[37]

So this short story clearly communicates its message to the reader. It teaches a fundamentally important point about morality from Jesus' perspective. Human behavior reflects who and what we are. Goodness and love radiate out from the human spirit. Of course, the heart here is not the biological organ, but a place within us that manifests itself through our thoughts and actions. Good and evil come from that location. That place defines who and what we are. The heart matters, not empty ritual.

CONCLUSION

Literary criticism is quite valuable. Narrative criticism, as one form of the literary approach, provides another avenue for reading texts. It does not have to avoid matters of history, but it focuses on the world of the text. In the readings above, I have tried not to engage in historical matters. Still, historical concerns can help the reader understand the story better. A historical understanding of the Pharisees and scribes and their traditions can lead to a deeper understanding. Still, a basic understanding is usually possible even without certain historical information.

Like other critical approaches, there are strengths and weaknesses to this approach. Powell discusses five criticisms that have been leveled against literary criticism and responds to each one.

1. Narrative criticism treats the Gospels as coherent narratives when they are actually collections of disparate material.
2. Narrative criticism imposes on ancient literature concepts drawn from the study of modern literature.
3. Narrative criticism seeks to interpret the Gospels through methods that were devised for the study of fiction.
4. Narrative criticism lacks objective criteria for the analysis of texts.
5. Narrative criticism rejects or ignores the historical witness of the Gospels.[38]

I do not plan to rehash his discussion here, but these criticisms raise important points.

The first point about disparate materials is not a problem unless one insists that literary criticism is the only way to read these texts. Historical approaches are designed to deal with this point quite well. Literary criticism has another purpose. It helps us see a larger picture, but it is just another way of viewing the literature.

The second criticism of imposing modern concepts is true of both historical and literary methods. It is inevitable. How can anyone today see past texts devoid of modern ideas and concepts? It is not possible. It is simply a limitation. Even making claims to read a text the way ancient audiences read them is impossible. We cannot put ourselves in their place because there is a gulf of time between them and us. No matter the method, we can only read texts from the present. Doing so reflects a modern concern.

The third criticism about fiction carries somewhat more weight. Much of the biblical literature is purporting to be an account of real events. Yet, the biblical stories in the Hebrew Bible and in the Gospels are stories and not word for word recordings of what was said and done. Therefore, they contain artistic aspects, and overly literal readings can be a disservice to the narratives. The storyteller may have taken liberties with the accounts to produce a good story. Literary criticism is able to help us appreciate and enjoy these artistic aspects. And some of the stories may just be stories told to entertain or teach a lesson.

The forth criticism about narrative criticism lacking objective criteria for analysis is in my view not serious. Claiming an objective status for any critical method is questionable if objective means a way of determining truth devoid of subjectivity. Literary and historical approaches may be able to set certain "parameters" on what a text can legitimately mean, but they cannot be completely objective.[39]

The final criticism is that a literary approach "undermines the historical grounding of the Christian faith."[40] To limit truth to the historical is narrow. The truth may come through myth, legend, metaphor, and fictional stories such as parables. There is ample room for historical and literary approaches. Both are needed if we hope to appreciate the riches of the biblical texts. The truth is not limited to what actually happened.

NOTES

1. Mark Allan Powell, *What is Narrative Criticism?* Guides to Biblical Scholarship New Testament Series ed., Dan O. Via Jr., (Minneapolis: Fortress Press, 1990), 19, 53–54.
2. Ibid. 23–25.
3. Baldick, *The Concise Oxford Dictionary of Literary Terms*, 145.
4. Meir Sternberg, *The Poetics of Biblical Narrative: Ideological Literature and the Drama of Reading*, (Bloomington: Indiana Press, 1985), xii.
5. Barr, 79. Also see pages 10–12.
6. Powell, 52.
7. Sternberg 129–185.
8. Ibid., 235.
9. Ibid., 369.
10. Ibid., 388.
11. Ibid., 388–389.
12. Ibid., 391–392; Robert Alter, *The Art of Biblical Narrative*, (New York: Basic Books. 1981), 100.
13. Chris Baldick, *The Oxford Dictionary of Literary Terms*, New York: Oxford University Press, 1990, 170.
14. David Rhoads and Donald Michie, *Mark As Story: An Introduction to the Narrative of a Gospel*, (Philadelphia: Fortress Press, 1982), 73.

15. David M. Gunn, "Narrative Criticism," 213.

16. Ibid., 214.

17. Erving Goffman, *The Presentation of Self in Everyday Life* (Garden City: Doubleday Anchor, 1959), 4–16.

18. Ian Burkitt, "Language and the Social Self." *Current Sociology* 39 (Winter 1991): 29, 38, 43, 52–53.

19. The Septuagint Lucianic Greek has added the words, *kata kuriou theou* (by the Lord God) as an explicative or an explanation of the oath. Simon J. DeVries, *1 Kings*, Word Biblical Commentary, ed. John D. W. Watts, vol. 12 (Waco: Word Books, Publishing, 1985), 4.

20. Alter, *Art of Biblical Narrative*, 98–100.

21. Ibid., 99.

22. Alter, *Art of Biblical Narrative*, 100.

23. I. Benzinger, *Die Bücher der Könige, Kurzer Hand-Commentar zum Alten Testament*, ed. Karl Marti, 9 (Freiburg: J. C. B. Mohr, 1899), 11; Tomoo Ishida, *The Royal Dynasties in Ancient Israel: A Study on the Formation and Development of Royal-Dynastic Ideology*, Beihefte zur Zeitschrift für die alttestamentliche Wissenschaft, 142 (Berlin: de Gruyter, 1977), 74.

24. J. W. Wesselius, "Joab's Death and the Central Theme of the Succession Narrative," *Vetus Testamentum* 40 (1990): 347–348.

25. Benzinger, *Bücher der Könige*, 11; and Johannes Fichtner, *Das Erste Buch von den Königen*, Die Botschaft des Alten Testaments: Erläuterungen alttestamentlicher Schriften, ed. K.-D. Fricke, vol. 12/1 (Stuttgart: Calwer Verlag, 1964), 155–156.

26. Wesselius, 348. Wesselius notes that Adonijah must have felt that he could easily exploit her for his own personal gain.

27. Rhoads and Michie, Mark As Story, 63.

28. Ibid.

29. Ibid., 73–77.

30. Ibid., 75–77.

31. Powell, 60.

32. David J. Rudolph, "Jesus and the Food Laws: A Reassessment of Mark 7:19b," *The Evangelical Quarterly* 74:4 (2002): 291–311.

33. Rudolph 295–299.

34. Ibid.

35. The quote follows more closely the Septuagint version.

36. Hugh Anderson, *The Gospel of Mark*, The New Century Bible Commentary ed. Matthew Black (Grand Rapid: Wm. B. Eerdman's Publishing Co., 1976), 187.

37. Powell, 60.

38. Ibid., 91–98.

39. Ibid., 95.

40. Ibid., 96.

Chapter Thirteen

Postmodern Approaches

Before continuing, some background related to an important cultural shift is necessary. This shift has affected all academic endeavors including biblical studies. The methods we have covered so far fall within the modern frame of reference. Modern approaches seek objectivity and neutrality. They do not value subjectivity. Whether a modern interpreter is using one of the historical or literary methods discussed so far, he or she is seeking an objective way of understanding the text. The historical critic seeks the "normative" or correct meaning in the author's intent. The narrative or literary critic seeks the normative meaning in a close reading of the text. In this reading, the proper interpretation entails reading the text correctly. For the historical critic or for the literary critic, the text can only have a limited range of legitimate meanings.

From a postmodern perspective, the limits no longer apply with the same force. All we have, according to this view, is interpretation. The German philosopher, Friedrich Nietzsche (1844–1900) says that "there are no facts, only interpretation."[1] From this viewpoint, David Jobling notes, "texts are always already interpretations; interpretations are new texts to be interpreted."[2] Even texts themselves derive from authors attempting to communicate their understanding or view of things in writing. Interpretation is always a subjective activity. And our interpretations of biblical texts then are merely interpretations of earlier interpretations.

Things do not seem so subjective in our daily experience, however, since humans often assume all human experiences and understandings are similar. Humans operate on common-sense assumptions that one person can understand another person's actions.[3] This assumption is necessary for a functioning society. Consequently, an author probably assumes people can understand his or her communications in the way he or she intended them to be

163

understood. Readers may also assume as a matter of common sense that they properly understand what is being said.

Postmodern views, however, do not accept these assumptions. There is no way to avoid subjectivity. We are not all alike, and we do not all see the world the same way. Therefore, our interpretations always reflect our personal biases and experiences. So what does this mean for biblical studies? While answering this question, it is important to explain the differences between modernism and postmodernism in relation to biblical studies.

THE MODERN SEARCH FOR TRUTH
VERSUS POSTMODERN PERSPECTIVES

Modern ways of knowing depend upon building a strong foundation. For rationalists, the foundation is based on reason and rationality. For others, it is built on reason and experience. Reason alone or reason and experience together become the means for obtaining an understanding of everything. It allows one to establish a baseline upon which a complete structure can stand. This foundation becomes the basis and support for all that can be known. If one can lay out a solid procedure for determining a certain truth and follow it to its conclusion, then a good result is likely. Modernization looks ahead pushing into the unknown with faith in human ability to know things with some degree of certainty.

The modern approach involves proper reasoning, logic, categorization, organization, and systematization. Historical approaches, new criticism, and narrative criticism are based on this modern worldview. The way to find meaning is to approach the text with the proper techniques. Modern thought is about discovering the "Truth" using reason and experience; they do so through proper method and technique. In most modern thought, the goal is Truth that is universal, which means that something is true for all places. It would also be true for all times (i.e., the past, the present, and the future). Truth on this account is not relative or subjective.

To discover this Truth, one needs to be devoid of passion and emotion. If not devoid of emotion, one has to keep the emotions and passions under control, so they do not interfere with one's objectivity and neutrality. The objectivity and neutrality of an individual ensure his or her single-minded dedication to the Truth. This way of studying things is crucial for one to reach a stable and absolute Truth.

For instance, in historical research, the interpreter wants to learn everything possible about the historical and social world of the author and the text. The knowledge gained provides many clues needed to understand what the author is trying to communicate through the text. The primary goal is not to apply the text to the modern world, but to understand what the author was saying to a historical audience. While researchers may acknowledge the lack of information and the imperfect nature of their interpretations in cases where information is lacking, the goal remains the same. One should do his or her best to fill in the gaps of information as objectively as possible. The goal is to recover the correct meaning.

In literary studies, the goal is to pay close attention to the text itself and read in sympathy with it. The goal is similar to the historical critic. Unlike the historical critic, the literary critic may not necessarily be interested in the author's intention, but he or she is interested in the correct interpretation of the text. In this sense, there is an objective meaning located in the text. They seek a meaning that can be reproduced by other competent readers.

There is genuine value in these approaches for those able to minimize bias and prejudice. "Minimize" is the key. From my perspective, I would conclude that total objectivity and neutrality is impossible. Still, anyone dedicated to the Truth above all else is to be commended. One who works hard to control his or her personal biases and seek the Truth whatever the cost has integrity. It still does not ensure success since one cannot completely detach oneself from his or her prior experiences and understandings. The temptation to find what one wants to find is great especially in religious contexts where one's personal beliefs may be at stake. The great Danish theologian, Søren Kierkegaard, once noted the "terrible despair" one would feel if there were no "God, who provides life with purpose and meaning. Since this situation would be so unbearable, Kierkegaard concludes it cannot be true."[4] While this attitude may be understandable, it is not admirable. To follow Truth, one must be willing to risk one's most cherished beliefs if they do not measure up.

Representation is another aspect of the modern view. Nietzsche prepared the way for postmodern thought with his rejection of such a view. He discusses the impossibility of being able to represent the views of others in an objective fashion. Today it is common to see the word representation with a hyphen between the "re" and the "presentation." Re-presentation written in this way emphasizes the view that what is being represented is not an identical copy of the real thing. Modernism cannot make things present to us; it can only re-present things to us through a partially obscured lens. Like dirty glasses that limit one's sight, our personal experiences and biases partially distort our views of everything we encounter. The text is filtered through the lens of personal experience and bias and what comes across on the other side is somewhat partial. No one is to blame for this situation; it is just part of the human condition.

The modern theory of knowledge says that a subject (in our case an interpreter) can represent an object (i.e., meaning of the text) to us as it really is (objectively). A postmodern viewpoint says that interpretation is not a representation or doubling of the object but a re-presentation of it. The representing of an object is a construction based on the subjective understanding of the interpreter.

The modernist view of representation could be described as follows: The psychologist can explain the work of Sigmund Freud in a way that represents his work to us accurately and so we might say that we know Freud, the psychologist. A teacher can resurrect Freud and make him present for us with his or her explanations and descriptions of him. What we are receiving is the very mind of Freud through the mouth of the teacher. We can come to know the real Freud in the same way that our teacher knows him. A teacher can present his work and thoughts objectively, and we can passively receive them and pass them on.

Now consider the same idea in relation to biblical texts. The New Testament scholar can explain the letters of Paul in a way that represents his thoughts to us accurately. As a result, we might say that we know the Apostle Paul. The scholar can resurrect Paul and make him present for us by explaining his ideas. What we are receiving is the very mind of Paul through the mouth of the interpreter. We can come to know the real Paul, in the same way, the scholar knows Paul. The New Testament scholar can present Paul's work and thoughts objectively, and we can passively receive them and pass them on.

However, can we do that? Nietzsche says no. We cannot present the essence of another person to an audience in a way that does not include our desires, feelings, emotions, views and perspectives. What we get is a re-presentation of the person through the eyes of a third-party. It is a somewhat new presentation containing the interpreter's insights that are colored by some elements. We get Paul through the eyes of New Testament scholars. The interpretation partially depends on the scholar's gender, class, the place where he or she grew up, the schools he or she attended, and his or her personality.

There is nothing wrong with that except that we should not deny that those things affect our understanding of the world. This process is what Nietzsche and postmodern perspectives define as mediation. Paul comes to us, for instance, filtered through culture, language, ideology, desires and life experiences. We cannot build a time machine and go back to meet Paul, and even if we did, we still could only know him through our own imperfect understandings that are shaped by our experiences, culture, and education. In short, we get a view of Paul that is mediated or filtered. The subject or interpreter of Paul, in this case, is never a blank tablet waiting to be inscribed by the thoughts and views of another person. Think of voices in a noisy room. We try to focus on one, but it is not clear and in some cases it is distorted by other voices. Voices here, of course, refer to our various life experiences, desires, and ideas. These voices can distract us and leave us with less than perfect clarity of what is being said. In other words, we come to understand Paul through a number of lenses that are unique to the interpreter. Therefore, there can be different portraits of Paul.

Postmodernism says we cannot know or represent a person as they are but only as they appear to us. Like it or not, our understanding is subjective. I can only understand what Freud or Paul says as one who was born in a particular place at a given time. Subjects can never know an object in any other way. And here is the crucial point: human understanding is always imperfect, partial, and biased.

CONCLUSIONS

So what does all of this mean for biblical interpretation? First, the biblical scholar works in a different environment today than fifty years ago when historical approaches were the only game in town. Today biblical scholars work in a pluralistic and interdisciplinary environment. Now one has to view things through different lenses or perspectives. The historian has to take postmodern viewpoints into consideration even if he or she rejects them. Scholarship today is much more inclusive. Women and minorities are much more involved, and this involvement has changed the playing field for biblical studies. No longer can we ignore the political implications of our interpretations. The interdisciplinary nature of biblical studies is evident from all the different views covered in this book.

Both modern and postmodern traditions have value. Objectivity is valuable even though it is not completely possible. Seeking the truth is also important even if it is not possible to gain it in an absolute sense. If a text is violent and promotes violence, it is not the task of the interpreter who strives for truth and objectivity to force a more palatable meaning onto it consistent with his or her values. Postmodern views that appreciate multiple possibilities are equally valuable. Texts have multiple ways of being interpreted. A subjective aspect of interpretation is not inherently a bad thing. One thing is clear, postmodern interpretations have significant potential. At their best, they promote openness, inclusiveness, and a healthy subjectivity.

The remaining chapters cover rhetorical criticism, reader-response criticism, deconstruction, ideological criticism, and theopoetics. These approaches fit fairly well within a postmodern worldview. They go beyond any strict concern for historical authors or editors. Neither are they wedded to the text as the sole location of meaning. Meaning or truth is not fixed or limited in any narrow way. They acknowledge and allow for subjective aspects of reading.

NOTES

1. Stephen Best and Douglas Kellner, *Postmodern Theory: Critical Interrogations*, ed., Douglas Kellner in Critical Perspectives: A Guilford Series (New York: the Guilford Press 1991), 22.

2. David Jobling, "Postmodern Pentecost: A Reading of Acts 2," ed., A. K. M. Adam in *Postmodern Interpretations of the Bible: A Reader* (St. Louis: Chalice Press 2001), 216.

3. See Maurice Natanson, "Introduction," in *Collected Papers I: The Problem of Social Reality*, ed. Maurice Natanson (The Hauge: Martinus Nijhoff, 1967), XXXV; Alfred Schutz, "Concept and Theory Formation in the Social Sciences," in *Collected Papers I: The Problem of Social Reality*, ed. Maurice Natanson (The Hauge: Martinus Nijhoff, 1967), 57–66.

4. Tony L. Moyers, *The Moral Life: Obligation and Affirmation*, (Lanham: University Press of America, 2011), 188.

Chapter Fourteen

Rhetorical Criticism

Rhetorical criticism as presented in this chapter has enormous potential. The approach of Patricia K. Tull[1] is particularly useful. Her approach can bring historical and literary concerns together in some important ways. Not only that, but it meshes well with reader response criticism. In short, the rhetoric of the text has a past; it resonates in the present, and it may have a significant impact on the future. It opens the text up to many possibilities. It is not just about what the author wants to accomplish, but it is also about how the words are received in the past and present.

A brief background on the use of rhetoric may help. Interest in rhetoric is not a recent occurrence; it goes back to the New Testament period and earlier. The Romans and Greeks were interested in rhetoric as the art of persuasion. Persuasion is not just about putting pen to paper. It requires talent; one must have a way with words and a way of constructing convincing arguments. Arguments may sometimes play well to an audience without having much real substance. Rhetoric is useful and significant, but it also potentially dangerous. Plato (427–347 BCE) recognized the potential for the misuse of rhetoric in his dialogues. He notes a type of rhetoric represented by Gorgias as a means to an end. The ends might be petty or selfish. The other type of rhetoric is a good faith effort to promote what is right and good.[2]

Aristotle (384–322 BCE) identified three types of rhetoric. The first type is judicial rhetoric, which takes place within the context of the judicial system. It entails making charges against someone or defending one from charges. One might imagine a defense lawyer's closing statement who tries to persuade a jury of his or her client's innocence. It may appeal to the emotions (pathos) or one's sense of right and wrong. A second type is called epideictic rhetoric. Epideictic rhetoric might use reason to appeal to one's moral sense or emotions focusing on a current event or context. In the public arena, a person may deliver a speech to promote the celebration of an event or to place blame on someone or something. A third type is deliberative rhetoric, which persuades others to do or avoid doing something. Again it may use reason, ethics, or emotion as a means to an end.

In short, then, rhetoric is using language to persuade. People use language in different settings to accomplish some purpose. It is part of everyday life. Children try to persuade their parents to let them do certain things and parents often try to persuade their children to pursue or avoid certain actions. The same is true of written documents, particularly biblical texts. They seek to convince the audience to act or refrain from acting. In the Psalms, the psalmist is often trying to persuade God to act on his or her behalf.

The use of rhetoric is as old as human communication. As stated above, the discussion of rhetoric was popular among the Greeks and Romans. The topic of rhetoric would also have been familiar to the apostle Paul and his audience. The popularity of the subject did not last. Its influence waned during the Enlightenment period. The fascination with reason and experience as the way of determining truth cast a bad light on rhetoric. Rhetoric employed reason, but it also depended on the communicator's ability to persuade others using emotion and sentiment. The effectiveness of rhetoric, which depended heavily on style discredited it as a means of discovering the truth in modern thought. Rhetoric could be nothing more than mere propaganda having little or no truth. The Enlightenment valued reason and logic along with empirical research over rhetoric.[3]

Rhetoric did make a comeback with a change in emphasis. Tull notes that "Classical rhetoric concentrated on prescriptions for effective speaking, the 'new rhetoric,' . . . deals more broadly with theories of discourse and epistemology."[4] The newer approach to rhetoric, therefore, looked at the connections between "language, knowledge, and social control."[5] The focus on these areas adds new dimensions to a rhetorical study of biblical texts.

POSSIBLE COMPONENTS OF A RHETORICAL READING

In biblical texts, persuasion may be directed at individuals, nations, kings, or even at God. For example, many prophetic texts implore people to reform their ways or face judgment. Lament psalms may implore God to assist an individual or the community in some struggle. The language of the prophetic text or the lament psalm may contain images, metaphors, themes, stories, warnings, and appeals as a means to convince the people or God to act in a particular fashion. Rhetorical criticism, therefore, studies style, technique, and language used by the writer to accomplish his or her goals.

Rhetorical criticism may incorporate both historical and literary concerns. One might focus on Paul's use of rhetoric in his letters. This approach would require attention to any literary techniques that Paul uses as well as a consideration of the historical realities. Why is Paul writing the letter? Whom is he addressing? What is the historical situation that prompts the letter? Both historical and literary concerns merge. If, however, one is interested in the modern audience, the study may look much like a reader response approach that focuses on how readers respond to particular texts. The audience could be the original audience, the modern audience, or an audience somewhere between the two. One might consider how the early church leaders of the fourth century CE responded to a text. So the possible applications are wide open.

Early rhetorical approaches focused heavily on matters of style. One could concentrate on such things as the text's literary structure and its use of language without much concern for the purpose of the language. It is important to remember that the style by itself is only a small part of the story. The style has a purpose. The purpose is to persuade the audience. Therefore, one needs to examine how the style and beauty of the text contribute to the purpose, which is to persuade an audience to act or think in a certain fashion. Rhetorical criticism may call attention to how an author uses repetition, the structure of the text, characterization, metaphor, images, and symbols to produce certain effects on the audience.

Consequently, rhetorical criticism is interested in how a writer uses language to accomplish a goal. For instance, Jeremiah's so-called temple sermon attempts to convince the people living in Jerusalem that they must "amend their ways" (Jer 7:1–15). One tactic of this sermon is a warning of pending doom. If they continue their present course, Jerusalem will meet the same fate as Shiloh. Shiloh was an important sanctuary, but it was destroyed. So the audience would have understood this reference to Shiloh as a warning of danger.

Jeremiah's sermon highlights another important aspect of rhetorical criticism. One needs to consider the rhetorical environment, which is the situation that calls forth text. The situation includes the "particular problem that the author is seeking to overcome."[6] The rhetorical situation for Jeremiah involved the threat of the Babylonians and the corrupt behavior of the people in Judah.

Tull introduces two other key considerations for a rhetorical approach: intertextuality and dialogism. Intertextuality is a property or trait of texts. A text is entangled in a web of associations. These associations are subjective in nature and differ from person to person. In other words, texts or communications come to us, but we understand it and respond to it based on prior experiences and understandings. There is no way of knowing if we make the same connections as the author. It is the notion that a text is not a monolog where the writer speaks, and the audience passively accepts his or her words. Dialogue is a notion introduced by Mikhail Bakhtin. It refers to the fact that texts are dialogues. Texts enter a world filled with other utterances or texts that affect the way we understand and respond to them. [7]

Intertextuality is a quality of all communication written and oral. It refers to the fact that all texts and communications are related. That does not mean one has intentionally linked them. They are linked because we as human beings read or hear them and make associations with various other texts or communications. It is impossible not to do so since this is the way we make sense of our world. We as the reader may make a connection to a text that the writer had no knowledge of, and the connection may color our understandings of this text. For instance, science texts may color and influence the way we understand and read the book of Genesis.

But how we make sense of our world differs from person to person. We do not learn words from a dictionary. As children, we hear words used in a particular setting, and we learn to use those words in similar contexts. The context in which one uses the word and not the dictionary definition shapes our understanding of what it means. It is also our context that affects the associations we make with these words. We associate a word to specific settings, and the settings inform our understandings. Such understandings, of course, are partial, and we may go through life without ever looking up many of the words in a dictionary for their exact meaning. The meaning of words depends in part on one's culture and social environment. The word salvation may mean one thing for a Christian and something quite different to a Hindu.

The associations we make with a word are important. The individual who has heard the word rhetoric probably has some feeling about it. One may associate the word with things that are positive, negative, or neutral. Some people may have heard the term used in relation to politicians. Someone may refer to a politician's speech as "mere rhetoric". This statement implies that the words are untrue or insincere. Such a view of the word rhetoric would be negative. Other words such as fundamentalist or liberal may create positive or negative associations in the mind of the individual. A fundamentalist who hears the word "fundamentalist" may see it as a badge of honor. An educated person who is called a fundamentalist may find it offensive.

The associations, therefore, are part of the process of interpretation. Our social environment shapes our understandings. Concerning texts, a reader who has read a wide range of material would respond to the text much differently from one who has a smaller range of reading experiences. Our personal and educational experiences affect our understanding.

Another important consideration of rhetorical criticism follows from the notion of intertextuality. Often, we think of reading as a monolog. Readers passively read the text and follow the author's train of thought. It is not that simple. In fact, what we have is a dialogue instead of a monolog. When writers and their texts attempt to persuade readers, they enter into dialogue with the reader. The author may try to anticipate the audience's responses with his or her response.

Readers may often resist the urgings of the text. He or she may hear the text and associate it with other texts and experiences. Jeremiah's audience heard his words of warning about the "Temple of the Lord," but they also heard others say that God would never allow Jerusalem to fall. These others may have been government officials, religious leaders such as priests, or common people. Who are they to believe? Jeremiah uses strong language to persuade his audience to repent and turn from their wicked ways. He engages in dialogue with them by alluding to a belief of his audience that Yahweh would never abandon Jerusalem. The people feel they are invincible since God would never allow Jerusalem to fall. Jeremiah provides them with a chilling example of Shiloh. The audience knew that God did not keep that city safe from its enemies. In short, the writer and audience are engaging in a dialogue in which Jeremiah hopes to win the people's hearts and minds. The people are resistant, but the example of Shiloh surely made a strong impression on them.

Likewise, when we read texts, we may decide to ignore what we do not like. We may try to downplay parts of the text or interpret them in ways more suitable to our tastes. Like Jeremiah's audience, we often do not like what the text says. Conservative Christians may not like to admit that they resist the message of biblical texts at times. Nevertheless, they may ignore or misinterpret a text to ease their discomfort. Liberal Christians may also reject the message of certain texts because it does not fit their views of what is good or bad.

When one hears the words of a text, he or she may think of other texts and not just biblical texts. For a fundamentalist reader of the book of Revelation, certain popular books such as the Left Behind series may affect them. For secular readers, one text may lead to associations with other texts in the areas of science, philosophy, literature, or theology.

The notion of dialogue is not just about the audience. It also includes the author. Both author and reader carry on this dialogue. The author imagines how an audience will respond to his or her message. The author shapes the words accordingly. Readers respond or react to the words based on their situation. Therefore, authors try to anticipate the reactions of their audiences. They do so in order to respond to their objections. These authors or editors attempt to persuade the audience to respond to their message in a particular way. In the case of Jeremiah, he wants his audience to repent, and the message he delivers is determined in some measure by his audience.

Rhetorical criticism, consequently, could take different forms. Based on the discussion above, there are at least three important areas, which are introduced and discussed by Tull.[8] I would add a fourth. One could begin with the language of the text and its use. This section would draw attention to literary concerns because the artistic aspects of the texts help fuel the rhetoric or persuasive aspects of the text. With narratives, a look at such things as structure, characterization, perspective, repetition, plot, symbols, and images are important. In poetry, structure, rhythm, images, metaphors, allusions, and symbols might play a more significant role. So it is not literature for the sake of entertainment, but literature as a means of persuasion. How do such elements enhance the persuasiveness of the text?

The second section deals with the rhetorical environment referring to the situation that calls forth the text. This part of the analysis may call for a historical understanding of the situation. For instance, we are able to fit the words of the temple sermon in Jeremiah to a particular historical period. In some cases, however, it is not possible to pin a text down to a specific historical period. Many of the psalms cannot be related to any specific historical period. In such cases, one can look at the language and determine the situation to which the text best speaks.

It is at least possible that the situation may not be historical but literary. If a work is a fiction, the situation may be part of the writer's imagination. Fiction can be a means to persuade readers as well as real historical settings. A parable, for instance, creates a story world that provides the hearer or reader with a context for understanding the action. This part of the analysis involves not only a consideration of the writer but also the audience. The dialogue takes place between the writer and his or her immediate audience. It also takes place between the author and subsequent audiences.

Part three of a rhetorical study could focus on issues of intertextuality and dialogue with the dialogue focusing on historical or modern audiences. It would consider the language of the text to understand how the author attempted to persuade his or her audience. As part of the dialogue, it could also consider how the audience may have responded to the text. Is there anything one could say about the success or failure of the text and the author's use of rhetoric? One might make a judgment based on the text. How convincing is the argument, and is there any indication in the text of success or failure? Did the words fall on deaf ears? Below I shall demonstrate this approach through a Hebrew poem (i.e., Ps 73) and a letter of Paul addressed primarily to Philemon.

PSALM 73

The Use of Language

As is the case with all methods, a close and detailed reading of the text is the best place to begin. In terms of language, the psalm begins with the exclamation "Truly" ('ak). Its use here is in the form of a creed.[9] Initially, this psalm begins with a contrast. The contrast is between the just and unjust. The creedal like statement affirms the conviction that "Truly God is good to the upright, to those who are pure of heart." Upright and pure of heart stress the declaration that God rewards the good. The unstated part of this statement is likely assumed by most people; God punishes the wicked.

Verses two and following express the writer's anguish over the fact that the wicked do sometimes prosper. In verse two, the reasons for the poet's distress are introduced by the conjunction "kî" meaning "for" or "because." Images of the poet's struggle are conveyed by stumbling and slipping. The poet no longer feels he or she is on solid ground. The good person stumbling and slipping in verse two is a far cry from walking in the way of the righteous and not standing in the company of the ungodly, which is found in Psalm 1:1. Psalm 73:2–14 expresses weakness and doubt whereas a similar poem, Psalm 1, shows strength and certainty. These images of stumbling and slipping are, however, reversed in 73:18. Now it is the sinner who is on dangerous ground. The wicked person is set on slippery places. Furthermore, God makes this person fall. The wicked person is "destroyed in a moment, swept away utterly by terrors!" (Ps 73:19)

We might also note the words used to describe the wicked. They are clothed in "pride" and "violence." Their eyes "swell with fatness." This statement probably indicates they are growing more prosperous. Their "hearts overflow with follies" (Ps 73:7). Their mouths (perhaps a metaphor for death) are set against the heavens, and they are waiting to devour the innocent. Verse 9 may echo Canaanite mythology. Mot, the Canaanite god of death, has jaws that reach to earth and lips reaching to heavens.[10] Such a myth may have been widely known, and the ancient reader would have understood the metaphor. The tongue strutting through the earth may also relate to the above myth "or it may refer to the arrogant as slanderers."[11]

And yet, the wicked prosper (Ps 73:3), and the psalmist has been "plagued" and "punished every morning" (Ps 73:14). This description challenges the common view held by the psalmist to this point. The psalmist seeks a way to affirm the traditional view. He or she searches for an explanation, which has a positive result. The writer finally "perceives their end" (Ps 73:17). The language in the second half of the psalm reverses the picture painted in the first half. The wicked are indeed set on "slippery places." The wicked are now put back in their traditional place. They are "far from" God while at the same time the psalmist now senses God's nearness (Ps 73:27–28).

The "truly" of verse 18 hearkens back to the truly of verses 1. Truly is used in verse 13 where it expresses the vanity or emptiness of keeping oneself pure. Again the psalmist uses the Hebrew particle 'ak (truly) in verse 18. The use here is to express his or her strong conviction that God puts the wicked in slippery places. Also, the conjunction noted in verse 3 (kî) occurs again in verse 21 now expressing a time before this revelation when the psalmist was sorely distressed. The writer compares himself or herself to a "brute beast." All of this leads to the realization that God was always there. The psalm concludes with the psalmist expressing a great and genuine desire for God above any other thing. As James Crenshaw puts it,

> Psalm 73 achieves fresh insight into the resolution of this vexing problem. It suggests that the issue has been stated falsely, and therefore the author restates the problem. In essence the psalmist contends that the goods of this world are wholly irrelevant to the matter of God's justice. Proof of God's goodness rests in the divine presence, not in material prosperity.

Such an unorthodox solution flew in the face of traditional teaching. [12]

In short, this psalm represents a step forward in the discussion of the problem of suffering.

The Rhetorical Environment

From a look at the language of the text, it is clear that the poet wants to present a case for a modified traditional view of rewards and punishment despite seeming contradictions. It is part of an ongoing dialogue within the ancient Israelite community. Many people had a hard time reconciling the conventional view of their circumstances. This writer struggles for an explanation of an obvious fact. Sometimes good people suffer and bad people do quite well. Surely such sayings as "no good deed goes unpunished" or "good guys finish last" are not just the conclusions of modern peoples. The writer enters this situation attempting to persuade his or her audience. The final message can be expressed in other trite sayings: "appearances can be deceiving" or "they will get theirs in the end". If Crenshaw is right, the writer steps away from a familiar view that the good receive material things and the wicked do not. The relationship with God becomes central, and earthly goods take a back seat.

We do not know the identity of the author or the time of the psalm's composition. The superscription, "A Psalm of Asaph" is not an identification of the author, but it may identify the collection to which this psalm belongs. One likely added the superscriptions to the Psalms years after their original compositions.

The date of composition is uncertain. There are no specifics that would allow for a firm date. Most scholars date it to the post-exilic period. [13] Erhard S. Gerstenberger thinks the most likely setting is in the Persian period. The "topics and theological outlooks" point in this direction. [14] These topics define the rhetorical situation of this psalm. The concerns about the fate of the wicked and the just, along with the suffering of the just, are vital for this period. Additionally, divisions between "antagonist groups," the "absence of a strictly temple-centered theology, [and] the strong identification with the (correct, orthodox) community of Israel"[15] lend support to this date.

Psalms 73 is a reflection on the consequences of good and bad. The conventional view is that good people are rewarded, and bad people are punished. The question of why good and bad things happen to individuals and groups is probably universal and timeless. The answers vary, but the question remains throughout the ages. No one has provided the definitive last word.

The conclusions the poet has drawn thus far depend largely upon 73:1. It says, "Surely God is good to the upright." The problem is that the Hebrew text actually says "Surely God is good to Israel." The Hebrew text, however, may reflect a copying error so that the first translation given above is the correct one.

Ernst Würthwein accepts the reading, "Truly God is good to Israel." He identifies the speaker as the king who is the representative of the people of Israel. For him, this Psalm is not primarily about the problem of theodicy (i.e., the justice of God). It is about the divine election and the enemies of Israel. Such a psalm makes sense only in the period of the monarchy. His argument depends on verse one."[16] The English reader can see what is at stake by comparing the NRSV with the KJV. The NRSV has "Truly God is good to the upright, to those who are pure in heart" while the KJV has "Truly God is good to Israel, even to such as are of a clean heart."

The more likely reading is "Truly God is good to the upright." The difference between the two readings is slight in Hebrew. It involves "dividing l^eyiśrā'ēl . . . into l^eyāšār 'ēl."[17] The second half of this verse, "to the pure of heart", supports the reading "Truly God is good to the upright" with "pure of heart" paralleling "upright." This reading would have "pure" referring to individuals and not to the nation of Israel.

Likewise, the rest of the psalm identifies the speaker as an individual instead of a nation. That does not negate the likelihood that it was used in worship, and the "I" who speaks, also represent the feelings of many within the faith community. An individual may recite the words, and others may identify with them. The author may very well have desired to speak for the community as a whole.

The remainder of this psalm does not provide any significant evidence of the speaker being the king of Israel. The constant reference to the third person plural pronoun "they" seems to refer to enemies that are all around. The wicked seem to be insiders who set a bad example for others. The context and language appear to reflect an ongoing discussion within the community of faith and not external enemies of the nation of Israel. If the Hebrew text is correct, one is not forced into identifying the psalmist with the king. Even if one accepts the reading of "Truly God is good to Israel," Israel could be a reference to the faithful community. The second half of the verse is an additional narrowing of the group to those pure of heart. The psalmist, therefore, would be speaking as one of them.

This psalm indicates that the poet is jealous of those who are insolent or arrogant but who are also prosperous. The poet's whole world is called into question. It seems reality itself witnesses against the traditional view. The wicked appear to be people living in the community who are of questionable character. They are healthy and in no trouble. How can this be? Because these wicked people are prospering, they are also prideful and sinful. The pride makes the poet's distress even greater. Still worse, other people view them positively and find no fault in their actions (Ps 73:10). This lack of congruence between good actions and reward is dangerous because it encourages evil thoughts and actions. The wicked do not think God knows what they are doing; so they can get away with their wrongdoings (73:11). The actions of the wicked seem to confirm such a belief.

It is clear that the situation has caused the poet to feel as though he or she is suffering unjustly. The poet cannot adopt the ways of the wicked for that "would have been untrue to the circle of your children" (Ps 73:15). The poet seeks to remain true to his or her convictions trying to make sense of what seems senseless. The poet's crisis has now built to a critical point.

The next verse represents a transition. A revelation comes to the psalmist in the sanctuary. We get a rare and brief glance here into the mind of the author. "When I thought how to understand this, / it seemed to me a wearisome task" (Ps 73:16). It is not common in biblical literature for the reader to get a glimpse, albeit a very brief one, into the thoughts of the writer. This personal revelation changes everything. Now the poet moves to instruct his or her audience. The poet has struggled to make sense of things and now seeks to convince others that the traditional view is correct after all.

The argument has added weight because the revelation came while the poet is at the sanctuary of God. At this point, the poet sees the end of the wicked. It may appear as though they are on top of the world, but it is only an appearance as well as temporary. In the end, they will receive due payment for their deeds. Verses 18–28 express the poet's reaffirmed confidence in conventional wisdom. The poet trusts in God and expresses the belief that God takes care of the faithful and punishes the wicked. The punishment in the Hebrew Bible is not punishment in an afterlife. The punishment may result in a distance from God's life-giving presence.

The psalm ends with the poet's reassurance that God is near to the faithful. Those removed from God's proximity will perish. The author has made a journey questioning the traditional view only to have a word from God reveal the answer. This psalm represents another stage in the argument central to Job. The books of Job and Ecclesiastes make it clear that the issue remains unsettled as many find it hard to reconcile their reality with the traditional view.

If this psalm dates to the post-exilic period, it will represent an attempt to understand the old views in light of new circumstances. The psalmist must feel there is a growing threat or challenge to the standard view. He or she must feel a need to deal with the questions and propose a response to it. The poem reflects the situation of the post-exilic community.

Intertextuality and Dialogue

The writer and audience likely feel the tension. The poet identifies with the traditional view, but he or she detects difficulties with this view. How can God be just if the wicked prosper and the just suffer? But in the real world, the just often suffer. How are we to understand this fact? The writer in the end attempts to show and convince the audience that ultimately the righteous are vindicated. Surely the audience is well aware of the problems associated with traditional views on good and evil. Anytime an innocent person suffers, he or she must wonder why.

On the other side, those who find themselves identified as the enemy or wicked may not see themselves that way. For them, these words may seem false. They may take offense at such characterizations. They may view those who speak these words as self-righteous or hypocrites. From their perspective, the sufferings of the so-called righteous may be deserved. We must keep in mind that there are always two sides to every story. We have also heard the saying that history is written by the victor. So the so-called wicked may feel that others have unjustly maligned them. Even the author of Job and Ecclesiastes does not affirm the views of this psalmist. So what we have here is an ongoing dialogue. Not everyone would be sympathetic to the psalmist's solution.

The audience, therefore, hears this psalm and some may be open to its message while others remain skeptical or resistant. Some people may identify with the language describing the wicked. They may find the words convincing. Others may find the words unconvincing and take the view expressed in Ecclesiastes rejecting any strict correspondence between one's deeds and the consequences of those deeds. Some may accept that sometimes good people suffer.

This psalm has attempted to affirm the traditional view although with a significant detour. It has not affirmed this conventional view directly as did Psalm 1. Yet, it does teach that the wicked will not escape justice indefinitely. At some time, the wicked will perish. Has the poet been successful in convincing the audience? The psalm certainly did not end the debate. For some worshippers, it may be successful in that it offers a deeper understanding of one's relationship with the divine. It is a step forward in the discussion.[18] In short, the poet is addressing people who already have opinions, and this psalm is addressing a concern and proposing a solution. The poet is not only aware of the various views of good and evil, but he or she is also battling for the audience's acceptance of his or her resolution of the dilemma.

Modern Audience

What about modern audiences? The conversation would differ from church to church or community to community. The subject matter is still of great concern and the success of the argument in this psalm depends on the audience. Theologians and philosophers have continued to struggle with the problem of evil. There is a vast body of literature and scholarly writings on the subject. For those familiar with some of this literature, the psalm has to make its case. The reader engages in the ongoing dialogue; this psalm represents one voice in the discussion.

PHILEMON

Many of the Books in the New Testament are letters. New Testament letters are good examples of writings designed to persuade. This short letter seems to be of a personal nature. Nevertheless, it is not only addressed to Philemon but also to Apphia, Archippus, and "to the church in your house" (Phlm 1:2).

Before turning to the use of language, a bit of general background is helpful. Many discussions of this letter focus on the issue of slavery. Commentaries provide information about Roman slavery as a background for understanding the letter. It is commonly stated that the supposed slave, Onesimus, is a runaway slave who may even have stolen property from his master Philemon. Paul has come to value Onesimus' service while in prison. Paul appeals to Philemon to either take Onesimus back as a brother (Phlm 1:16) or permit him to stay and assist him. Some interpreters see Paul's appeal as an attempt to win Onesimus' freedom from slavery while others view this letter as an attack on the institution of slavery.

Marvin R. Vincent sees Paul as being silent on the institution of slavery. He thinks it is wrong to assume that Paul set out to destroy this institution. Paul "addressed himself to the regulation, and not to the destruction, of existing relations."[19] In the end, however, Vincent concludes that the "principles of the gospel not only curtailed the abuses … [they also] destroyed the thing itself" (i.e., slavery).[20] It is also true that some advocates of slavery used this letter to support slavery. One argument viewed Philemon as a slaveholder and a member of the church that Paul had established. On this view, Paul does not state any opposition to slavery nor does he try to eliminate it.[21]

Interestingly, not everyone thinks this letter is addressing slavery. Is Onesimus a runaway slave? It is possible that the recipients of the letter had sent Onesimus to help Paul.[22] Allen Dwight Callahan argues that Onesimus is not a slave at all. He is Philemon's brother in the flesh, a member of Philemon's own family.[23]

So what can we say about the historical background for this letter? The letter is written sometime during the mid-50s to early 60s.[24] The church is also part of the audience Paul addresses even though the letter is directed primarily to Philemon. In my view, Philemon is most likely a letter about a slave named Onesimus. However, there is no compelling reason to assume Onesimus is a runaway slave let alone a thief. He may have assisted Paul with Philemon's permission.

Whether Onesimus is a slave at all cannot be known with certainty. Verses 15–16 say that he is a slave. Nevertheless, Callahan argues that the reference to slave or servant in verse 16 should not be taken literally. He notes Paul's request for Philemon to receive Onesimus back as a "beloved brother." Callahan quotes a nineteenth century abolitionist, George Bourne. Bourne expresses the view that Onesimus is a "natural brother" of Philemon."[25] The statement in verse 16, "no longer as a slave but more than a slave, a beloved brother—especially to me but how much more to you, both in the flesh and in the Lord," adds weight to his argument. "In the flesh" supports his view by suggesting that Onesimus is Philemon's real brother as well as his brother in Christ.

One can say that the letter is about reconciliation. Cain Hope Felder says the fundamental point of the letter, even more fundamental than the issue of slavery, is the "power of the gospel to transform human relationships and bring about reconciliation."[26] Is it reconciliation of a slave to his master? If so, it might suggest that Paul accepts the institution of slavery, a common practice in that day. But if, as the letter states, he should become "more than a slave, a beloved brother", Paul is likely calling either for Onesimus' freedom or for his total equality in the community of faith. A third possibility is that Paul is calling for a reconciliation of true brothers.

The request is also disclosed to the Christian community meeting at Philemon's house. So Paul is confronting the issue on two fronts. If the community is persuaded, then it would put pressure on Philemon to acquiesce to his request. In this case, Paul may very well be calling on Philemon to free Onesimus, therefore, allowing Onesimus to assist him in his mission to the Gentiles. The language supports this view.

One other thing is clear. In the Christian community, there should be no division between master and slave. Galatians 3:28 says that in Christ there is neither "slave nor free." In the Christian community, therefore, one could no longer treat another person as property. The radical equality expressed in Galatians 3:28 was likely part of a baptismal formula, which means it was central to the faith in all communities.[27] It does not necessarily imply, however, that Paul is calling for the end of slavery. It would mean that slavery has no place in the Church.

The Use of Language

The structure of this letter is consistent with Paul's other letters. There is the salutation (Phlm 1–3), thanksgiving for Philemon (Phlm 4–7), the body of the letter (Phlm 8–22), and the final greetings and benediction (Phlm 23–25). While most of his letters are to the church, this one is primarily directed to Philemon. The letter is public in some sense, but it is also personal. Paul's words "I hear of your love," could possibly indicate that Paul "does not know the persons or communities at first hand."[28] Other aspects of the letter indicate that the two men are friends and co-workers.

There are a number of statements, words, and phrases that have significance and carry great feeling and passion. The language is intended for the church as well as Philemon. In verses 1 and 8, Paul refers to himself as a prisoner of Christ. In verses 10 and 13, he talks about his imprisonment. So the letter is written during a time when he is imprisoned. Still the references may affect Paul's audience, winning him sympathy and support for his plea.

Paul also expresses his deep appreciation for Philemon. Verse 4 opens, "when I remember you." "You" in verses 4–21 is singular referring to Philemon. So the one being addressed is Philemon even though there is a larger audience. Paul begins by building Philemon up. He thanks God for Philemon's love and for his work. He tells Philemon that he prays for the effectiveness of his work. Paul expresses the joy and encouragement he receives from Philemon's love and faith. All of these comments may be genuine, but they also prepare for Paul's request in verses 8–22. Paul's words here are diplomatic and soothing.

Verse 8 represents an abrupt shift from the flattering language. The shift may have the effect of grabbing the recipients' attention. He says that "I am bold enough in Christ to command you to do your duty," referring primarily to Philemon. Paul chooses instead "to appeal" to Philemon out of love. Paul is appealing to Philemon on behalf of his "child, Onesimus." Now that Onesimus' has become part of the Christian community, Paul views himself as his father. Paul plays on the name Onesimus, which means useful by saying that "formerly he was useless to you but now he is indeed useful both to you and to me" (Phlm 11). Paul wants to keep him, but he sends his own heart, meaning Onesimus, back to Philemon and leaves the decision in his hands. It must be a willing consent to return Onesimus to Paul. Nevertheless, Paul makes it hard for him or for the congregation to ignore or refuse his request.

Paul asks Philemon to receive Onesimus back not as a slave but as a "beloved brother." If he is to remain with Philemon, it seems that Paul is asking for him to be considered an equal, a true brother in Christ. Verses 17–22 add additional weight to his request. Paul uses the notion of partnership. If they are partners, then he calls "upon Philemon to honor all that partnership involves and implies: acceptance, trust, regard, divisions of responsibility in a common purpose, and equality of sharing."[29] If they are partners, Paul would in effect be a co-owner of Onesimus.[30]

Paul also addresses the issue of wrongdoing. He does not say that Onesimus is guilty of any wrong, but he expresses his commitment to take care of any wrongdoing if it occurred. He promises to make good on anything Onesimus might owe. He shrewdly, however, reminds Philemon of his own debt: "I say nothing of you owing me even your own self" (Phlm 19). He then expresses his confidence that Philemon will do the right thing. If that is not enough, he announces his intention to visit. This visit implies that Paul would confront those who refuse to receive Onesimus back as a brother in Christ. Thinking of 1 Corinthians 4:19–21, the mention of a visit takes on an ominous and threatening quality. Similarly, is this mention of a visit a subtle notice that the audience will have to confront Paul face to face?

The language shows that Paul is working hard to persuade Philemon and the church. It is clear that Paul is making a conscious effort to be diplomatic and assertive. He seems unwilling to command Philemon but rather calls upon him to do the right thing willingly. He is deliberately vague, and this vagueness is a source of frustration for interpreters. The seriousness of the language and the topic certainly suggest that Paul is not at all sure that Philemon will agree. Modern audiences, who view slavery as wrong, might see Paul's request as more than reasonable; they might see Philemon as a villain. For Paul's day, however, slavery was just part of one's mental landscape. The church members meeting at Philemon's house may themselves have had slaves. Paul's request to Philemon may have implication for the other members as well.

The Rhetorical Environment

As stated above, the situation that calls forth this letter is Paul's relationship with Philemon, the church, and Onesimus. Paul has come into contact with Onesimus while he is in prison. How this meeting occurs is uncertain. Did Philemon and the church send Onesimus to support Paul? The first part of the letter, verses 1–3, does not provide any information about Onesimus. Therefore, the "recipients of the letter, Philemon, Apphia, and Archippus, already know that Onesimus is with Paul, indeed probably that they had sent him."[31] It is commonly thought that Onesimus is a runaway slave, but this assumption is uncertain.

Modern interpreters are at a disadvantage. The recipients know things we do not. Paul's letters require outsiders (i.e., modern interpreters) to make inferences from what is said to deduce the details of the situation. In this case, ambiguity in the language makes the task difficult. Getting the situation wrong, therefore, could lead to a misunderstanding of Paul's request. Unfortunately, however, one must draw conclusions based on incomplete information. In this letter, Paul is calling people to live and act in certain ways. Richard A. Horsley says Paul sees the Christian community as an "alternative society."[32] For Horsley, Paul has an apocalyptic understanding of the role of the Christian community. He attempts to resocialize the Christian communities under his watch. In these communities, there should be no slaves. Paul is calling for alternative communities that are "counter-imperial." They would have an "international" or "multicultural" character being made up of people from different "ethnic and cultural backgrounds". The counter-cultural character derives from their "loyalty to Christ." These alternative communities represent societies where people live their lives without being involved in mainstream Roman society. They seek to win others to the faith and enlarge the "Christian movement (esp. 1 Corinthians 5; 6:1–11; 7:29–31; 10:14–22) during the time remaining before the *parousia* [i.e., second coming] of their Lord."[33]

Consequently, one can conclude that Paul likely rejects the institution of slavery and says it has no place in this community. Onesimus is free and equal in the body of Christ. This view is supported by Paul's statement in 1 Corinthians 7:22–23 where he says that a slave who has a chance for freedom should take it.[34] It is less clear that Paul actually sought to eliminate slavery in the Greco-Roman society since he believed the end was near.

Intertextuality and Dialogue

As Horsley points out, we cannot assume that Paul's request will find sympathetic ears. He is attempting to resocialize his audience. Often Paul meets with resistance. It seems that he anticipates some reluctance on Philemon's part. Paul's language is flattering in some places and forceful in others. It expresses Paul's intent to visit them, possibly an implied threat. As mentioned earlier, Paul announces a visit to Corinth where he plans to confront the congregation. Here too the visit implies any disobedience might be challenged. In short, the overall tone of Philemon indicates that Paul is being careful. He is trying not to offend but to make the most compelling case possible.

The audience may certainly become alarmed with the language of verse 8. Bold, command, and duty are serious words. The audience may begin to feel uneasy. What does Paul want? They may even begin to feel some resistance. Then he appeals to them, which may soften the blow since an appeal is certainly not a command. Still, they may feel they cannot really refuse his appeal. It is interesting that Paul does not mention his apostleship in the letter. He addresses them as a prisoner. He addresses himself to a "dear friend and co-worker" as well as the church meeting at Philemon's house.

His message to treat Onesimus as a beloved brother and not as a slave would seem irregular for people socialized into a Roman society where the institution of slavery is taken for granted. Also, one might wonder if Onesimus is the only slave in question. Did Philemon have other slaves who prepare food and other things for his household? The other church members may also have slaves. If so, the message would affect them as well. A member who owns slaves might take the letter as a call for the other members to free their slaves as well. And if slaves are members of the church, are they treated as equals? A Roman citizen may feel that Paul has no right to make such a request. Roman citizens may have had considerable discomfort treating a slave as an equal. Potentially, this letter is controversial.

Finally, Paul promises to pay any debt Onesimus might owe to Philemon. He is calling in a favor by reminding Philemon of his own debt. He is anticipating possible reasons why Philemon might resist his request. He puts pressure on Philemon to respond favorably. In the end, we do not know the results of this letter, whether it was successful or not. One might conclude that it was successful because the letter made it into the canon. Another interesting rhetorical study of this letter could investigate how it functioned in relation to American slavery.

In short, rhetorical criticism is concerned with the text as a means of persuasion. As demonstrated above, it focuses on three aspects. First, we have looked at the language and how it is used to persuade an audience. Next, we looked at the rhetorical environment, which focuses on the situation that calls forth the text. Finally, this discussion looks at intertextuality and dialogue. This aspect focuses on both author and audience. Both are involved in a dialogue. We can consider how ideas and words are understood and experienced in a particular historical and social context. This approach shows that meaning is a two-way street. Audiences do not passively receive and accept information. The author knows this and attempts to anticipate areas of agreement and resistance, which in turn shapes his or her message. In this way, the author and audience are engaged in a dialogue.

This approach is appealing in large part because of its flexibility. It benefits from the historical and social analysis as well as literary examination. It is particularly useful in biblical literature. Biblical texts are almost always trying to persuade. So the approach is appropriate. Finally, the flexibility of this approach allows one to look at how a text might speak to any audience past or present.

NOTES

1. Patricia K. Tull, "Rhetorical Criticism and Intertextuality in *To Each Its Own Meaning: An Introduction to Biblical Criticisms and Their Application*, ed. Stephen R. Haynes and Steven L. McKenzie (Louisville: The Westminster Press, 1999), 156–180.

2. Moyers, 12–13.
3. Tull, 157.
4. Ibid.
5. Ibid.
6. Ibid., 161.
7. Ibid., 266–267.
8. Ibid., 166–175. She provides more details and would be an excellent resource.
9. James L. Crenshaw, *A Whirlpool of Torment: Israelite Traditions of God as an Oppressive Presence*, Overtures to Biblical Theology, ed., Walter Brueggemann and John R. Donahue, no. 12 (Fortress Press: Philadelphia, 1984), 94.
10. A. A. Anderson, *Psalms (73–150)*, The New Century Bible Commentary eds. Ronald E. Clements and Matthew Black (Wm. B. Eerdmans Publ. Co.: Grand Rapids, 1972), 531–532.
11. Ibid., 532.
12. Crenshaw, 96–97.
13. Ibid., 529.
14. Erhard S. Gerstenberger, *Psalms, Part 2, and Lamentations*, The Forms of the Old Testament Literature, eds. Rolf Knierim and Gene M. Tucker vol. XIV (Grand Rapids: William B. Eerdmans Publishing Company, 2001), 74.
15. Ibid.
16. Ernst Würthwein, "Erwägungen zu Psalm 73," in *Wort und Existenz: Studien zum Alten Testament* (Goottigen: Vandenhoeck und Ruprecht, 1970), 161–178 and Von Helmer Ringgren, Einige Bemerkungen Zum 73sten. Psalm. *Vetus Testamentum*, 3, no 3 (July 1, 1953), 265–272. Both Würthwein and Ringgren assume the speaker is the king.
17. Anderson, 530
18. See Crenshaw's chapter on Psalm 73 in his book, *A Whirlpool of Torment* cited above.
19. Marvin R. Vincent, *A Critical and Exegetical Commentary on the Epistles to the Philippians and to Philemon*. The International Critical Commentary on the Holy Scriptures of the Old and New Testaments eds. Samuel Rolles Driver, Alfred Plummer, and Charles Augustus Briggs (Edinburgh: T. & T. Clark, 1979), 166–167.
20. Ibid., 167.
21. Clarice J. Martin, "'Somebody Done Hoodoo's the Hoodoo Man': Language, Power, Resistance, and the Effective History of Pauline Texts in American Slavery," *Semeia* 83/84 (1998): 218–219.
22. Richard A. Horsley, "Paul and Slavery: A Critical Alternative to Recent Readings," *Semeia* 83/84 (1998): 180.
23. Allen Dwight Callahan, "Paul's Epistle to Philemon: Toward an Alternative Argumentum," *Harvard Theological Review* 86:4 (1993): 357–376.
24. Cain Hope Felder, *2 Corinthians, Galatians, Ephesians, Colossians, 1 & 2 Thessalonians, 1 & 2 Timothy, Titus, Philemon* New Interpreter's Bible Commentary, ed. Leander E. Keck, vol. 11, (Nashville: Abingdon Press, 2000), 884.
25. Callahan, 362–363.
26. Felder, 885.
27. Elizabeth Schüssler Fiorenza, *A Feminist Theological Reconstruction of Christian Origins: In Memory of Her*, (New York: Crossroads, 1995), 208–220.
28. Ralph P. Martin, *Colossians and Philemon*, The New Century Bible Commentary, ed., Matthew Black (Grand Rapids: Wm. B. Eerdmans Publ. Co. 1973), 160.
29. Felder, 899.
30. David L. Barr, *New Testament Story: An Introduction*, 4th edition ed. (Belmont: Wordsworth, 2009), 108.
31. Horsley, 180.
32. Ibid., 162–167, 176.
33. Ibid., 176.
34. Ibid., 196.

Chapter Fifteen

Reader Response

Reader response approaches typically tend to focus on the reader as an active player in the determination of meaning. Not all reader response approaches, however, concentrate on a real flesh and blood reader. Some focus on the implied reader, which is the reader being addressed in the text. One might also focus on an ideal or a typical reader, one who is representative of readers from a particular social context. There are several viable reader response approaches.

Reader-response critics discard the notion of a "disinterested reader." Readers have interests and desires that color their understandings. The use of scientific strategies in the pursuit of "verifiable knowledge" about the text does not lead the reader to complete objectivity.[1] For reader-response critics, the reader brings baggage with him or her to the reading process. Determining meaning, therefore, is an active process performed by a reader. The "text as a privileged autonomous object is displaced."[2] Instead, the knowledge and experience of the reader and his or her active response to the text becomes fundamental.[3]

One form of reader response criticism is based on an interactional model. Wolfgang Iser has developed such an approach with his concept of implied reader. Iser's notion of an implied reader involves an interaction between the reader and the text. For Iser, the "implied reader is the reader implied by the text."[4] It is the "product of the encounter *between* the text and the reader, a realization of potentialities *in* the text but produced *by* a real reader."[5] So, the text does not have any meaning apart from the actual reader.

This interaction model is not dependent upon Iser's notion of an implied reader. It works just as well with the concept of real or ideal readers. When John picks up the Bible and reads the story of creation in Genesis 1, he is encountering a story within a certain social context, and he must seek to make sense of it. His encounter, however, would be different from a Hindu reader encountering the same story for the first time. Both have to make sense of it from their frame of reference. I find the interactive approach to be the most desirable because it focuses on both reader and text without giving either one a dominant position.

Therefore, the reader has a real part in determining its meaning. The reader is not a self-contained isolated self. As a reader, I was once struck by Alfred Lord Tennyson's line in Ulysses, "I am a part of all I have met."[6] This thought sums up the notion of reader response for me. Cumulative life experiences shape the reader consciously and unconsciously. One cannot remove the subjective aspects of reading.

Readers draw upon various resources when attempting to make sense of a text. This process entails making connections between texts, which produces a network of texts. These other texts inform and shape our readings. The reader is making sense of a text and incorporating it into what he or she already knows. Since what readers know differs greatly, the understandings of the texts differ as well. I can never experience the letters of Paul as his contemporaries experienced them. I can only experience them as one living almost two thousand years later.

One might ask: Is there a correct meaning? If one takes the reader as an individual seriously, the answer is no. Everyone reading a text would differ in one way or another. There would be some agreement since individuals share common notions and experiences. Still, that would not lead to one reading. Certain communities may reach agreement on proper readings, but that may be in large measure due to social pressure to conform. Is meaning completely subjective then?

Literary critics have often viewed communication as traveling in one direction—from the text to the reader. Historical critics go in one direction as well beginning with the author, then moving to the text, and finally to the audience. With reader response, it is not necessarily one direction. Encounter indicates that the exchange between the text and reader produces the meaning. The reader has to navigate the text based on what he or she knows or can learn. The author speaks through the text. After that, the meaning is ultimately in the hands of the reader, so it is to some degree dependent on the reader.

Stanley Fish has introduced the notion of reading or interpretive communities into the discussion. For him, the interpretive community regulates the reader to some degree and puts a check on individual subjectivity.[7] As noted above, communities can put social pressure on members to conform to certain readings. This concept is important, but one does not have to limit it to professional reading communities that share certain reading strategies as it is for Fish. It can include reading communities who share common ideologies and worldviews. A religious group might in this sense constitute a reading community. Consequently, there always will be competing communities of interpreters.

Concerning the reader's identity, there are several possible ways to proceed. One approach could be to focus on the psychological or subjective aspect of reading.[8] This view theoretically allows for as many different readings as there are readers. The reader could be an expert or ordinary reader. The expert reader might be one who has been educated in the area of reading and interpreting. The ordinary reader might be the casual reader who has no special training.

A different approach would be to see the reader as part of a larger social network. Reading is primarily related to the reader's place in society. This approach considers the social location of the reader. It would be consistent with a reading community. The community might be made up of ordinary or expert readers.[9]

An interactive model for reading constitutes a middle ground between the psychological and social approaches.[10] The interactive model involves the reader's social location as well as his or her psychological or personal traits. Interpreters who take this interactive approach could go in either direction. It also limits the subjectivity of the individual or the community in that the text can rule some readings out or show them to be defective and unsatisfying.

Iser's interactive approach considers how the actual reader encounters a text and makes sense of it in relation to his or her experiences.[11] For Iser, reading is a linear process. The reader moves from one literary unit (i.e., a sentence) to another. Meaning is built up over this process. Expectations and understandings emerge and evolve. Readers encounter gaps in this process and must resolve them. His approach avoids complete relativism by giving priority to the text, which "controls the subjectivity of the reader."[12] Of course, this would not work the same way once one has heard or is familiar with the text. One is then not moving into an unknown.

So far, I have mentioned the real reader and the implied reader. Now I would introduce the notion of an ideal reader, which one can define in relation to the social sciences. An ideal or typical reader is analogous to Max Weber's notion of ideal type. Here one could focus on either modern or historical readers. The ideal reader is a typical reader within a particular social context. The reader might be the typical reader in ninth century ancient Israel or a contemporary feminist reader.

Consider, for instance, a typical Corinthian reader of Paul's day. How might she understand the issues discussed in 1 Corinthians? To answer this question, one would need to understand the worldview of that society. A typical reader or audience would share a "common stock of knowledge"[13] with other readers from the same or similar social setting. In this case, there is a dual layer of reading going on. There is the so-called typical reader, which is a historical construct, and the actual reader who may be a historical or literary critic.

This kind of analysis looks at a typical reader from a socio-historical context. The readers are part of a reading community. A reading community could be any group of readers who share important commonalities. For example, a fundamentalist church's reading of the story of Jonah would differ from a historical critic's reading of that text. Each community has beliefs and practices that govern its interpretation. Factors such as ideological sympathies, gender, race, and class are factors.

Reading communities introduce a repressive element into the interpretive process. Communities may be oppressive to their members and outsiders. There can also be tension and conflict between different reading communities. There is potential for both positive and negative readings when one is considering reading communities. Reading communities produce continuous unresolved conflict, but it is possible that dialogue between communities could lead to positive outcomes.

APPLICATION

Reader response is "doing what comes naturally," which is the title of a book written by Stanley Fish on the subject.[14] It is entirely natural for a reader to make sense of what he or she is reading. We do it every time we pick up a book or newspaper. Individuals draw upon their collective experiences and knowledge to make sense of the encounter. It is so natural that one is hardly ever conscious of doing it unless difficulty arises in understanding.

There are three basic steps that can help one use this approach. First, one needs to identify and describe the reader. The reader may be the real reader, an implied reader, or typical reader. It is best to make this clear up front to avoid confusion. When the reader is an implied or ideal reader, there is a dual reading taking place. For instance, the interpreter might focus on the implied reader or the historical reader, which constitutes one level of reading. Nevertheless, the interpreter is also reading and contributing to the understanding of the text forming a second level of reading. Consequently, it is a subjective exercise. Awareness of this situation is important because the interpreter cannot ever capture the exact reality of how a reader would respond. It is an approximation.

Second, one might describe how the reader sees the world. One could describe the worldview of the reader in question so as to understand how he or she might respond to the text. This understanding contains social and psychological aspects. Still, it is not really possible to know what derives from nature versus nurture (i.e., one's social environment). Understanding the reader helps to understand how the reader may interact with the text.

Finally, one should engage in a close reading of the text with a clear notion of the reader's identity and mental background. What would the reader respond to and how would he or she respond? If the reader in question is sympathetic to feminist issues, the interpreter would ask how that reader might react to the metaphors, symbols, and images in the text. How might he or she respond to the characters, their motives, and actions? Historically, one may ask how the events recorded might affect a particular reader. From a literary perspective, one may focus on the effects the language might have on the reader. One could go in many different directions as long as the focus remains on the reader's response.

For the sake of simplicity in the two readings below, I shall be the reader. At one time, this would have seemed a little self-absorbed to me. But at one level or another I am always the reader. As stated above, even if I focus on a typical reader or engage in a form-critical analysis of a text, I am still the one producing an interpretation. In some sense, I am always the reader. As a matter of explanation, therefore, I offer a brief description of what conscious influences guide my readings.

I find all the methods discussed in this book valuable. I do value some more than others, but that is a personal choice. I affirm them all. My reading is influenced by various critical perspectives. I prefer the historical or social approaches even though I am not sure why. I do not value fundamentalist readings because they tend to allow their own presuppositions to dominate the text while believing or claiming to be true to the text alone and therefore to God. They do not adequately recognize the human element involved in the interpretive process.

For me, the bottom line is the meaning of the text and not trying to find a meaning to my liking. My main concern is for the author's intent and the text as the conveyor of that intent. I am also interested in the potentialities of the text, potentialities that may exceed the author's intent. Moreover, I am concerned with past and present readers or audiences of the text. I try to let the text speak for itself and then I make my own judgments. I do not feel a need to read in sympathy with the text.

In short, I desire freedom and openness to the text and oppose narrow readings that promote intolerance. I want to be open to the Other (those different from myself) although I am not always able to understand or identified with the Other especially if this Other is narrow and judgmental. The Other is not always saintly or defenseless. All of these observations affect how I read. This description is certainly not exhaustive, but it can suffice for the purposes of illustration.

Along with this brief personal profile, I operate on a few basic assumptions. First, objectivity, neutrality, and the search for Truth are things I pursue even if they are never fully obtainable. I accept the view that all I know and feel comes filtered to me through numerous kinds of life experiences.

Meaning is always mediated through language, culture, and a multitude of other things. Reading is never merely a linear process as Iser notes. It is not a process of building information as if starting from zero. Texts enter our consciousness, and our consciousness is continually being shaped so we can make sense of things. It is to a degree a linear process but not really. A text such as Jeremiah is not the beginning point for the reader even if the reader has never read the book before. For my reading of biblical texts, I cannot experience any first time with a text since they are part of my life from childhood. A context for reading them has always been there for me as far as I can remember.

One other thing, the present is a fiction. By the time the present moment comes into existence, it is instantaneously receding into the past. A reader is constantly influenced by the past and the projected future. By projected future, I mean the future I imagine when reading a text. It is what I anticipate. But the present by the time it registers with me becomes the past. I do not accept the view of reading as primarily a linear process. It is similar to taking a step backward and then forward. Our understandings derive from our past influences and experiences. As we become conscious of reading, we at the same time fit the words we read into our prior experiences. All of this comes together to forge a particular reaction to the text.

Deuteronomy 7 and Luke 15:11–32 are the passages for consideration in this chapter. The readings do reflect my interests and concerns. The first passage is of interest not because of its difficulty but its ideas. It contains instructions to "utterly destroy" the people living in the land of Canaan, and it issues warnings about the results of disobedience. This passage has certainly haunted me over the years. Add Jesus' response to the Canaanite woman in Matthew 15:21–28 to the words of Deuteronomy 7 and the picture is disturbing. Jesus' change of heart and response to the Canaanite woman in Matthew 15:28 soften his reply to her found in verse 26, but Jesus' attitude is surprising.[15] The second text discussed below is Luke 15:11–32, which I have always found to be inspiring. It reminds me of a love so great that it embraces the worthy and unworthy. It is a love that is quite unconventional by human standards.

DEUTERONOMY 7:1–11

As a reader, I come to this text having read it and related texts several times before. For this reading, I am not interested in the historical aspects of the text. The text does not represent what happened since it is highly unlikely that there was a total conquest of the land. My concern is about the ideas and implications of this text for past, present, and future audiences. So my reading focuses on its ideological implications.

On reflection, I am struck by the contrast between God who delivers an enslaved people from Egyptian bondage and God who instructs these same peoples to conquer and destroy the peoples of the land of Canaan (Dt 7:8). Historically, this picture is flawed. The ancient Israelites were themselves indigenous peoples living in the land of Canaan. The text, however, justifies taking the land and perpetrating extreme violence toward these peoples. Such actions are justified on religious grounds. That is what we have in verse 4. Since the people of the land may corrupt ancient Israel's children and turn them away from following God, they must be annihilated. The Hittites are one of the peoples they are to destroy. Thinking back to Abraham's buying of a burial place for Sarah in Genesis 23, the Hittites appear generous and welcoming. Now they are to be destroyed because of a promise of land made to Abraham by God (Dt 1:8, 6:10, 7:8, 9:5, 27, 29:13, 30:20, 34:4).

There are two concerns in these verses. First, there is the destruction and second obedience to God. The two are connected in that the peoples of the land might cause ancient Israel to disobey God's commandments. The command by God to "utterly destroy them" must mean killing these peoples, which is an act of genocide. A vivid picture of "utter destruction" is given in Joshua 6:17–19, 21. The story of Achan in Joshua 7:1–26 tells what happens when Achan disobeys God's commands.

These stories have always disturbed me. Years ago I saw a reference to an article entitled "Canaanites, Cowboys, and Indians,"[16] which caught my attention. The connection between Canaanites and Native Americans along with various other peoples who have been pushed off their lands is clear. Why has this subject not received more attention? Oppressed peoples have suffered the loss of life and property to an aggressor. What is remarkable is the reversal where the ancient Israelites go from slaves to oppressors. Unfortunately, these biblical stories have been used to justify acts of violence on others.[17]

Viewing this text through the eyes of others is important. The words of Deuteronomy 7:1–2 are dangerous to Canaanites of all times and places. Verses 1–5 contain an ethnocentric attitude where the other person's religion, children, and people are impure and a threat to the in-group's way of life. The solution is destruction.

Ancient Israelites shall "make no covenant with them and show them no mercy" (Dt 7:2). A covenant is an agreement or contract. They are not to enter into any negotiation or treaty with these peoples. They must not "intermarry with them" (Dt 7:3) or be contaminated by them. Contact with them might cause ancient Israelites to follow and serve other gods, an act that would move God to destroy them. Consequently, they must destroy them along with their altars, pillars, sacred poles, and idols all associated with the Canaanite religion. They must remain pure since they are God's chosen (Dt 7:5–6).

It is clear from the outset that the text depicts God as the one who is responsible for ancient Israel's success. These other nations are "mightier and more numerous" (Dt 7:1). Verse 8 tells why God is acting on their behalf. God loves them and has sworn an oath to their ancestors to give them the land of Canaan. The ending of this section can certainly be understood as a warning to these chosen people. God is loyal to the covenant people so long as they reciprocate with love and obedience. However, God stands ready to punish the disobedient Israelites who fail to keep the "commandments, statutes, and ordinances" (Dt 7:11).

The covenant mentioned in verse 9, therefore, is conditional. God's favor depends upon the actions of the people. The language used in Deuteronomy 7:7–11 is similar to language in Exodus 19–20. This understanding is supported by Deuteronomy 1:8, and 6:10–19 which explicitly mentions the oath sworn to Abraham, Isaac, and Jacob. The covenant in Deuteronomy 7:9 is also related to the Sinai covenant (Ex 19:5) and the Exodus tradition.

The themes of destruction and obedience introduced in these eleven verses continue in Deuteronomy 7:12–26. The text promises rewards to the obedient. The nations will be destroyed "little by little" (Dt 7:22). Foreign kings and images of foreign gods shall be destroyed (Dt 7:24–26). And again, God will not overlook the people's failures to comply. So the themes of destruction and obedience are repeated and emphasized.

Deuteronomy 7:1–11 is a human interpretation of what God wants. It is a pattern that occurs too often in human history. Oppressed peoples may become oppressors as soon as the situation is reversed. As stated above, this theme of conquest is probably not historically accurate, but the fact that a sacred text calls for the utter destruction of a people should not be overlooked. The writers or editors were likely elites in the religious community. They felt that obedience to God was critical and that disobedience could lead to their destruction. They may have felt that their own survival or the survival of a pure form of their religion was at stake. Canaanites represented a threat, not to the average Israelite but more likely to the religious elites and their worldview. Regardless of the justification given, there is no ethical justification for such an act. Just because a Canaanite people represent a possible threat to the ancient Israelites' religion is not a justification for their elimination.

LUKE 15:11–32

This passage presents a far different view of God than Deuteronomy 7 and Matthew 15:21–28. For me, it has always been a story about a loving father. Readers tend to identify with one character or another. I have great admiration for the father, but I may be more like the younger or elder brother in the story. I certainly understand the elder son's point of view. Nonetheless, the parable is also about the father who inspires me to be more than I am.

So for me, reading exposes a tendency to be sympathetic to the conventional point of view, and yet it pushes me past this human tendency to keep score. It is the excess in this story that disturbs my complacency. I am both lifted up and wounded by this parable. What kind of God can take back an unfaithful son and treat him better than one who had been faithful all of his life? How can a father just forgive the past that way? As the dutiful individual, this is a concern. I must remind myself, however, that I might sometimes be more like the younger son. This parable exposes a self-centered perspective. When I am the younger son, forgiveness is a wonderful thing, but when the shoe is on the other foot, I exhibit a certain sense of self-righteousness.

However, I am eternally thankful for the father. Not just thankful, the parable moves me at times to think how my own father forgave me when I did not really deserve it. I have often been reminded of that as a parent. I have learned that a father is not free to just give up on his children. The father, therefore, is an inspiration and in him I see the best of humanity, and in the elder son I see myself. I have often felt as if others should pay for their actions, and yet I have been in situations where I needed forgiveness. All of these emotions come to the fore in this story.

The parable is part of three parables about being lost and found. Luke 15 begins with a familiar scene. The scribes and Pharisees are upset at Jesus. In this instance, they are upset because Jesus "welcomes sinners and eats with them" (Lk 15:2). Tax collectors are specifically named in verse 1 along with the sinners in general. Jesus first tells the parable of the lost sheep and then the lost coin. The point is that God is concerned with the lost and is profoundly happy when the lost is recovered. In both cases, the story ends with reuniting the lost with the one searching. The meaning is revealed in Jesus concluding statements where he says there is joy in heaven over sinners who repent.

The story often referred to as the "Prodigal Son" begins in verse 11. The final parable of this trilogy focuses on the family, a father and two sons. What is significant about the sons is the age and character of the two. One is younger. He wants to get out and experience the world. The other is the elder son. Being the elder son in this society would have been significant. He would have a certain prestige and privilege.

This story contains several oppositions. The obvious is the younger versus elder. But we also have the irresponsible opposed to the dutiful. The younger son experiences abundance and famine. The younger son's actions also introduce the notion of honor and shame. Other contrasts include dead and alive along with lost and found all of which emphasize the message of the parable. Lost and found ties this parable to the other two in Luke 15.

The younger brother's request and the father's response contrast sharply with conventional wisdom. Seen within commonly expected practices, the father and younger son are out of touch. The younger son wants what will someday be his so he can leave home and begin a new life. The father does the unthinkable in giving him what he wants, which seems irresponsible. He did not try to hold back. His willingness to let the son go reveals a deep love that wounded the father. Had I not known the story ahead of time, I would have expected the father to disown the son, to declare him dead, meaning he is no longer welcome or has any claim on him. In fact, the parable does say the son was dead, but he returns and the father is waiting with open arms and outstretched hands. For some readers, this acceptance of the wayward son might point to weakness. Should he not have sent him away? Instead, he embraces him and reverses his fortunes.

Another contrast is the younger son's shift in perspective. At first, the son uses the imperative form of the verb "to give." The father can refuse this demand, but he gives him what he wants. At this point, the reader hears nothing of the elder son's reaction. A short time later, the younger son leaves, and we hear nothing about what he did except that he "squandered his property in dissolute living" (Lk 15:13). Dissolute would mean "reckless"[18] which is generally taken in the sense of immoral behavior. It also can be viewed as wasteful behavior. Exactly what this behavior entails is left to the imagination. Regardless, he spends everything and finds himself in a shameful place for any Jew; he feeds the pigs. The reader is not told what he received in return for this shameful job, but apparently it was not enough for he is "dying of hunger" (Lk 15:17).

The story turns when the younger son "came to himself." He now sees what he must do. Is he sincere when he decides to return home and ask his father to take him back as a "hired hand"? (Lk. 15:19) The reader does not know whether he has truly repented. He confesses his sin against heaven and his father hoping his father will allow him to return. He is desperate, and his father now has him at his mercy. And so, this son sets off to enact his plan.

Upon his return, he repeats the confession verbatim, but the father acts unexpectedly. He interrupts the son before he can repeat his offer. In fact, the father does not have to be persuaded at all. I am struck by the words, "while he [the younger son] was still far off, his father saw him, and was filled with compassion, he ran and put his arms around him and kissed him" (Lk 15:20). Did he stand daily and watch for his son's return? It would seem so since he saw him coming from a distance. As a father, I can only imagine the joy that consumed him upon that very moment of recognition.

The father allowed his son to leave, which must have been painful, and now the pain has transmuted to joy, relief, and celebration. He kisses and embraces his son in his exuberance. Besides the robe,[19] the father puts a ring on his finger and sandals on his feet. Then he instructs the servants to prepare the fatted calf to celebrate his son's safe return for his son was dead and is now alive and was lost but now is found. Nowhere is there talk of condemnation or punishment. There is no preaching or demanding of an apology. There seems to be no desire at all from the father to hear the son admit to his callous and selfish behavior; there is just open arms and joy.

Now, what about the elder son? He had been in the field—working and being responsible. As he came back to the house, he hears a celebration. When he finds out what is going on, he is not happy. He is angry. He confronts his father, and the father pleads with him. The elder brother feels hurt and unappreciated. This brother tells his father, "'Listen! For all these years I have been working like a slave for you, and I have never disobeyed your command; yet you have never given me even a young goat so that I might celebrate with my friends" (15:29). He feels cheated. He is upset about the fatted calf, although he does not mention the robe, ring, or sandals. He refers to his brother as that "son of yours" therefore stressing his separation from him. Even though the text did not specify how the son had wasted his inheritance (15:13), the older son imagines he spent it on prostitutes. (Lk. 15:30)

Interestingly, his father reverses this separation by referring to his younger son as this "brother of yours." The father reaffirms his devotion and connection to the elder son and tries to explain his actions to him. The explanation returns to the theme of the parable: dead and alive, lost and found.

Scholars have pointed out that the parable may address Jesus' ongoing dispute with the religious leaders of his day. The elder son represents the scribes and Pharisees. While this may be the case, the power of this story for me is not in Jesus' conflict with the religious establishment. It is in the challenge to human self-centeredness and self-righteousness. Its counter-cultural character is also immensely important. For whatever reason, the father is the shining example to me of what we should be like. The sons are the reality of how many people feel from a conventional point of view.

My confession as a reader is this: when I find myself in the situation of needing forgiveness, I identify with the younger son. When I feel smug and good, my first reaction may be to find fault in the one who breaks the rules. I want to be like the father. The father is the ideal; he is the one who is counter-cultural. He does not keep score. He gives us freedom even though this gift may seem like an irresponsible gift. When we mess things up, the father welcomes us back, and the father in the parable welcomes his son back without caring about the son's true motives. The message seems to be that the father faces humanity with arms open wide. Humanity and conventional wisdom, on the other hand, depends upon keeping score and balancing the books. This parable calls human notions of justice into question. The father's love is unconditional not based on human notions of honor or duty.

NOTES

1. Aichele, George et al. "Reader-Response Criticism," in *The Postmodern Bible: The Bible and Culture Collective*, (New Haven: Yale University Press, 1995), 42.
2. Ibid.
3. Ibid.
4. Charles E. Bresslere, *Literary Criticism: An Introduction to Theory and Practice*, 5th ed., (Boston: Longman-Pearson, 2011), 79.
5. Ibid., 31.
6. Alfred Lord Tennyson, "Ulysses," in *Literature: Structure, Sound, and Sense*. 3d ed., (New York: Harcourt Brace Jovanovich, Inc., 1978), 636–638.
7. Aichele, George et al. 30.
8. Ibid., 27–30.
9. Ibid., 27, 29–31.
10. Ibid., 27–29.
11. Bresslere, 79.
12. Aichele, George et al., 41.
13. This phrase comes from Alfred Schutz.
14. Stanley Fish, *Doing What Comes Naturally: Change, Rhetoric, and the Practice of Theory in Literary and Legal Studies*, in Post-Contemporary Interventions ed., Stanley Fish and Fredric Jameson (Durham: Duke University Press, 1989).
15. Miguel A. De La Torre, *Reading the Bible from the Margins*, (Maryknoll, New York: Orbis Books, 2002), 65–66.
16. Robert Warrior, "Canaanites, Cowboys, and Indians," https://canvas.instructure.com/courses/872266/files/ [accessed December 12, 2014].
17. Torre, 64–65; and Robert P. Carroll, "Cultural Encroachment and Bible Translation: Observations on Elements of Violence, Race and Class in the Production of Bibles in Translation," *Semeia* 76 (1996):41.
18. Timothy Freiberg, Barbara Freiberg, and Neva F. Miller, Analytical Lexicon of the Greek New Testament (Victoria B.C.: Trafford Publishing, 2005), 80. The Greek adverb *asotos* refers to "living in a wild, abandoned manner *recklessly, riotously, loosely.*"
19. I am reminded somewhat of the story of Joseph where Jacob had a robe made for Joseph (Gn 37:3). Similarly, there are elder sons who become jealous of their younger brother due to the father's behavior.

Chapter Sixteen

Deconstruction

Jacques Derrida is considered the founder of deconstruction. He clearly says that deconstruction is not a method or tool.[1] So where does that leave us? Is it possible to define what deconstruction is or is not? Initially, it is important to recognize that deconstruction is not an act of destruction as some have supposed. It does entail the undoing of various kinds of structures or ways of thinking in a systematic fashion. It focuses mainly on texts. Deconstruction depicts how these texts are initially constructed.[2] Since all systems are human constructions, deconstruction sets out to dismantle them, which opens things up for new interpretations and ideas. It may give birth to new ideas. Concerning texts, it keeps them open to new readings and prevents them from becoming stagnant.

What I attempt below is to describe the background from which Derrida's work emerges before moving on to illustrate how this way of reading can provide constructive and responsible meanings. The discussion shows how deconstruction, whatever it is, might affect one's understanding of biblical texts. Without trying to define or describe it as a method, the account below focuses on the main terms and ideas related to deconstruction.

KEY IDEAS

The earlier chapter on postmodern approaches prepares for this discussion. It distinguished between modern and postmodern thinking. Modernism focuses on neutrality and objectivity. It views the individual as a self or an "I". The "I" is an autonomous individual capable of building on previous foundations to work toward a knowledge of everything possible. This goal is unrealistic from a postmodern perspective. Knowledge is always limited because the human subject is limited. Deconstruction is typically associated with this kind of postmodern view. The "I" is never a fixed or static entity. The self is always in flux. It may have a degree of autonomy, but it is never completely separate from its embeddedness in culture, assumptions, worldviews, and language. We understand ourselves based on these elements and perhaps others such as personality type. The self is divided and complex. I can only attempt to understand myself through the ideas and concepts made possible by human language.

This view of the self also has implications for the notion of an author. The concept of an author as a creator or originator is impossible. An author is not an originator but a medium or filter through which ideas and views pass. Certain cultural ideals and values find expression through individuals. In a postmodern view, authors are transmitters of ideas. Everything we know comes filtered to us through such things as language, education, experiences, and religion. The author/subject is not independent of these things. He or she is a node (i.e., a point that intersects) in a large network.

Besides the author, deconstruction also speaks to the subject/object dichotomy. In modern thought, a subject is thought to be able to present the thoughts of others (i.e., an object) in a reliable way free from bias and prejudice. Deconstruction does not view this effort as having any chance of success. The reader or interpreter always re-presents the object to others meaning that the subject's desires, biases, feelings, education, culture are always shaping his or her perspective. What one gets is not a true view of an object, but a view filtered through the life experiences and overall worldview of the subject.

Another key component of deconstruction is the notion of language. For deconstruction, language is at best an imperfect means of communicating. There is no way to know an object or the "thing in itself" to use Immanuel Kant's words. The only way to know what the word signifies is to describe it in other words. Dictionaries, for example, define the meaning of a word by the use of other words. Therefore, words defer their meanings from one word to the next making absolute or final meaning impossible.[3] We are left with rough approximations. The words following a word in a sentence or larger communicative transaction limit the possible range of meanings, but it does not fix the meaning. Derrida coins the term "différance" to describe this situation. Différance is an intentional misspelling of difference.

Similarly, German philosopher, Martin Heidegger, began the practice of crossing out a word known as erasure. In simple terms, the practice means that a word denotes a necessary concept, but it is not completely adequate.[4] Words and concepts may be required for communication, but they are never final or perfect for the reasons discussed above. As a result, pursuing meaning depends upon interpretation.

Life is about human interpretation. We live to make sense of our world. Some people may simply accept a view of life that simplifies existence for them. But most people face instances where they have to make sense of their world. Nietzsche sees everything as interpretation.[5] Interpretation is part of every human interaction, and it is an essential part of being human. Interpretation comes between the stimulus and response.[6]

Interpretations can also be connected to power and authority. Nietzsche had much to say about power. Life is a struggle for power. Consequently, interpretations may authorize certain ideas and may give some people an advantage over others. Power struggles occur on every level of society, and not all are violent. For Nietzsche, power is about overcoming resistance. His main focus is on self-overcoming or self-mastery. This use of power is about conscious self-control and self-determination. Of course, power is often an attempt to control others.

One can see this point in Derrida's writings. Deconstruction rejects any monopoly on meaning. Claiming one and only one legitimate interpretation is to seek the power to undercut different possible interpretations. Deconstruction, therefore, counteracts the desire of those who try to establish one absolute meaning as the standard for everyone to follow. Deconstructionism draws from Nietzsche the view that Truth is truth from one's perspective, from one's own little piece of the world. Deconstructionists often quote Nietzsche words—"Truth is a mobile marching army of metaphors, metonymies (figures of speech) and anthropomorphisms. . . . Truths are illusions of which one has forgotten that they are illusions." Truth then is not absolute. It is truth from a particular vantage point and from a human perspective.

So deconstruction is not about Truth. We cannot step outside this world to get a view that is objective and free of interpretation. "Truth" is always mediated through culture and language. It is like living in a city with a wall that is too high to cross. We cannot send anything over the wall, and we have no way of knowing what is beyond it. We may have heard that there lives a race of great people on the other side, but we do not know. We cannot peer over the wall. Any speculation about what is beyond the wall is speculation that has our fingerprint on it.

But suppose we could transport ourselves to the other side? How could we ever hope to understand a realm so different from our own? We cannot approach that world without projecting our understandings of this foreign land. It is humanly impossible to know that world as it truly is apart from our world.

So if Truth in an ultimate sense is not possible for humans, how are we to understand our world? A view of language as metaphorical may provide a way forward. Sallie McFague says that a metaphor "is" and "is not." Something is like something else, but it is not that. There are similarities and differences.[7] Language is never able to capture the "is" without the "is not." Language and communication are incomplete. A metaphor is one way of trying to transcend the limits, but it cannot provide us with the "thing in itself" either. Human knowledge is incomplete and imperfect. Paul says so much in 1 Cor 13:9–10, 12 "For now we know in part, and we prophesy in part, but when the perfect comes, the imperfect will pass away. … For now we see in a mirror dimly, but then face to face. Now I know in part; then I shall understand fully…" In large measure, this view is what I am arguing. I do not deny absolutes. I deny the human ability to rise to the level of God. Humans always inhabit this world and are limited by our human, all too human perspectives to use Nietzsche's phrase.

Another key concept of deconstruction focuses on binary oppositions where people generally value the first word in the opposition over the second one. Some of these oppositions are male/female, public/private, subject/object, us/them, speech/writing to name a few. The speech/writing dualism can serve as an illustration since it is particularly related to the subject of this chapter.

Derrida is not trying to reverse the opposition in order to value the second term over the first. He is not seeking to value writing over speech in opposition to Western thought going back to Plato. Plato assumed that speech is natural and writing is secondary or derived from speech, so it is artificial or secondary. This modern preference based on Plato goes back to another opposition of valuing nature over culture. Plato's view sees the speaker as being present in his or her speech. One's consciousness is conveyed directly to another person. When I write, however, I am not present in the same way. I am absent in one sense because I am not communicating with another face to face.

Derrida, however, shows that the two are not opposites.[8] The conditions that make writing a limited and imperfect means of communication applies equally to speech. Whether I am trying to understand the person speaking to me or reading a poem does not matter. I simply cannot understand the communication apart from it being mediated through my personal life experiences as discussed above. Speech and writing are both embedded in the same processes.

This insight also raises the issue of text. So far I have not bothered to define text. I have assumed to this point that a text simply refers to the writing of one or more persons. But to understand deconstruction, this view of the text is inadequate. With Derrida and deconstruction, one needs to think much larger. A text is not limited to the Gospel of Matthew or the Book of Genesis. When Derrida says, "there is nothing outside of the text" it is apparent he is not using text in a confined sense of a definable written work such as the Book of Genesis. In some sense, everything is a text.[9] Speech and writing together constitute the text. Everything, our entire world, makes up this text. Human thought, perspectives, culture, experiences belong to it. It is a "'general text' or 'archi-text.'"[10]

According to John D. Caputo, Derrida does not reject a traditional view of meaning. He does not oppose the notion of commentary or doubling the thoughts of a writer. Explaining what the author meant is for him a legitimate exercise, but it does not exhaust the potentialities of the text. For Derrida, "deconstruction is not a license to circumvent it" (i.e., fundamental interpretive techniques to capture the message of the text). The doubling is a starting point. Deconstruction, therefore, does not justify "saying whatever comes into your head about the text, however, absurd and ridiculous."[11] But a deconstructive reading goes further. It "explores" what a doubling commentary leaves out. It seeks what the writer did not recognize or know—what is "going on in the text, as it were, behind her [the author's] back."[12] Therefore, deconstruction accepts doubling and perhaps may begin with it, but it moves toward something more.

DECONSTRUCTIVE READINGS ILLUSTRATED

As stated above, deconstruction is not necessarily a method, but there are key concepts that can provide guidance. A deconstructive reading should keep the text open. It does not seek to offer the final word. In fact, it is this openness that conserves a work making it relevant for the present and prevents it from being a relic of the past.[13] It begins with the author's ideas and views, but it does not accept them as the final arbiter of authoritative meaning. It unravels these ideas showing what is going on in the text not recognized by the author. It goes beyond any doubling to something more, open to something more. It is these aspects that inform our reading of Psalm 1 and Matthew 6:1–4.

Psalm 1

I begin with a discussion of binary oppositions. One of the many opposites found in the Bible is the righteous/wicked opposition. Psalm 1 operates on that and related oppositions. Even the psalm's structure is based on an opposition of the righteous and wicked. The structure is as follows:

1. Happy are those who do A (1:1–2), and unhappy are the others (i.e., wicked) who do B.
2. Those who do A prosper (1:3) and those who do B perish (1:6)

The writer of this psalm finds it self-evident that the righteous have nothing in common with the wicked. Moreover, the consequences of one's lifestyles lead either to reward or punishment. Something that is self-evident is what postmodernists refer to as presence, meaning that its truth is clear and unquestionable for the reader, hearer, or observer. The truth is present and clear for all. It is present in the sense that it is a reality. The opposition of righteous/wicked connects to a fundamental principle; consequences are associated with lifestyles. In wisdom literature, the principle often rests upon on universal laws, laws that govern how the world works without specific reference to a deity even though God stands behind this order.

This poet never once exhibits any doubt about the fate of the righteous or the wicked. Their fates are fixed. The righteous prosper in all they do while the wicked perish. The psalmist is firm and resolute in this belief. In the face of such certainty, it seems the only thing left is for the reader to enjoy the language and images of the text. The simile or comparison of the righteous to a tree with deep roots may capture the reader's imagination.[14] This thriving tree can tap into an ample water supply resulting in a healthy tree with an extensive and sufficient root system providing a firm foundation for the present and future.

This picture of fertility ("yielding its fruit in its season") and thriving (its "leaves do not wither") contrasts sharply with the imagery related to the wicked who are like dry bits of material that cover the grain. When the grain is threshed, the waste product is scattered and blown about by the wind. In short, it is clear to anyone that the righteous will thrive, and the wicked will perish. So the moral of the story is that one should follow the example of the righteous to reap happiness (1:1). In fact, it is an extremely rosy picture: "In all that they do, they prosper" (1:3). This message sets the tone for the book of Psalms. Psalm 1 is an introduction to this collection of psalms. So the instruction is crucial.

But how might one call this presence or self-evident view into question? This presence must surely be built upon suppressed doubt. In Psalm 73, that doubt is fully acknowledged. Surely the ups and downs experienced by the Israelite communities had led many to doubt this conventional wisdom. Qoheleth, the writer of the Book of Ecclesiastes, observes that in fact it is sometimes the case that the wicked prosper over the righteous (Eccl 2:14–23, 4:1–3, 6:1–6, 7:15–18, 8:10–15, 9:2–3, 9:11–12).

The amount of attention Qoheleth gives to this topic seriously undermines conventional wisdom regarding reward and punishment. He deconstructs the dichotomy between the righteous and wicked.[15] In Ecclesiastes 9:11, Qoheleth rejects any positive correlation between deed and consequence. "Again I saw that under the sun the race is not to the swift, nor the battle to the strong, nor bread to the wise, nor riches to the intelligent, nor favor to the skillful; but time and chance happen to them all." Being able to control one's fate is an illusion and thinking that the righteous will always prosper is wishful thinking.

But how does the writer of Psalm 1 recognize the righteous and wicked? The poet obviously expects readers to recognize the wicked so they can avoid following in their footsteps. They need to know the good from the bad before they can identify those who can provide proper council (1:1). Is wickedness always on the outside so that people can see it and steer away from those people? And is everyone agreed on just what constitutes wickedness? Such a view makes the individual an infallible judge even though he or she can only see the outward—that is how one behaves. In verse 5, the poet says that the "wicked will not stand in the judgment nor sinners in the congregation of the righteous." Again, the individual must be the judge. In Ecclesiastes 8:10, Qoheleth observed the wicked are going in and "out of the holy place, and [they] were praised in the city where they had done such things." Surely, those who praised them considered them righteous casting doubt on their judgments. If, then, the judgment is suspect, the whole opposition is suspect.

The tension raises the question: what distinguishes the righteous from the wicked? The writer says only that the righteous delight in the "law (Torah) of the Lord." Not only do they delight in it but they meditate upon it "day and night" (Ps 1:2) Nevertheless, there is no way for the observer to distinguish between sincere and insincere devotion. And just who can delight in and meditate upon it day and night? Is that limited to those with the means? Is it just for those who read, who have access to the law, or who have time for such activities? Of course, one can hear and remember the law, reflect upon it, and meditate on it without direct access (cf., Ps 40:8).

But who really knows or can identify the righteous? Do we as mere mortals know the heart of others? Can we know if the outward deeds reflect inward purity? The righteous person's inclusion or exclusion from the congregation (1:5) apparently depends upon human judgment. For if the wicked/sinners will not stand in the congregation, then someone must do the discerning job of excluding the other, those who do not measure up. Yet who can really measure up? Does considering oneself righteous make one self-righteous and is self-righteousness true righteousness or is it hypocrisy?

How can one recognize the wicked? Is it one who does not spend day or night meditating on the law? The wicked are also scoffers. The Hebrew participle translated "scoffers" comes from the verb meaning to scorn. Scorn derives from a sense of self-righteousness. One scorns others out of a sense of pride, and he or she may delight in the act for it may make him or her feel morally superior. The wicked then may be righteous in their eyes just as the righteous might really be wicked. Opposites may in fact not be opposite, but they depend upon human identification, recognition, and definition. Naming righteous and wickedness does not come from on high without human contamination; the naming is embedded in human language and culture. Righteousness is not something that confronts one from outside of language, but it is tied up in language. Its meaning takes shape based on conventional usage.

In short, the righteous are righteous because they are not wicked. The wicked, if one may call them wicked, may see themselves as righteous and may be righteous according to their definition. What seemed clear and certain at the beginning of Psalm 1 now becomes less certain. Does obsession with the law constitute righteousness? Is it an obsession or obedience that matters? Neither obsession nor obedience is an unqualified good; in fact, both can lead to great evil. Even obsession to the law or Torah does not ensure moral behavior or motives. If obedience is what matters most, does it matter whether the obedience is heartfelt or based on following a rule book. Is one's desire for the law sufficient as a way of excluding others who lack this extreme desire?

So is it a simple matter of being either righteous or wicked? What about those who are righteous and wicked or a little of both? Will they be spewed out because they are just lukewarm? (Rev 3:16) So where does one fit in this scenario of extremes? And how do the righteous explain not prospering. How do the wicked explain their good fortune? Such extreme distinctions may seem neat and safe, but in reality they fall apart.

The concluding two verses raise a question. The wicked people sitting in the "seat of scoffers" (1:1) cannot stand in the judgment (1:5). God watches over the righteous, but the wicked will perish. God cares for and protects the community or congregation but not the sinners. But what if the excluded ones, those who do not delight or meditate on the law day and night, make their way into the congregation of the righteous? Perhaps they can slip by the censors and fool the guards. Will they have God's protection because they gained entrance to the congregation of the righteous, which then is no longer a righteous congregation? Will they still prosper? Some may see the judgment here referring to a future judgment, but this interpretation is not by any means certain.[16] It seems more natural to interpret it within the confines of the post-exilic community. And regardless of the author's intention, the questions remain open as does the entire interpretation of this text.

Deconstruction has often been described as destructive and negative. One may see this interpretation of Psalm 1 as negative because it muddies the waters for the reader. What I have tried to do is nothing more than what other biblical texts have already done. Many texts question this conventional wisdom. I have attempted to disturb the bliss and make problems for this view, to look at it from a mundane human perspective. In fact, the view of Psalm 1 taken in isolation from other texts is dangerous because it promotes the view that one group is pure and another impure. In fact, it is never that clear cut. The wicked may have some good in them, and the good may have some bad. Extremely rare would be the one existing without the other.

Matthew 6:1–4

In the New Testament, Jesus' teachings are often deconstructive in that he turns oppositions on their head. For instance, he says, "many who are first will be last, and the last will be first" in Matthew 19:30. Notice this is not a simple reversal. It says, "many." It is not a blanket statement that the first will be last, and the last will be first. Jesus is often overturning normal expectations. In Matthew 6, Jesus calls attention to behavior that is done for others to see and praise. He urges against making a show of one's goodness for others to see and admire. This caution indicates that it is not about outward deeds. But in this instance, the logic of the text begins to unravel.

These verses appear on one level to address motives. Why does one do good things? In western thought, there is a long history of this discussion centered on the notion of altruism. Is unselfish behavior possible? I will not attempt to retrace this discussion, but the question confronts us: Can we act unselfishly? On one level, it would appear this text is calling for unselfish behavior. One is not to do good works or pray in public for the praise of others. These acts should be done in private. If one gives money for a good cause (giving alms), it should be done in extreme secrecy, so the right-hand does not know what the left hand is doing.

This wonderful expression of doing good things and avoiding the praise of others, however, is clearly undermined by the promise of reward. To act unselfishly toward another is to offer a true gift to the other. Altruism is a gift without return. Giving alms to the other, perhaps the poor and needy without strings attached is a gift to this other. Giving without the attachment of debt or gain defines what a gift is.

Derrida has written a good bit about the gift and the double bind that accompanies it. What we call gift or altruism implies something given without cost or return. The discussion of altruism is similar or corresponds to any discussion of gift. Is it possible for a person to give something to another without the attachment of debt or reward? If I give the poor person money anonymously or secretly, not letting my right hand know what my left hand is doing, is the gift safe? Is it unselfish? No one else will know and provide me with a return on my investment. However, the joy received from helping another person even in secret is a return. I can pat myself on the back and feel good about my generosity or expect my reward later in heaven.

The other aspect of this gift is debt. One of the first things we feel when we receive a gift is a debt that must be repaid. No matter how much one may protest that there are no strings attached, it is human nature to want to cancel the debt in some way by reciprocating. The student who receives help in paying for school may feel a debt to the donor. This student may try to repay the debt by doing well and making the donor feel he or she invested his or her money wisely. Debt is part of the gift, but it also cancels the gift. Consequently, one must question any gift/debt opposition.

Matthew 6 and other biblical texts illustrate this predicament. Ephesians 2:8 opposes gift to works saying "For by grace you have been saved through faith, and this is not your own doing; it is the gift of God—not the result of works, so that no one may boast." Nevertheless, it is a gift that requires something. A gift must be accepted negating its status as a gift. So is the trap of language.

Matthew 6 likewise tells one to avoid seeking rewards from others so that he or she may receive a reward from God. Here we have the public/private, worldly/other worldly oppositions. Still the private can ooze into the public and the worldly into the heavenly. The private giving is to end in heavenly reward. But some manuscripts say that "when you give alms, do not let your left hand know what your right hand is doing, so that your alms may be done in secret; and your Father who sees in secret will reward you openly" (6:3–4). In other words, some manuscripts have an additional word, "openly."

Here there are two possibilities. Either the scribe deleted the word openly from some manuscripts that now lack the word, or they added it to some manuscripts that did not have the word. So is the text saying that one will receive a reward from God that will be seen by everyone? If so, this view clearly undermines the instruction to do good in secret, which implies doing things for the right motives. But even if the original text lacked the word "openly," it is still implied. It makes a nice contrast; God who sees what one does in secret will reward him or her before everyone. Regardless, the gift is entangled in the reward.

Because of this entanglement, the gift giver puts the recipient into his or her debt and at the same time earns a double reward. He or she gains the good feeling of doing something good and, at the same time, places the other under a debt. If the debt is not repaid, the gift giver has the satisfaction of knowing that the other person is in his or her debt, a debt that can be collected if needed. The receiver by virtue of receiving the gift feels obligated to repay it.

Matthew 6, therefore, becomes entangled in this play between the ideal of gift and the reality. Even if the gift giver avoids being like the "hypocrite," he or she cannot avoid the return or profit connected to the giving. Righteousness and piety practiced for others to see and admire have no heavenly reward but only earthly ones. The praise is the reward. This behavior is the behavior of hypocrites. A hypocrite is an actor but not in a positive sense. In this passage, it refers to a person who pretends to be moral or religious.

So what is the goal or target? One is not to seek the praise of others concerning his or her acts of piety. Jesus is calling for one to be good for the right reason. Acting for heavenly rewards seems to be acceptable even when it ends with open adulation. However, the heavenly reward casts doubts on the purity or motive of the acts in the first place since they are still motivated by a return. In short, giving a good gift without return may not be possible in this life. At best, it is a goal to which one may aspire. Giving for the sake of doing the right thing and nothing more is admirable. Such extreme altruism may be beyond human ability. It also seems to be beyond the ability of human thought and language.

The main opposition in this text involves doing what is right for the sake of reward versus doing what is right for its own sake. Other oppositions include public/private and sincerity/hypocrite. But these opposites are not opposites. In the first instance, the notion of profit is solidly intact. Only the location has changed. God rewards the individual in heaven rather than on earth. And if the text contains the word "openly" the reward is earthly and heavenly. Neither does the public/private opposition stand up. Both rewards are public. The heavenly reward is either stated or implied.

But what about doing what is good for its own sake with the calculation of reward. Would that not be better? Surely this is better than pursuing a reward. Is this idea not present in this text in some way? The whole notion of doing in private indicates the notion of sincerity—doing things for the right reason. This conclusion is implied strongly by the use of the word hypocrite. Hypocrites pretend to be what they are not. So the opposite of that would be genuine. The text implies that a good person acts in accordance with his or true character not for a reward. This suggests virtue for virtue's sake with virtue becoming its own reward.

This view, however, is undermined by the text. The heavenly reward is not a gift but something that is earned. The text conforms to human expectations. The only reason to be good is for a reward. While the text may imply that genuineness is what God desires from people, this genuineness is undercut by the promise of reward in heaven.

In the book of Job, there is a rhetorical question in 1:9. The Satan asks: "Does Job fear God for nothing?" Here one could ask: Does one enter into his or her closet to pray or help the poor for nothing? The answer would seem to be no; it is all about the reward at the end. Still, this text and Job 1:9 raise the specter of more, of an excess that overflows the normal boundaries. Imagine a place where people could act not for reward but for the betterment of self and others.

I have just discussed the first 4 verses of this chapter, but this discussion continues down through verse 21 repeating the same themes. It concludes in verses 19–21 with the warning to lay up one's rewards in heaven. The reoccurring theme, therefore, makes it clear that reward is expected. What is rejected is hypocrisy and insincerity. The text does not say that one should do good only to be rewarded. The emphasis is on the opposite of hypocrisy. Even this is not really an opposite because even good and sincere people have a few hypocritical bones in their bodies. As stated, the gift is never really free, and our actions are never really selfless. We try to make good impressions and pretend to care when we do not or flatter when it is mere words. We live by a social contract that is filled with pretending. Being sincerely good and just, as well as authentic, is a goal that few ever obtain for long. Moreover, being authentic and sincere does not necessarily mean being good. One may sincerely be greedy or thoughtless.

This text points to a supreme ideal of sincerity but reflects the human situation that makes such an ideal almost impossible. In Matthew 6:1–21, the reader is pointed toward sincerity. Hypocrisy is rejected, and sincerity would seem to be the alternative. The text is firmly grounded in this earthy reality, but it may point to something much more.

NOTES

1. John D. Caputo, *Deconstruction in a Nutshell: A Conversation with Jacques Derrida*, Perspectives in Continental Philosophy, ed. John D. Caputo (New York: Fordham University Press, 1997). 9.

2. Aichele, George et al. "Poststructuralist Criticism," in *The Postmodern Bible: The Bible and Culture Collective*, (New Haven: Yale University Press, 1995), 120.

3. Black, *Dictionary of Literary Terms*, 58.

4. Madan Sarup, *An Introductory Guide to Post-Structuralism and Postmodernism*, 2d ed. (Athens: The University of Georgia Press, 1993), 33.

5. Stephen Best and Douglas Kellner, *Postmodern Theory: Critical Interrogations*, ed., Douglas Kellner in Critical Perspectives: A Guilford Series (New York: the Guilford Press 1991), 22.

6. Ruth A. Wallace and Alison Wolf, *Contemporary Sociological Theory: Continuing the Classical* Tradition, 2d ed. (Englewood Cliffs, New Jersey: Prentice Hall Inc., 1980), 201–203.

7. Sallie McFague, *Metaphorical Theology: Models of God in Religious Language*, (Philadelphia: Fortress Press, 1982), 14–29.

8. Aichele, 123–125.

9. Caputo 77–82.

10. Ibid., 80.

11. Ibid., 79.

12. Ibid., 78.

13. Ibid., 78–79.

14. McFague, 38. McFague says the simile in contrast to a metaphor lessens the "shock of the linkage through its 'like,' reducing an awareness of the dissimilarity, and hence allowing us to slip into literalistic thinking."

15. Mark Sneed, "Qoheleth as a 'Deconstructionist,'" *Old Testament Essays* 10/2 (1997): 303–311.

16. A. A. Anderson, *Psalms (1–72)*, The New Century Bible Commentary eds. Ronald E. Clements and Matthew Black, (Wm. B. Eerdmans Publ. Co.: Grand Rapids, 1972), 62–63.

Chapter Seventeen

Ideological Approaches

Ideological approaches are not based on a specific method of criticism so much as on different perspectives. In general, one could view ideology as an organized set of beliefs or ideas held by a particular person, group, or culture. These ideas would tend to shape one's general outlook on life. Liberation and feminist perspectives are two such outlooks that have received a good bit of attention in the area of biblical studies. These approaches are not methods of biblical interpretation. One could use historical methods to focus on a text from a feminist or liberation perspective. The method used such as form or source criticism might situate the passage in its historical context so that the interpreter can see if it addresses the issue of gender discrimination or oppression. Literary approaches can also be used to focus on these themes as they relate to a biblical text. So any of the methods discussed so far could be employed from a feminist or liberation perspective.

In the area of literary theory, Terry Eagleton has sought to discount the naïve view that literature has nothing to do with politics. According to Eagleton, "Literary theory has a most particular relevance to this political system [western political system]: it has helped unwittingly or not, to sustain and reinforce its assumptions."[1] Likewise, the Bible has often been caught up in political agendas, which should not be a surprise. Biblical texts have often had political significance. They are often interpreted and used to support social and personal agendas. Such use is not necessarily negative. One needs to understand that biblical interpretations are not just spiritual matters; they affect human behavior that matters in this everyday world. The use of power, therefore, is a crucial issue for ideological approaches.

Liberation perspectives call for freedom from oppression that is based on ethnicity, class, or gender. Such ideological perspectives are not merely about the religious or spiritual realm. It relates to everyday life. Biblical interpretation cannot be divorced from issues of class, gender, politics, and ethnicity. For the sake of this chapter, I focus briefly on the issue of gender.

FEMINIST BIBLICAL CRITICISM

Feminist criticism could be pursued in either a historical or literary context. Moreover, it could be used in modern or postmodern ways. A modern historical approach might seek to uncover and understand how women lived in the past along with the contributions they made to their societies. A literary approach might look at how women characters function in a literary work or how they are portrayed. This interest could be connected to a personal or group concern of readers interested in the issue of gender. Postmodern or deconstructive approaches might attempt to undermine or deconstruct stereotypical binary oppositions associated with gender such as strong/weak, public/private, or rational/emotional. In such oppositions, the latter is typically considered inferior to the former. Deconstruction seeks to unmask assumptions about gender based on these oppositions.

Discussing feminist criticism under the notion of ideology is not to imply anything negative. While Karl Marx may view approaches deemed non-scientific as an ideology, this book makes no such assumptions. Oppression in Marx's view is based on an ideology that favors the owners of the means of production over the poor and oppressed. This ideology serves to justify an oppressive system and keep the oppressed playing roles that benefit the wealthy.

Regardless of Marxist oppressor/oppressed opposition, one can see that ideology is widespread and quite human. It is part of us and colors our perceptions of the world. Our perceptions have a powerful hold on us, and I doubt we can ever completely leave them behind. The discussion below focuses on how power and oppression have adversely affected the lives of women. Traditional religious views and scriptures of the world's religions often contain a bias against women. Biblical texts typically reflect a patriarchal view of the world consistent with various traditional and pre-modern societies. These traditional views about gender continue today, particularly within certain religious communities.

Feminist criticism focuses on political, social, and economic rights of women.[2] One of its focuses is on equality. As stated above, feminist criticism is not a method; critics who are concerned with this topic have drawn upon historical, literary, and deconstructive readings. These critics believe that biblical texts are important since they may be used to justify or question gender inequality. Since many people see biblical texts as divine revelation, these texts represent a powerful source of authority for many people. This authority influences people's attitudes and actions along religious, social, cultural, political, and economic lines. Patriarchal views can have a deleterious effect preventing equality particularly in the realm of certain religious communities.

Literary critic Steven Lynn says that feminist criticism assumes that "a literary work is shaped by our reading of it."[3] One's reading, therefore, is influenced by one's own social location and gender. Gender matters in how one understands and responds to texts. A reader's understanding of a text is guided by his or her socialization. Women in patriarchal culture are taught or encouraged to read texts in certain ways.

This observation is specifically true with regard to reading biblical texts in certain religious communities. Women have not been allowed to read texts with their own interests in mind. Biblical critics need to encourage all readers, especially women, to read texts and allow their own social and political concerns to shape their response. Many women have been taught to share the patriarchal worldview to such an extent they do not read a text in this manner. One might even say that the patriarchal view has frequently been spiritualized resulting in an elevated status that is beyond question in some religious communities. In other words, one might feel that they are questioning God when they question certain readings that undermine gender equality.

The ultra-conservative or fundamentalist attitude toward the Bible has aggressively held on to traditional patriarchal biases. Fundamentalists view the Bible as the inerrant and infallible "Word of God". Such a view requires a literalistic and overly spiritualized reading of biblical texts. Such readings are roadblocks to a positive use of the Bible for women. Fundamentalists take certain passages as master texts. They superimpose the views found in certain texts on others thus finding one unitary voice in the Bible. They focus on those texts that exclude women from playing key roles in religious life.

So what might a feminist perspective contribute to the field of biblical criticism? Some feminists believe the Bible is hopelessly patriarchal. Those unwilling to abandon the study of the Bible, however, must determine what role the Bible should play for women. Should critics seek to reinterpret biblical texts from a feminist perspective? Should they try to liberate these texts from patriarchal control?[4] Should they seek counter-texts that are supportive of equality and reject patriarchal texts? Just how is one to proceed?

According to Danna Nolan Fewell, many feminist critics try to "rehabilitate the text's gender code, making the story more palatable to modern women."[5] Some focus on women's roles and female characters in the Bible. How do biblical authors define and describe feminine qualities in a work? Such an approach allows the critic to focus on the multiple perspectives associated with the text. Such perspectives include the viewpoints of the author, audiences past and present as well as the perspectives present in the text. For example, what do the characters in the text believe about the role of men and women? In the end, a feministic interpretation might try to find and interpret biblical texts that affirm gender equality.[6] Some readings may focus on female biblical characters presented in a positive light. Other approaches may identify and critique texts that demean or devalue women. Some texts may present both positive and negative views.

Elizabeth Schüssler-Fiorenza takes an interesting approach. She locates a hermeneutical key for interpreting texts.[7] She does not say that all biblical texts have the same authority or any authority at all. For her, only texts that affirm equality such as Galatians 3:28 become central and authoritative for faith.[8] On this model, the "Bible no longer functions as an authoritative source but as a *resource* for women's struggle for liberation."[9] Texts that promote inequality, therefore, have no authority; they can no longer define women's place or justify the exclusion of women from places of service. She also uses historical methods to interpret texts, and she seeks to uncover the attitudes of writers and texts with regard to issues of gender.

My personal experiences on this topic come from conservative religious environments. The feminist interpreter in many cases is swimming against the stream in this context. Many readers, male and female, need to be resocialized before they can understand the importance of pursuing a reading sensitive to women's issues and needs. Gender is part of the socially constructed world in which we live. Readers would need to allow the text and their personal experiences to be shaped by a feminist sensitivity. This process would undermine the patriarchal mindset.

Reading biblical texts is most frequently done in religious communities. These communities may need to be sensitized to the concerns of women. In some communities, beginning a dialogue about the concerns of women and their relation to biblical texts would be helpful. Often women and sympathetic men find themselves isolated in their own religious communities.

More could be said about this topic, but I now want to discuss the application. As stated above, feminist criticism is not a method comparable to form criticism or rhetorical criticism. It is more of a perspective. The concern with oppressive elements in a text might lead an interpreter to pursue readings that focus on issues of gender.

One way to read any text from a feminist perspective is to listen to what a text says or does not say regarding gender. Silence can tell us much about a text and its message. Lynn has several good strategies for this type reading.

First, the critic can consider the significance of the author's gender as well as the gender of the characters in the text.[10] The interpreter needs to pay close attention to how characters are described. Are there gender stereotypes in the text? Are these stereotypes explicit or implicit? How do they affect one's interpretation? Next, one might focus on how texts depict, change, or "complicate the place (or the construction) of women (and men) in society?"[11] What are the implications of such depictions, alterations, or complications? Finally, male readers might try reading the work as a woman?[12]

This imaginary leap may help one be more open-minded. I use these and other strategies in my brief discussion of Proverbs 31:10–31 and Galatians 3:28–29.

PROVERBS 31:10–31

In this discussion, I focus on the author's description of the good wife to determine its significance for the interpretation of this passage. The interpretation of this passage discovers both positive and negative aspects on the topic of gender. It provides a positive role model for women in some respects. On the other hand, it functions to uphold the traditional family structure. The woman's worth in this text is primarily related to family life even though it takes her into the public sphere.

Many people are familiar with the text about this ideal housewife. It is an acrostic poem. For many, this poem presents a positive view of a wife who is strong and highly efficient. She is industrious and always looking out for the welfare of her family. This text begins with the question: A capable wife who can find? According to this description, this wife is rare. The Hebrew adjective translated "capable" by the NRSV is ḥayīl, which refers to her as a wife of strength, power, and efficiency. Certainly this wife is all of those things. She is a strong and influential woman who brings great benefit to others, primarily her husband. Her use of power is "neither oppressive nor exploitative nor manipulative."[13]

The description is consistently glowing from a traditional sense. She is a treasure that is "more precious than jewels" (Prv 31:10). Wisdom, portrayed as a woman in Proverbs, is also described as a treasure (Prv 3:15). This link connects the two characters and adds weight to the worth of this wife.[14] Therefore, her husband has complete trust in her. She works on behalf of her family night and day. Her life is spent in service to others. She gives to the poor and needy (31:20), she provides for her household, (31:21, 27), and she is wise (31:26). Her husband is well respected and well-known because of her; he takes his "seat among the elders of the land" and his status is greatly enhanced (31:23, 31). It is hard to imagine a more positive description.

And one last thing, she has "high social and economic standing (vv. 21f.), [and her] . . . husband occupies a position of importance within the community (v. 23). She appears to make business decisions independently (vv. 16, 18)."[15] We can see, therefore, that she has power and status. She has truly excelled. "'Many women have done excellently, but you surpass them all.'" Letting "her works praise her in the city gates" connects her to Lady Wisdom in Proverbs 1:21 who speaks at the city gate.[16] So the text has nothing but good things to say about her, and it also acknowledges the worth and value of other women as well.

This model wife, however, is an ideal of a patriarchal society. Descriptions of women in Proverbs are mostly negative portraying women in positions of subordination. Women are potential snares, and, as such, they pose a danger for men. The Hebrew adjective zārāʰ meaning strange describes a woman who is a threat to the family. This strange/peculiar woman is one who is an outsider. She could be a foreigner but not necessarily so. She could be a stranger to the household or family. The NRSV and the RSV translate the word strange to mean loose. In Proverbs 6:24–29, the woman in question is a neighbor's wife. The good wife, on the contrary, is of high value to her husband. [17]

In short, the poem on the ideal wife and the Book of Proverbs as a whole are somewhat mixed in their depiction of women. Unmarried or unfaithful women, as well as foreign women, are a threat to the life of a man. The poem of the ideal wife is an ideal of a patriarchal society. Nevertheless, this ideal wife is portrayed as one who has some power and is a strong leader. She commands servants and takes total control of the household. The husband may reap much of the rewards, but she is a quite impressive woman.

Her connection to lady wisdom enhances her status. Lady wisdom is an extraordinary character in the book in Proverbs 1:20–33, 3:13–18, 4:6–9, 8:1–36. It is altogether possible that lady wisdom was an Israelite goddess. [18] Wisdom (ḥokmaʰ) is a feminine noun and is personified as a woman. It is reasonable to believe that many Israelites were not in reality monotheists. Many would have accepted the existence of other gods, and it is entirely possible that wisdom or ḥokmaʰ reflects a history where she was not just a personification but a divine figure. Proverbs, at least in part, presents a positive view of the feminine.

GALATIANS 3:28–29

These verses are important for understanding Paul's attitude toward women. For many, Paul is seen as an enemy of women. This view of Paul, in part, relates to the discussion of authorship. If Paul is not, as most scholars believe, the author of the Pastoral letters (1 and 2 Timothy and Titus), then the view of Paul is more positive. Fiorenza and others have reassessed Paul's view on women. Fiorenza's discussion of Galatians 3:28–29 is important for an understanding of Paul's attitudes on the subject.

This short passage concludes a discussion of the Galatians who have turned to a "different gospel" (Gal 1:6). The different gospel is likely associated with a "circumcision faction" (2:13). In Galatians 2:15–3:27, Paul makes it clear that one is "justified by faith" and not by "works of the law" (2:16). Galatians 3:1–27 continues this discussion. Those who believe and have faith are descendants of Abraham and share in the blessing (cf., Gen

15:1–6) given to him by God (3:7–9, 15–18). The law served a purpose, but now that Christ has come, the law is no longer necessary (3:23–26). Verse 27 leads to the subject of baptism: "As many of you as were baptized into Christ have clothed yourselves with Christ."

The discussion of verses 28–29 draws upon the essay of Fiorenza. In this essay, Fiorenza argues that Galatians 3:28 is part of a pre-Pauline baptismal formula. Paul takes this formula and modifies it a little. The original formula reads as follows:

i. 3:26a For you are all children of God
ii. 3:27a For as many of you are baptized into Christ have put on Christ
     b have put on Christ
iii. 3:28a There is neither Jew nor Greek
     b There is neither slave nor free
     c There is neither male or female
iv. For you are all one[19]

There is a debate over the meaning of this pre-Pauline verse. Many exegetes have spiritualized Galatians 3:28 arguing that this verse relates only to a spiritual sense and does not address the role of women in church, politics, or society.[20] Fiorenza strongly rejects such views. Based on her interpretation, "no structures of dominance can be tolerated."[21] She further concludes that "Gal. 3:28 is, therefore, best understood as a communal Christian self-definition rather than a statement about the baptized individual."[22]

In its pre-Pauline form, baptism not circumcision becomes the primary rite of initiation into the church.[23] Therefore, women can become full members. A new kinship in Christ becomes the basis of the Christian movement. People who are biologically unrelated are now brothers and sisters in Christ. Galatians 3:28 rejects any distinctions based on ethnicity (Greek nor Jew), class (slave nor free) and gender (male and female).

Galatians 3:28–29 is key to understanding other passages in Paul's letters about women such as 1 Corinthians 7:1–16, 11:2–16, 14:33b–36. Many of the instructions concerning women in these passages can be seen as "practical elaborations on Gal 3:28c."[24] Fiorenza's examination of these passages concludes that Paul's instructions are to wives and not women in general. Paul's instructions to women in 1 Corinthians 11 are referring to unmarried or widowed women. By contrast, his instructions in 1 Corinthians 14:33b–36 address wives only. Moreover, these verses are probably not from Paul at all. They seem to be an interruption of Paul's thought, and they were likely added by an editor. I Corinthians 14:34 says "women should be silent in the churches. For they are not permitted to speak, but should be subordinate, as the law also says." This statement is clearly inconsistent with 1 Corinthians 11:4–7 where women and men are instructed on how to pray and prophesy.

The inconsistency is resolved, however, if Paul's instructions in 14:34 are addressed to wives and not women in general.[25]

To be blunt, one must face the fact that biblical texts are largely patriarchal. Biblical writers are shaped by the views of their day. Historical and literary approaches can help explain when authors and passages reflect traditional patriarchal views and when they endorse gender equality. Reader response and deconstruction open up other possible readings. Feminist critics may apply any of the approaches discussed in this book to the issue of gender. The discussion above has argued that even though some texts are patriarchal, counter voices provide a different perspective. While feminist readings are needed, every reading needs to be sensitive to issues of gender and power.

NOTES

1. Terry Eagleton, *Literary Theory: An Introduction*, 2nd ed. (Minneapolis: University of Minnesota Press), 171.

2. Danna Nolan Fewell, "Reading the Bible Ideologically," in *To Each Its Own Meaning: An Introduction to Biblical Criticisms and Their Application*, ed. Stephen R. Haynes and Steven L. McKenzie (Louisville: The Westminster Press, 1999), 268.

3. Steven Lynn, *Texts and Contexts: Writing About Literature with Critical Theory*, 4th ed (New York: Pearson, 2005), 31.

4. Fewell, 270–279.

5. Ibid., 272.

6. Ibid., 270–272

7. Elizabeth Schüssler-Fiorenza, *Bread Not Stone: The Challenge of Feminist Biblical Interpretation*, (Boston: Beacon Press, 1984), 6–7

8. Elizabeth Schüssler-Fiorenza, *A Feminist Theological Reconstruction of Christian Origins: In Memory of Her* (New York: Crossroads, 1994), 205–241.

9. Schüssler-Fiorenza, Bread Not Stone, 14.

10. Lynn, 31.

11. Ibid.

12. Ibid.

13. Dianne Bergant, *Israel's Wisdom Literature: A Liberation—Critical Reading*, (Minneapolis: Fortress Press, 1997), 91.

14. Ibid., 92.

15. Ibid., 92.

16. Ibid., 93.

17. Ibid.

18. David Penchansky, "Is Hokmah an Israelite Goddess, and What Should We Do About It? in *Postmodern Interpretations of the Bible: A Reader* ed., A.K. M. Adams (St Louis: Chalice Press, 2001), 81–92; Bergant, 98. Bergant still sees wisdom's characterization as a "device to further male objectives.

19. Fiorenza, *In Memory of Her*, 208.

20. Ibid., 207.

21. Ibid., 231.

22. Ibid.

23. Ibid., 210.

24. Ibid., 219.

25. Ibid., 230–231.

Chapter Eighteen

Theopoetics and the Renewing Power of Metaphor

By Robert A. White[1]

"There are some truths that are too big to enter by the narrow slit of reason."
Plato
"The heart has reasons that reason does not know." Pascal

Four children had been displaced by the war. They found themselves in a strange and unfamiliar place. In a spirit of adventure, play and imagination they explore this large and old home where they now live. While exploring the house and playing hide and seek with her siblings, Lucy entered a room that had nothing in it but a large wardrobe. Lucy opened the wardrobe and pushed past the coats that hung in the closet into the snowy woods of Narnia and a great adventure begins.

Of course, the reader will recognize this as the beginning of C.S. Lewis's *The Lion, the Witch and the Wardrobe* from the *Chronicles of Narnia*. Discovering theopoetics and the renewing power of metaphor is like opening the door of that wardrobe and walking into an entirely different world or at least a new way of seeing and interpreting the world.

Theopoetics opens the door to a new way of seeing and understanding the world around us—giving us new lenses to see beyond a one-dimensional, reductionist approach to life. This is especially true when applied to religious language.

WHAT IS THEOPOETICS?

Theopoetics is an interdisciplinary approach applied to theology that draws from the disciplines of postmodern philosophy, narrative theology, and literary criticism. The implications of theopoetics for theology are significant and exciting. Theopoetics suggests that instead of trying to develop a scientific theory or a purely rationalistic approach to God, we allow room for mystery and imagination. Instead of developing a systematic approach to theology, we are urged to embrace a more poetic approach. Theopoetics is not interested in inventing another system of theology but in discovering the beauty of the transcendent.

Theopoetics has a great potential since it openly embraces mystery and questions, uses narrative and poetry, values parable and prayer, merges imagination and faith in ways that allow one to see and understand things differently. We are invited to explore the vastness, mystery, otherness and the glory of creation. Theopoetics is a call to reclaim the potential of imagination and language.

The present moment in history seems to recognize the gifts that theopoetics can offer. Amos Wilder says: "A creative theopoetics is called for, therefore, not only to vitalize a traditional theology but also to relate our Christian experience to the new sensibility of our time and its images and cults."[2]

THE PLACE OF METAPHOR IN THEOPOETICS

One of the primary ways to use theopoetics in our use of language is to unleash the renewing power of metaphor. Metaphor offers a chance to recognize the familiar and obvious yet also pointing to a reality or possibility not yet realized. Seeing beneath the facts of the obvious into the mythological nature of truth, metaphor becomes the door into the heart; it becomes a way of knowing what the heart knows.

Metaphor allows us to take religious language seriously without reducing it to literalism. When metaphor is overlooked or dismissed, it is easy to turn the Bible into an idol. Without metaphor, the text is concretized, and we are told that there is only one way to read and understand a particular passage.

The understanding and use of metaphor not only enables the reader to resist a one-dimensional understanding of the text, it also calls for imagination in the interpretive act. Metaphor requires a symbolic sensibility.

While metaphor has been taken more seriously recently in philosophical and theological discussions, the use of metaphor is often overlooked and relegated to the language of the poets. The real challenge for postmodern theology is to recognize and understand the importance of metaphor. Metaphor can help people make sense of their world by connecting the ancient story of faith with the postmodern experience. Theopoetics employs metaphorical theology as a way to help make the connection between the biblical text and lived experience.

A Seismic Shift—Postmodernity, Theopoetics and the Work of Deconstruction

We have experienced a seismic shift in human history—from the modern era of history into postmodernity. This change is like living through an earthquake. The seismic shift has left many things in a heap of rubble. David Aubrey described this prevailing sense of uncertainty that is characteristic of our times: "In short, deconstruction—a feeling of the center collapsing is what the Germans called the Zeitgeist (spirit of the time)."[3]

The collapsing of the center and its recurring aftershocks create a spirit of fear and hopelessness for many. If we have already experienced the worst of the seismic changes associated with moving from one era to another, then we certainly are left to live with the aftershocks.

The ground we stand on seems much less secure than before. The crumbling of once secure institutions and the fast pace of change have created an atmosphere of insecurity. It is as if the center has collapsed, and we are called on to make sense of what is left. Confusion and uncertainty are common.

The effects of a collapsing center can be felt especially among people of faith. People react differently when faced with change and crisis. Some withdraw or retreat into the past, holding on to what they believe or have been taught. The drastic changes occurring in our time are threatening for many people who claim to be people of faith. The move from belief to fundamentalism and fanaticism can be traced in the world of religion. This tendency to literalize the language of faith has led to incredulous and divisive claims by religious people. These claims continue to polarize and divide us.

The other reaction to the seismic shifts is the reluctance if not refusal for many to live inside a religious system or structure. Instead of retreating inside the walls of literalism, this approach calls into question all truth claims.

The collapsing of the center and the recurring aftershocks have left institutions and ideologies, once believed to be invincible, shaken and vulnerable. This aftermath of the collapsing of the center has certainly impacted the religious and theological world. If the structures are still standing, they are suspect, and many refuse to live inside the walls of a theological system or institution they once called home.

The potential damage of these tremors of a changing time requires that every structure and idea be tested for its structural soundness. Nothing goes without testing in postmodernity. The task of checking the reliability and trustworthiness of a system or structure is the value and work of deconstruction.

The truth claims that are often made in the name of religion remind us of the importance of deconstruction. Postmodernity insists that we acknowledge that all truth is relative, subjective and partial. This discipline known as deconstruction becomes the first reality to deal with in theopoetics. Deconstruction is constantly questioning what is real and true. In postmodernity, we are often challenged to see there is no such thing as absolute or universal truth. If there is a truth, it is always with the lowercase "t."

Speaking of the value of deconstruction, John Caputo wrote:

> That is a methodological irony, a strategy of "reversal," meant to expose the contingency of what we like to call the "Truth," with a capital T-deconstruction being a critique of long robed totalizers of a capitalized Truth, of T-totalers of all kinds. I have no intention of sending that strategy into early retirement or claiming that it has outlived its usefulness. We will need that strategy as long as there is hypocrisy, as long as there are demagogues pounding on the table that they have the Truth, which means forever."[4]

Deconstruction is an important and essential discipline for postmodern theology. Otherwise, we forget that all systems and structures are human constructs. They were developed and promoted by someone and that someone has a particular perspective and agenda. All structures and systems are partial and temporary. An effort to make a system or structure as the only way to view God or read and interpret the Bible leads to a misplaced faith. We end up deifying systems of belief or structures of interpretation and miss the God who can make this word living and active. We end up worshipping the idols of systems to use biblical language.

Theopoetics begins with an understanding that any theological claim to truth is subjective and partial. This is the benefit of deconstruction. Frederich Nietzsche reminds all of us that we approach and understand life from our own perspective. Any truth we claim can only be made for ourselves. Each of us has our own perspective. This perspective shapes the way we see the world around us and our understanding of truth. Each of us brings our own perspective and deconstruction is the way that perspective is recognized if not revealed. There are no universal truths; there are no absolute theological systems.

This is especially true when it comes to religious language. The language of faith is metaphoric by necessity—especially in our references to God. Any effort to literalize religious language attempts to reduce mystery to formula. Theopoetics calls us to pay attention not only to our choice of language but how we read and interpret the words on a page.

Theopoetics begins with the recognition that all systems and structures are human constructs. This is recognition that at best any system is partial and temporary. There are no creeds or confessions that have the final say. Religious language reduced to the literalism of systems and creeds becomes an opening to the world of parable and poetry, narrative, hymn, and prayer. This refusal to concretize the metaphors and literalize the language calls for deconstructive work.

Interpretation and Imagination in Theopoetics

Change has created an atmosphere of fear and suspicion that left many trying to latch onto what they have always perceived to be true. Deconstruction has left many wondering if there is anything to hold onto at all. The tendency for many is to literalize the religious language of a text and attempt to hold on to one interpretation. The sentiment is often expressed in an either/or fashion with the text. If it is not literal, then it cannot be true according to this perspective.

This approach has added fuel to the fire of interpreting the Bible. People hold dogmatically to their understanding without a willingness to be open. This is a one-dimensional and reductionist approach. This approach has no room for imagination in the work of interpretation.

The tendency to take everything in scripture literally has created a crisis of interpretation for people of faith. This crisis of interpretation is fueled by the insistence that everything true and real, especially in the Bible, be taken literally. Truth is relegated to a system of interpretation as opposed to being a living reality. The tendency to read and reduce the mystery of faith to a set of propositions that can be charted is leading to the starvation of the soul and the impoverishment of the imagination.

This crisis has been the cause of debate and division, especially among the church. Of course, most people who hold this literalistic view are fairly selective of the passage they choose to take literally. In Alabama, a local news reporter did a story on snake handlers and announced that they believe the Bible and interpret it literally. It was a fairly convincing report as they held the snakes. Yet even among the most ardent proponents of biblical literalism, one discovers an inconsistent and selective approach.

The real danger that this approach presents is that truth is always literal. The language is flat and one dimensional. This view claims simplicity on this side of complexity. It does not take into account that truth is a living reality and cannot be reduced to a system or to a doctrinal proposition. Truth can be probed, explored, challenged, and embraced. It cannot, however, fit neatly into any theological system. The other problem that exists with theological systems is that they are human constructs—anything human in construct is only partial and temporary at best.

This is the difference in a one-dimensional viewpoint of the world around us and a three-dimensional view. Increasingly, we see a desire for more than one-dimensional understanding. Most movie theaters now provide a 3-D experience. Theopoetics encourages us to move from a one-dimensional viewpoint to a 3-D understanding. We are called on to learn the value of 3-D when it comes to the language of faith.

Oliver Wendell Holmes once said; "I wouldn't give a fig for the simplicity on this side of simplicity, but I would give my right arm for simplicity on the far side of complexity." On this side of complexity, religious language is often concertized and one dimensional, as though truth can only be explained in concrete terms. It fails to work through the complexity to reclaim some sense of simplicity. This is often referred to as the second naïveté.

Theopoetics challenges us to move beyond this first simplicity to the second naïveté—especially in our use of religious language. Through the use of religious language, theopoetics can help us consider the improbable by igniting the imagination.

If faith can be reduced to a system of belief or interpretation, then all one has to do is remember the points. We can summarize faith to the five points or seven theological concepts or whatever the particular view calls for. This allows us to interpret and explain without ever having to wrestle with the complexities of life and of the text. If religious language and scripture are reduced to a literal view, the potential for new possibilities is forfeited for the security of familiarity.

Creating New Possibilities—The Potential of Metaphor in Theopoetics

The breaking down of the Cartesian worldview of modernity has left a philosophical and theological void that metaphor is uniquely qualified to address. James Miller reminds us: "For Descartes, the cosmos was divided into two radically different substantial domains; that of matter, and that of mind or spirit."[5]

The dualism created by this worldview has crumbled in the contemporary world. Postmodern writers seek to bridge the gap between the physical world and the world of mind and spirit. Metaphor is capable of assisting in this effort. The bridging of the gap between mind and heart as well as reason and spirit requires an imaginative act. This bridge is the real value of theopoetics and the use of metaphor.

Sally McFague reminds us:

> The old Cartesian dichotomy between mind and body, objective and subjective, thought and feeling is not relevant to a radically metaphorical pattern of human movement and growth; human beings are organisms, not machines, and like other organisms they 'grope,' but in a special way, a conscious way, which means that their ability to make novel connections and associations within their familiar environment, dislocating it sufficiently so that the old, the stale, the ordinary, 'what is ' is seen in a new light as what might be.[6]

She warns that "the main difficulty with post-Cartesian epistemologies is that they do not figure in the figurer; they split mind and body, reason and imagination, subject and object, nature and history and end with something other and less than *human* knowing."[7] Indeed, theopoetics takes into account the human knowing—the heart knows things the mind will never understand.

Metaphor is uniquely qualified in helping create a new hearing. Walter Bruggemann called for the use of a more poetic form of speech. "By poetry, I do not mean rhyme, rhythm or meter, but a language that moves like Bob Gibson's fastball, that jumps at the right moment, that breaks open old worlds with surprise, abrasion and pace. The use of metaphor has the ability to break open old worlds with surprise, abrasion and pace and create a new hearing."[8]

Metaphor makes things happen by comparing and contrasting two different subjects. Metaphor takes two subjects and combines them in unusual and unlikely ways that develop interest and sometimes creates new shades of meaning. New understandings can be generated by examining the similarities and differences with respect to metaphors.

In spite of the hardships imposed on those living in a world where the center has collapsed, the contemporary person is faced with unparalleled opportunity to rediscover the use of metaphor and the value of theopoetics. The changing landscape, what is being referred to as the postmodern age has led many on a search for a deeper personal and spiritual life. The renewed interest in spirituality, angels, and life after death are just some of the indicators of the search many are undertaking to find a more meaningful life. This spiritual quest creates tremendous opportunities for us to explore the meaning and power of metaphor as it relates to theopoetics.

The possibility of igniting the imagination and stirring the soul of the listener exists with the use of metaphor. A metaphor can help those who have heard it all before hear an old and familiar word in a new and refreshing manner. Frederick Buechner reminds us that religious language often grows stale. "Words, especially religious words, words that have to do with the depth of things—get tired and stale the way people do."[9] So often this staleness of language becomes a barrier. This happens when we forget the metaphoric nature of religious language. Words and concepts are concretized and turned into creeds and systems that allow no room for imagination. This not only makes our language stale but also robs the words of their potential power to cross the boundaries of time and space and speak to the present moment.

McFague explains the potential of metaphor in the following statement: "The poet sets one metaphor against another and hopes the sparks set off by the juxtaposition will ignite something in the mind as well."[10] The tension generated by comparing and contrasting metaphors often creates new ways of looking at the world. A new reality of understanding can emerge from the tension created by an unusual combination.

The comparison and contrast of "this" with "that" can open new vistas of understanding. "This" may be considered the principal subject and often represents the secular, common, and earthy." "That" can be viewed as the subsidiary subject which points to the complex, ambiguous and unknown. "This and that" are words or subjects which retain their normal meaning but are used in a unique way that creates an unusual combination. The unusual combination of "this and that" produces opportunities for new understanding.

The exploring of the likeness and otherness of two subjects can reveal a new understanding when reflected and probed. An example of this can be seen in the metaphorical use of "death as a door." Occasionally, one hears of someone being at "death's door." This metaphor is filled with potential for a new and different understanding of death. From the perspective of life, death's door seems to be the door of exit. From the viewpoint of eternity, one could say death's door is the door that opens into eternity. This kind of comparison/contrast is certainly a part of the Ezekiel passage that we look at later in the chapter.

Theopoetics attempts to explore and create new possibilities by maximizing the potential of metaphor. When we discuss metaphor, we could also talk about poetry, parable, and narrative.

Making the Connection—Theopoetics Utilizing Metaphor

The nature of metaphor to take the known (present situation) and combine it with the unknown (not yet) creates a moment filled with possibility. In the comparison and contrast of the metaphor, the hearer is called upon to consider the connection with their own experience. This recognition often comes as a surprise—shock.

McFague challenges us to recognize the evocative nature of metaphor: "Metaphoric insight never takes us 'out of ourselves' but it returns us to ourselves with new insight; it is not a mystical, static, intellectual vision, but an insight into how ordinary human life and events can be made to move beyond themselves by connecting them to this and that."[11]

Again, She also states that "reality is created through this incredibly complex process of metaphorical leaps, of seeing this as that; we use what we notice about one thing to 'name' (describe, call up, evoke, elicit) another thing where we notice something of the same, and hence for the first time we see it that new way."[12] This became the reality for those in exile who heard Ezekiel's vision for the first time. There was a shock of recognition.

Theopoetics at its best takes the known and familiar combining metaphors in ways that help us make new connections. McFague writes: "What poets do is to take our literal words, our dead metaphors, and by combining them in new ways, make them capable of expressing new insight."[13]

Pointing Beyond the Obvious

The real potential of theopoetics is to look beyond the obvious, to envision the possibility of something more. It demands that we never accept things as they are without considering the what—if question. What if there is more than meets the eye? What if there is more than one way to read and interpret a text?

Metaphor enables us to point beyond the obvious in a way that stirs the heart and mind and moves us in the direction of hope. Theopoetics encourages us to look beyond the obvious to new possibilities.

In short, theopoetics engages in a poetic approach that can enrich religious and spiritual sensitivities. Sometimes the heart knows things the mind can never comprehend. It invites us to let go of our systems and limited vision of simply what makes sense and is in front of us. We are encouraged to see beyond the obvious into the sometimes hidden depth and beauty of things.

APPLIED THEOPOETICS—CAN THESE BONES LIVE?

This part of the chapter attempts to demonstrate the renewing power of metaphor in the area of theopoetics. The focus is on Ezekiel the prophet. This section explores theopoetics and the potential of metaphor through the biblical story of Ezekiel's vision. It is a vision of a valley filled with dry bones found in Ezekiel 37. The structure of the project emerges from the movement of the biblical text beginning with chaos and despair moving eventually to a re-imagined potential.

Surveying the Landscape—A Collapsing Center (Deconstruction)

> The hand of the Lord came upon me, and he brought me out by the spirit of the Lord and set me down in the middle of a valley; it was full of bones. ²He led me all round them; there were very many lying in the valley, and they were very dry. (Ez 37:1–2, NRSV)

As distant and strange as this passage may sound it is fairly descriptive of our times. The view of life both inside and outside the church is similar to the view Ezekiel had as he surveyed the valley of dry bones. Like Israel in Ezekiel's time, people today are confronted with the breaking down of all that is familiar and face the challenges of finding their way in a strange new land.

Ezekiel's vision begins with a survey of the landscape and what he saw was the devastation of a world he had been familiar with. The bones of Israel's hopes were scattered on the canyon floor. What Ezekiel saw was the scattered bones of Israel's army crushed in battle. The defeat in battle left Israel's future uncertain at best. It was as if the center had collapsed, and there was no certain place to stand. The defeat had called into question not only the political future but the theological foundation of Israel.

Ezekiel's words convey a sense of desperation if not despair. The valley was scattered with bones, and they were very dry. The emphasis seems to be placed on an uncertain future. This existential reality for Israel created a crisis of faith.

Considering the Improbable—A Crisis of Interpretation

> He said to me, 'Mortal, can these bones live?' I answered, 'O Lord God, you know.' Then he said to me, 'Prophesy to these bones, and say to them: O dry bones, hear the word of the Lord. Thus says the Lord God to these bones: I will cause breath to enter you, and you shall live. I will lay sinews on you, and will cause flesh to come upon you, and cover you with skin, and put breath in you, and you shall live; and you shall know that I am the Lord.' (Ez 37: 3–6)

Ezekiel and Israel were called upon to consider the improbable, can these bones live? Bones do not live; the very mention of bones implies death and hopelessness. The merging of the word bones with live in the same sentence creates an unlikely union that calls for a new hearing. When these two words are put together, they become a metaphor for the resurrection and renewal of the people of Israel. Ezekiel's metaphor ignites Israel's imagination and resurrects their hope.

The question before the prophet demands that he employs the power of metaphor. If Ezekiel had taken the question in a literal sense, this vision would be impossible. The words of God pertaining to the dry bones open the imagination and possibility for life beyond the present crisis.

Theopoetics finds meaning and power in the possibility of the metaphor. When the two words—bones and living—are brought together, a new possibility is envisioned. This possibility would not exist in a literalist approach.

The only way to ignite the imagination in ways that would look beyond the obvious is to allow the metaphor to speak. "Can these bones live? The obvious answer is no. Yet theopoetics invites us to consider the improbable. We are asked to look beyond the obvious.

Creating New Possibilities—A Potential Rediscovered

So I prophesied as I had been commanded; and as I prophesied, suddenly there was a noise, a rattling, and the bones came together, bone to its bone. I looked, and there were sinews on them, and flesh had come upon them, and skin had covered them; but there was no breath in them. Then he said to me, 'Prophesy to the breath, prophesy, mortal, and say to the breath:* Thus says the Lord God: Come from the four winds, O breath and breathe upon these slain, that they may live.' I prophesied as he commanded me, and the breath came into them, and they lived, and stood on their feet, a vast multitude. (Ez 37:7–10)

How does one offer hope to those who feel that their lives have crumpled around them? That is the challenge that theopoetics takes seriously. The times call for a rediscovery of the potential of metaphor to help create possibility and instill hope.

The question put to Ezekiel is an example of the potential of theopoetics and the power of metaphor. "Can these bones live?" How can the words bones and live be used in the same phrase to inquire about a situation? The combining of these two words creates an unusual union that calls for a new hearing. Bones do not live; the very mention of bones implies death and hopelessness. Yet, when these two words are put together, they become a metaphor for the resurrection and renewal of the people of Israel. Captivity in Babylon had dashed Israel's dreams and destroyed their hope. From the ruins of exile the prophet brings a word of renewal and hope. Ezekiel employs a metaphor to ignite Israel's imagination and resurrect their hope.

The power of metaphor can be seen in the text—"I prophesied as he commanded me, and the breath came into them, and they lived, and stood on their feet, a vast multitude." Ezekiel is told not only to prophesy to scattered bones but also to the spirit/breath. As he prophesies, a new potential comes into view. What had been a hopeless situation now becomes a new possibility.

Making the Connection—The Shock of Recognition

> Then he said to me, 'Mortal, these bones are the whole house of Israel. They say, "Our bones are dried up, and our hope is lost; we are cut off completely." (Ez 37:11)

Israel experienced the power of Ezekiel's vision as they made the connection between their experiences of exile with the valley of bones. As they considered the devastation and hopelessness of that valley with the words of the prophet, something deep within them stirred. They knew what it meant to be cut off from hope. As they considered Ezekiel's vision, the connection was eventually made—perhaps before Ezekiel pointed it out to them. In the moment of understanding, there was a shock of recognition.

Theopoetics invites us to not only consider the improbable but also makes connections that we may not have seen otherwise. That is certainly true of this text. Israel had lost hope in the despair of exile and declared, "Our bones are dried up, and our hope is lost." The power of the connection made is the recognition that the dry bones had become living bones. As they heard the words of the prophet, there came a moment where something in their heart stirred that their mind could not comprehend.

Pointing Beyond the Obvious—A Renewal of Hope

> Then he said to me, 'Mortal, these bones are the whole house of Israel. They say, "Our bones are dried up, and our hope is lost; we are cut off completely." Therefore prophesy, and say to them, Thus says the Lord God: I am going to open your graves, and bring you up from your graves, O my people; and I will bring you back to the land of Israel. And you shall know that I am the Lord, when I open your graves, and bring you up from your graves, O my people. I will put my spirit within you, and you shall live, and I will place you on your own soil; then you shall know that I, the Lord, have spoken and will act, says the Lord.' (Ez 37: 11–14)

When one dies, he or she is dead. That is obvious. The facts are the facts. The obvious is hard to ignore—so hard that many will never see beyond it. But what if? What if death is not the end? What if? What if death became a doorway to envision something more—something beyond the obvious?

Physical death is not the only death we experience. All of us experience many deaths across a lifetime. The deaths of a relationship or a job are obvious examples. Death is typically viewed as the end.

Theopoetics invites us to explore religious language and the use of imagination as a way to see what could be. Imagination empowers us to see beyond death to the possibilities of something new about to be birthed. This something may be completely unforeseeable.[14]

This becomes the potential of theopoetics—to point beyond the obvious, to envision the possibility of something more, to ask what if. Ezekiel's vision does exactly that for the people of Israel. Ezekiel takes what has become a common phrase that grows out of the obvious context of exile and reframed it in the potential of metaphor. Ronald E. Clements observes that a "reader sensitive to the vitality of speech and to the relationship between word and picture will find that Ezekiel is here able to turn a popular saying into a memorable vision."[15] Ezekiel's vision points beyond the obvious despair of the people in exile. This is the power of metaphor and the purpose of theopoetics.

This Ezekiel passage envisions a new reality, pointing beyond the obvious. Israel felt hopeless in exile, cut off from any chance of survival. They considered themselves dead as a people—as those with no hope. Ezekiel announces an amazing thing—dead bones are raised to new life! Clements reminds us: "Yet standing against this hopelessness is the ability of the prophet to awaken a belief in hope, established on an awareness of God's reality and power."[16] He also notes: "It is hard to find any more sharply defined and exalted word picture of the power of human speech than that given here."[17]

NOTES

1. A version of this chapter was presented at the American Academy of Religion November 2015.

2. Amos Wilder, *Theopoetics* (Lima, Ohio: Academic Renewal Press, 2001), 7.

3. David Awbrey, *"Dawn of the Postmodern,"* *The Huntsville Times,* Sunday, January 3, 1993, sec. C, p. 1.

4. John Caputo, *What Would Jesus Deconstruct?* (Grand Rapids: Baker Academic Press, 2007), 30.

5. James Miller, *"The Emerging Postmodern World,"* in *Postmodern Theology,* (San Francisco: Harper and Row, 1989), 8.

6. Sallie McFague, *Speaking in Parables* (Philadelphia: Fortress Press, 1975), 58.

7. Ibid.

8. Walter Brueggemann, *Finally Comes the Poet* (Minneapolis: Fortress Press, 1989), 3.

9. Frederick Buechner, *Telling the Truth* (New York: Harper and Row, 1977), 17.

10. McFague, *Speaking in Pararbles,* 39.

11. Ibid., 48–49.

12. Ibid., 52.

13. Ibid., 50.

14. John Caputo editor with commentary, *Deconstruction in a Nutshell: A Conversation with Jacques Derrida* (New York: Fordham University Press, 1997), 156–164.

15. Ronald E. Clements, *Ezekiel* (Louisville: John Knox Press, 1996) 166.

16. Ibid., 166.

17. Ibid.

Chapter Nineteen

Reading Responsibly

To begin, I feel obliged to say that my conclusions largely stem from a Judeo-Christian perspective.[1] I do not claim to speak as an expert ethicist or philosopher. Neither am I trying to be neutral or unbiased in this chapter. My argument is not an appeal to reason and rationality, although I would see my argument as reasonable. In a sense, it is more of a plea or an appeal to the heart as well as to the head. I do, however, value reason and objectivity. The discussion below attempts to be sensible, pragmatic, and as objective as possible.

So what would a responsible reading look like? This question is complex since there cannot be one simple answer to the question. One might argue that the text is the one thing all readers have in common, but that is not really true. The text is based on copies of earlier manuscripts that stretch back over long periods of time. The manuscripts are not all the same. When variations occur, there is often no way to determine with absolute certainty which manuscripts or readings are most reliable and faithful to the originals. Additionally, the text most people read is a translation of ancient manuscripts into their own language. Just comparing different translations of the same text is enough to show that we are not all reading the same words on the page.

As a result, all readings are provisional. The search for one and only one proper interpretation of a text is futile. Still, the text is the starting point for all approaches. Even historical critics who seek the author's intent are dependent upon finding that intent in the text. Obviously, without the text there would be no author or literary features for one to discuss.

Reading is a human activity that entails making sense of a text (i.e., interpretation). It also entails making decisions about a Hebrew or Greek text that could contain errors. That we may be wrong does not make a reading irresponsible, just human. The tasks of making sense and making decisions are part of every reading. And, there is always the chance of being mistaken. When we encounter a text where there is more than one possible reading we have to decide which is more likely. The same is true when making decisions about textual variations, which leads to another. We may be wrong no matter how careful we are because the sources of our information may be flawed or limited.

The main area of concern, however, has not been a primary focus of this book to this point. Interpretations are important because of the harm they can do. Looking to Ezekiel for information on UFOs may be a far-fetched and perhaps even irresponsible activity, but it does not necessarily lead to harmful results. However, such abuse is minor. The use of interpretation is of great concern.

Irresponsible interpretations produce harmful consequences. However, it is also the case that responsible interpretations can be used to promote harmful or violent actions as well. For instance, a historical critic may correctly interpret a text. He or she may conclude the passage is calling for the destruction of a people. The historian is not necessarily condoning such actions. Still another person may use such an interpretation to justify extreme violence toward another person or nation. In such cases, the blame is with the author, the text, and the one making the application. If an author or text has been misinterpreted, then the author or text is not necessarily to blame. [2] In short, it is important for one to distinguish between the interpretation and the use made of that interpretation.

To begin this discussion, I would argue that diversity of interpretations is inevitable and healthy. It is inevitable because we are human, and we do not always agree. First of all, the text we work with is not the same for every person. People who read Hebrew and Greek have an advantage since these are the main languages of the Bible, but even these scholars must deal with variations in different manuscripts. Additionally, texts exceed the boundaries of what one type of reading can provide. The form critic may do a good job, but the text has much more to say than the form critic can uncover. Other reading strategies are beneficial because they alert one to other possibilities. The possible meanings help readers stretch their imaginations and open their minds since the possibilities exceed the limits of one approach or one person. Freezing the meaning to one thing would ensure its irrelevance [3] for many people.

Secondly, I would contend that the interpretations or methods covered in this book are responsible. The only possible exception would be an extreme reader response interpretation that has no corroboration from the text itself. The approaches discussed in this book vary widely, but they all provide guidelines, strategies, or concepts that safeguard the text from total relativism. None of the practitioners of these approaches is free to say whatever comes to mind. [4]

Fish's notion of reading communities is helpful. Historical approaches, for example, are pursued within a certain type of academic community. This community puts a significant premium on locating a text within its proper historical setting. What constitutes a responsible reading would find general agreement within this community. Here the term competent may be more appropriate. That does not mean, however, that someone might not use one of these interpretations to promote irresponsible actions. By itself, however, the notion of reading communities does not discern responsible from irresponsible since some communities promote disrespect or violence toward others.

We are still left with the question: What makes a reading irresponsible? There is always a danger of reading things into the text. This is a risk for academics as well as laypeople. We all have pet views, ideas, and beliefs. We also may look to the Bible for support of these views. The historian who is a responsible member of the academic community must seek evidence for his or her theory and consider opposing views. Critics may have to modify or even dismiss their theories if they are proven false or if the evidence is lacking. It is a critical process. The text is the key element in the discussion. Has the critic been faithful to the text as far as possible? If the answer is no, then he or she has failed. Being faithful to the text simply means one has given the text its due consideration. If so, the interpretation may be flawed in some way but the interpreter has acted in a responsible manner and has produced a responsible interpretation.

What about the person who has allowed certain doctrines of the church to govern his or her interpretation of a text? Here I would say the interpreter may very well be acting irresponsibly. If the starting point is external and unrelated to the text under consideration, then the outcome will likely be suspect. One popular method of this type is proof-texting. The texts are not considered in context, but verses may be singled out in isolation from a larger context just to prove a point. They may be used to support a Church or denominational doctrine or personal belief. Bits of texts quoted or cited to convince, control, dominate, or manipulate others is misleading and open to extreme abuse. The text becomes secondary and of little importance in this process.

In the academic world, responsible readings are judged by a group of practitioners or experts. But is there any mechanism at play in non-academic or religious communities? Again Fish's use of reading community may be expanded to include religious communities. What about interpretations that occur within these communities? Certainly, there are religious communities with expectations or perhaps well-defined criteria for the evaluation of how a religious text is interpreted. Some may expect interpretations to be based on historical, literary, or theological approaches. Such expectations mean that these communities may share common concerns with academic communities. Other communities may make their own rules, and the community may, in fact, be controlled by a few select people who do not answer to anyone outside their group.

This whole business of distinguishing between reading communities is messy to say the least. The lines become blurred when one moves into the area of denominations or non-denominational communities. As a result, there is a need to address the ethical concerns involved in the act of interpretation. Are there some understandings or guidelines that can prevent irresponsible readings and more importantly irresponsible actions based on such readings? One can make arguments to oppose certain types of readings and applications. My major premise is that readings should allow for various peoples of different backgrounds and beliefs to live and work together peacefully. This priority provides the context from which one's readings and applications must be judged.

ETHICS OF INTERPRETATION

I have not been able to sever the ties with modernity; I still desire foundations and safe ground. It has been hard to venture into uncertainty. Nevertheless, sticking one's head in the sand is not a good option. Most everything we do depends on interpretation. It is one of the most important aspects of human existence. How one makes sense of the world matters. It matters to me as an individual, and it matters to us as a people. It determines whether we treat each other with respect, contempt or indifference. Furthermore, how one interprets the Bible matters in terms of how it influences our thoughts and actions. I do not worry about people having different views or beliefs, but I do worry about beliefs and attitudes that lead to harmful consequences.

By harmful, I suggest several areas of concern. Some people might use the Bible to justify the abusive treatment of women and or children. Attacks on gays and other minority groups may stem from misuse of the Bible. Disrespect and hatred of one's enemies could be supported by selective use of the Bible as well. Harm, therefore, may come in many forms ranging from verbal, mental, and physical abuse.

So now I find myself in the realm of ethics and morality. In ethics, there are those who consider themselves consequentialists and others who are non-consequentialist. Non-consequentialists do not judge acts good or bad based on the consequences they produce. They might say that a lie is bad regardless of the consequences. It is one's duty always to tell the truth. Consequentialists may see most any act as being good or bad depending upon the consequences it produces. A lie may be good in certain circumstances if the good consequences outweigh the bad ones. Both views have strong and weak points. Consequences are important and so are principles. Neither approach is entirely adequate. In fact, I do not believe there is one approach that is foolproof. Some would call upon conscience as an infallible guide, but it is perhaps more fallible and uncertain than the other two. What people generally think of as conscience is largely based on human socialization. And even if there is a conscience that reflects a moral impulse, it still would not tell us exactly what to do even though it may urge us to do something.[5]

Where does this leave us if ethics does not provide any absolutes? It leaves us without the certainty and safety that we might desire, but it does not leave us empty-handed. Closely tied to the notion of ethics is an obligation and some might add duty. I prefer to stick to obligation. People feel obligations to others. Sometimes that is because I feel indebted to someone. Other times, however, I may not even know the other person. I see a stranger in need, and I feel an obligation.

Obligation, however, does not mean that we know what to do in any given situation. One may feel an obligation without knowing how to respond. Drawing upon one's reason, experience, religious beliefs, and ethics may help one figure out what to do. One simply has to make a decision based on what is known. Obligation, however, is not sufficient. While it may depend partly on a moral sense, it is largely related to one's social upbringing and conscience. In the end, one is left with tools but no absolutes for making correct moral decisions as if there were only one decision. In cases known as moral dilemmas, there is no one correct answer.[6]

Tied to obligation is the response. What will one do when faced with an obligation? Will one refuse to respond? Is this refusal possible? Is it not in fact a response? Or will one be behaving responsibly just by responding? And what does acting responsibly actually entail in terms of reading biblical texts? Here, I would recommend a book by Eric A. Siebert entitled *The Violence of Scripture: Overcoming the Old Testament's Troubling Legacy*. Siebert proposes three essential reading habits: "(1) to read actively, (2) to question the text, and (3) to engage in an ethical critique of violent ideologies."[7] Siebert also acknowledges that what he says about violent Old Testament texts also applies to violent texts in the New Testament.

By reading actively, Siebert means that readers should not passively accept the text. In other words, he resists the notion that readers should be "compliant readers". One should not affirm or reject something just because the biblical texts affirm or reject it. Readers need to exercise a certain distance and independence. He is calling for an active engagement. Second, one should be willing to raise the tough questions that follow from an active reading of the texts in question. Finally, he contends that texts, which are "morally questionable, need to be ethically critiqued rather than uncritically approved."[8]

Siebert then proposes three guiding principles for this critique. The first is the "rule of love." This principle is based on the "two greatest commandments to "love God and neighbor."[9] The second principle concerns an obligation to act justly toward others. The final rule is to act upon a "consistent ethic of life."[10] One's readings need to affirm the life of everyone not just those in our own little circles. All life is to be valued. These ethical principles are based on Christian ethics, and I find them to be consistent with my own views with some minor elaborations.

First, I return to the notion of an active reading. From a historical perspective, one must first establish a baseline. This baseline is not exactly a passive reading of the text. It simply attempts to understand it on its own terms rather than to critique it. This endeavor should be taken seriously. Once the initial analysis of the text and its baseline meaning is established using historical approaches, one can proceed to a more active reading. The same is true with narrative criticism and deconstruction. Some narrative critics may not actually get to the active reading because of their notion of reading in sympathy with the text. I agree with Seibert, however, that it is a good thing to push beyond passive readings and become critical readers. Deconstruction like historical approaches may begin with the text, but it goes beyond it. Derrida may begin with the doubling commentary of the traditional approaches whether historical or literary ones, but he does not allow that to be the final word. Seibert is not cutting out this first step, but he is interested in how one deals with a violent text.

Second, I would argue that even if Seibert's ethical principles are good ones, they are not established in any sense or grounded in absolute truths. They are generated out of a reading of the same Scripture that he is critiquing. As he notes, the Bible contains texts that call for violence and texts that call one to love others and treat them justly. He takes the latter texts as containing the guidelines for his ethical critique. One might consider these as divinely revealed guidelines, and I would not disagree, but they are not universals in the sense that they can be established beyond question by ethicists. They represent a particular Christian perspective, but not everyone would accept the view or its implications, not even all Christians.

Another interesting question concerns psychological and social forces. What causes one to respond to texts in ways that lead to violence or disrespect for others? It is not a simple matter. One simply cannot say that the "Bible made me do it."[11] The text is just one part of the equation. One might say there are pre-disposing factors that may make one susceptible to a violent or disrespectful response. Two people from different backgrounds and upbringings may encounter a text calling for us to love everyone. One of the two may ignore its call to love whereas the other allows this principle to govern his or her life. Personality, upbringing, and associates may all play a part in the person's response. D. Andrew Kille's contribution to the book, *The Destructive Power of Religion*, deals with these kinds of factors. This work and its topic need to be considered seriously by religious communities.

If we want people to be loving and responsible readers then it may take much more than a book on the topic of biblical interpretation. Readers often need help in overcoming some of the baggage they bring to the text.

If ethics is not sufficient to define what a responsible reading would be like, then where do we go? I urge the reader not to despair. Nothing in this world is perfect including ethics or religion. Certainly we are not. To settle for a pragmatic substitute for the perfect is the best we can do. This imperfect substitute contains the notions of obligation and responsibility. They are imperfect in that they are based as much on feeling as on reason and experience.

By imperfect obligation and responsibility, I mean that they cannot be defined exactly or placed within a nice neat system that tells us how to be responsible and how to meet our obligations. Sometimes these things are messy; that is life. Obligation and responsibility along with justice, stand outside our grasps and beckons us to strive for them, that is, to strive for perfection. Still, justice is not an ideal that we can approach. It is not something that we can define, program, or capture in earthly systems. Justice is open; it exceeds what we can anticipate or plan for.[12] Unique situations exceed what has been anticipated and programmed ahead of time. Some things occur that are not foreseeable and justice requires one to make decisions, to decide what justice calls for in this particular situation.

In short, perfection is not something we can expect to obtain no matter how much we might progress. There is always going to be unforeseeable developments. So what I am proposing is provisional and can never be more than that. Justice and love always intrude on our certainties, plans, and feelings. Any responsible reading answers to this love and justice that is always prompting us for a decision.[13] Responsible readings never call for one to act unjustly or unlovingly toward others inside or outside our circle. Does this mean that violence or struggle against others is never justifiable?

Again, the decision has to be based on the specifics of the situation. In ethics, there are cases known as moral dilemmas. In such cases, the whole point is that there is no clear cut right or wrong. At times, an act may be good for one person or group and bad for others. No matter what one decides, someone is harmed. I conclude that the best we can do is to read the text and decide what to do with it. What we should do with it is to act responsibly, which means to act justly and lovingly in any given situation as far as possible and for as many as possible. The general notion of doing no harm may serve as a guide as we consider our options.

PROPOSED GUIDELINES FOR RESPONSIBLE READINGS

I offer the following as a guide for responsible reading. First, the reader should deal seriously and faithfully with the text as an independent whole. The interpreter should allow the text to speak for itself before ever trying to incorporate it into a larger structure such as the canon. Incorporating it into a larger structure afterward and understanding it within that structure is not a problem. Such an approach may be fruitful, and it should open up new possible meanings.

The basic interpretation of the text entails description. Historical approaches attempt to provide descriptions of the text and what it means in relation to its author. Literary critics may attempt to describe the literary features of the text without concern for the author. Deconstruction may begin with the doubling commentary before it moves on to another level. It is important to deal with what the text is all about before going on to consider just how an individual or group might use it. Understanding the basic meaning is important because it provides an anchor, and it can call into question other readings and uses made of the text. In a sense, it places limits on how one should use the text.

Therefore, in my view it is necessary to begin with the basic text. This means I would at least familiarize myself with the historical and literary readings of the text before attempting to move beyond it. It is not responsible simply to use a text without regard for its overall context. To redirect philosopher Immanuel Kant's famous categorical imperative away from moral absolutes to texts, I might say responsible readings do not use the text as merely a means to an end. Proof texting is wide open to abuse.

Next, the reader needs to deal with a second level. Many interpreters may end their study after the first step, and this cessation is perfectly acceptable. Stopping after the examination of the text leaves the text open to other readers. The second level, however, requires great care from a moral perspective. It centers or turns upon the dynamics of love and justice. These two open-ended forces speak to the receptive reader, and they influence one's response to a text. At minimum, love and justice entail respect and concern for others whether individuals or groups. How one reads and responds to the text should be shaped by these dynamics. This does not guarantee that everyone will respond, in the same way, but it does mean that readers will not just read uncritically. They must consider how the text and their readings affect others. Does it build others up or destroy them? It calls for us to be critical readers, not compliant ones. [14]

This second step or level comes in the interpretation process. In historical approaches, this second step involves the application of the meaning for the present day. This step entails more than just applying what the text means in the current context. It would be extended to a critical analysis of how the meaning should be implemented or if it should be applied at all. This part entails an active reading, which entails the interpreter's concerns and questions about the text, its meaning, and its implications. If a text reflects a patriarchal attitude, for instance, the interpreter may question or reject its authority for the Christian faith. If a text calls for genocide, one should certainly reject it as a guide for any action.

One might see this as arbitrarily selecting texts that are agreeable and rejecting those that are disagreeable. In fact, we all do this. The phrase "a canon within a canon" refers to how people function with a selective group of authoritative texts whether recognized or not. Fiorenza identified Galatians 3:28 as a hermeneutical key meaning it becomes the key verse for judging which texts have authority and which do not. And before rejecting this idea out of hand, one might consider Martin Luther's rejection of the Book of James in the New Testament. He says that James' "purpose is to teach Christians, but in all this long teaching it does not once mention the Passion, the resurrection, or the Spirit of Christ."[15] As a result, he did not accord it the same status as the other New Testament writings.

Literary approaches also need to move beyond the text so they can engage a second level of analysis. It cannot simply rest on reading in sympathy with the text. To apply the text, one needs to engage the text critically. While the reader may try to jettison his or her modern biases to enter into the story world of the biblical texts, he or she need not accept the values of this world without question. Therefore, literary readings should not cause one to be a submissive reader.

Rhetorical criticism, reader response criticism, deconstruction, and ideological approaches all move beyond what the text meant or means to a deeper level. They can begin with the doubling commentary so to speak and move to something beyond that. This point should be evident from the discussions of these methods. Questioning of these texts and considering how they might be used are important activities. Considering the benefit and harm produced by a given interpretation is a crucial part of evaluating biblical interpretations. The Bible still has the power to transform and save lives from the depths of despair and destruction. At the same time, it contains texts that can be used to call for genocide and violence toward others. As a result, it is truly a book of life and death. The power and potential of the Bible as Scripture is tremendous. The only responsible way to handle such a book is with care. Reading through the lens of justice and love is necessary.

It is true that people disagree about what constitutes love and justice. That is why I would add a couple of notes in conclusion. Justice and love are not separate or opposites. One goes with the other. Love longs for and calls out for justice while justice is the enacting of love. They form a deep unity, and they are universal in their scope. They are not universal in that one size fits all; instead, they extend to every individual. Love is directed toward self and others.

Justice is not about exacting revenge or getting even. Justice is not about an eye for an eye but turning the other cheek (cf., Mt 5:38–39). Justice is a radical notion, and it breaks down walls such as rich/poor, black/white, and male/female. It overturns our normal sense of reward and punishment or our feelings about being deserving and undeserving. It is consistent with treating everyone whether Christian, Jew, Muslim, agnostic, or atheist as lovingly and justly as humanly possible. It is compatible with the notion that God loves everyone and not just a handful of obedient servants. God even loves the unlovable, which may seem offensive to us. All I can say or do in response is to try to read and act responsibly. For those who think otherwise and long for judgment and destruction of their enemies, the Bible may be a dangerous book.

NOTES

1. I am indebted to John D. Caputo's notion of the "jewgreek." See Moyers, *The Moral Life*. 190–193; John D. Caputo, *Against ethics: Contributions to a poetics of obligation with constant reference to deconstruction.* Studies in Continental Thought, ed. John Sallis Bloomington and Indianapolis: Indiana University Press, 1993, 53–68.

2. Moyers, *The Moral Life*, 99–104. In this book, I discussed this issue in relation to the irresponsible use some Germans made of Friedrich Nietzsche's work. In what way if at all can an author be held responsible for the misunderstandings or deliberate distortions of others?

3. Caputo, *Deconstruction in a Nutshell*, 79.

4. This criticism as mentioned earlier has been leveled at deconstruction. Caputo notes that is simply not the case. Caputo 78–79.

5. Moyers, *The Moral Life*, 26–33. In particular see my discussion of Zygmunt Bauman on pages 31–33.

6. Ibid., 222–230.

7. Siebert, 62.

8. Ibid., 65.

9. Ibid., 67.

10. Ibid., 68.

11. D. Andrew Kille, "The Bible Made Me Do It": Text, Interpretation, and Violence." In *The Destructive Power of Religion: Violence in Judaism, Christianity, and Islam* ed. J. Harold Ellens, vol. 1 *Sacred Scriptures, Ideology, and Violence* (Westport, CT: Praeger, 2004), 55–73.

12. Caputo, *Deconstruction in a Nutshell*, 129–140.

13. Ibid., 137–140; Moyers, *The Moral Life*, 223–225.

14. Siebert, 54–57.

15. Martin Luther, *Luther's Works: Word and Sacrament I*, ed., E. Theodore Bachmann, vol. 35 (Philadelphia: Fortress Press, 1960), 396.